Triathlons
for women

Triathlons
for *women*
4TH EDITION

SALLY EDWARDS

VELO.
press

BOULDER, COLORADO

1830 55th Street
Boulder, Colorado 80301-2700 USA
303/440-0601 · Fax 303/444-6788 · E-mail velopress@competitorgroup.com
Distributed in the United States and Canada by Ingram Publisher Services

Library of Congress Cataloging-in-Publication Data
Edwards, Sally, 1947–
Triathlons for women / Sally Edwards.—4th ed.
    p. cm.
Includes index.
    ISBN 978-1-934030-40-0 (pbk.: alk. paper)
1. Triathlon—Training—Handbooks, manuals, etc. I. Title.
GV1060.73.E395 2009
796.42'57—dc22

                          2009015189

For information on purchasing VeloPress books, please call 800/234-8356 or visit www.velopress.com.

This book is printed on 100 percent recovered/recycled fiber, 30 percent post-consumer waste, elemental chlorine free, using soy-based inks.

Cover design by Erin Johnson
Cover illustration by Christina Ung; back cover photograph by Timothy Carlson
Interior design by Anita Koury
Interior illustrations by Charlie Layton (pp. 30, 80–84, 90–93, 100, 103, 109, 118, 122–124, 177, 225, 228, and 232)
Photographs courtesy of Aquasphere (pp. 167–170); Shaun Botterill, Getty Images (p. 17, top); Tom Marek (frontispiece and p. 251); Paul Mozell, AP Images (p. 16, left); Robert Murphy (p. 17, bottom); Pearl Izumi (pp. 186 and 190); Mike Powell, Getty Images (p. 16, right); Timex (p. 163); and Trek (pp. 101, 175, and 259)
Excerpt on pp. 245–246 reprinted by permission of the author

10 11 12/10 9 8 7 6 5 4 3 2 1

Let her swim, climb mountain peaks, pilot an airplane,
battle against the elements, take risks, go out for adventure,
and she will not feel before the world that timidity.

—SIMONE DE BEAUVOIR

Contents

Foreword

by Karen Smyers

First, allow me to say how excited I am that you are reading Sally Edwards's *Triathlons for Women*. If you are reading this book, you are either taking the first step toward becoming a triathlete or you are working on improving your race performance.

Like Sally, I have been competing in triathlons for many years. Both of us started racing in triathlons because they are fun and challenging, and then we ended up making our careers in the sport.

Also like Sally, I am passionate about encouraging more women to discover their inner athlete by *trying a tri*.

When I first started participating in triathlons in 1984, there were very few sources of information about the sport. Like most triathletes, I learned things the hard way—through trial and error. All on my own, I discovered what not to eat the morning of the race, how to lose your bike in the transition area, and how much training before a race is too much. Luckily, everything you need to know about training for and racing in a triathlon is in this informative and inspiring book.

There is no question that entering your first triathlon can be intimidating. Because of the three-sport format, it is as if there are three times as many questions. When you glance around before the start of a race, it may appear that everyone else is a seasoned, extremely fit veteran with the most expensive high-tech equipment available; however, if you look closely at the transition area of your local triathlon, you will find equipment ranging from mountain bikes to touring bikes to the latest racing bikes. Although you also will see a wide range of body types and levels of fitness, every woman will have the same gleam in her eyes, reflecting a determination to meet her personal goals.

You will discover that your feelings of intimidation are unfounded when you do your first race. There tends to be a lot of camaraderie in triathlon, especially in all-women races. One of my fondest memories during my 18 years of racing is from my first all-women race. As I was leading the charge on the last mile of the out-and-back 5K run, many of the other women were just starting their run as we crossed paths. Every single woman cheered for me as I went by. When I finished, I went back to the course, as did most of the top women, and returned the favor by encouraging the women who were still racing. Although each woman was focused on achieving her own goal, each still had the energy and awareness to support every other competitor in the race. It was an incredibly positive and motivating atmosphere in which to compete.

When I attended the pre-race meeting for first-time triathletes at a Danskin race in Boston, I listened as Sally, one of the best motivational speakers I have ever heard, enthralled a very nervous bunch of women. Step by step, she took them through everything they could expect to encounter during the race. At the same time, she inspired palpable feelings of confidence and empowerment. She made every one of those women believe in herself and her goal and at the same time laugh at her jokes, which made the tension melt away. I wanted to turn back the clock and become one of those first-timers because I envied their sense of anticipation and the feeling of accomplishment they were going to experience the next day.

Sally's dedication to making the Danskin Triathlon Series a success has been evidenced by her participation. Sally swims, bikes, and runs with the last woman in the race, giving her constant encouragement and positive reinforcement and saving every woman from the most prevalent first-timer worry: finishing last. Sally gladly accepts the last-place position and in turn does every woman in the race the favor of removing that anxiety.

Sally drew on her vast experience in the sport of triathlon to write this book. Her insight into which questions people need answered; her ability to explain the basics of swimming, biking, and running in an understandable way for novice and experienced racers alike; and the inspiration she provides along the way are what make this fourth edition of *Triathlons for Women* indispensable. With this book, you are armed with all the information you need to train for and compete in a triathlon.

Now, go forth and "tri" your best!

Karen Smyers *is a seven-time U.S. National champion (1990–1995, 2001), Hawaiian Ironman champion (1995), ITU Olympic World Triathlon champion (1990, 1995), ITU Long-Course World Triathlon champion (1996), and Inaugural inductee to the USA Triathlon Hall of Fame.*

Foreword

by Maggie Sullivan

If you are considering participating in a triathlon, *Triathlons for Women* is the book for you. Read this book because you want to learn, grow, accomplish, and enjoy the sport and the triathlon lifestyle. Read this book because it is written by a master of the sport.

I know firsthand because I've had the privilege of working side by side with Sally for the past 20 years as we—along with a talented team—built triathlon's groundbreaking series for women. I have seen hundreds of thousands of women of every age, shape, and level of athletic ability get to the starting line of their first triathlon and cross the finish line because of Sally. For most women, finishing a first triathlon is transformational. Just as a caterpillar becomes a butterfly, the first-timers in our national triathlon series become triathletes for life thanks to Sally's help.

This transformation occurs because of Sally's sound, scientific approach. Add to that her motivation and energy, which help inspire women to get off the couch and to the starting line. Sally has crisscrossed the country for decades to speak at training seminars and pre-race pep talks. Hundreds of times I have seen the way women walk in as doubters and leave as believers, each one knowing "I can do it." Sally possesses an amazing charisma; she is authentic to the core as a minister of health and fitness.

Sally's uncanny ability to convert and transform is present in all she does—books, seminars, blogs, DVDs, and keynote presentations. She communicates and inspires us to take a chance on ourselves: to push the boundaries that at times confine us, to question the terms that define us. Indeed, she gives us the courage to begin to redefine ourselves. She helps us destroy the myths and negative beliefs that hold us back. She gives us the strength and the desire to shake things up in our lives and take a chance on doing something new, becoming someone new—maybe even becoming a fit and happy triathlete.

Sally is well qualified to be the author of many books on the subject of women and triathlon because of her knowledge as an exercise scientist and her own athletic accomplishments as a professional triathlete. She is a 16-time Ironman finisher and the former masters world record holder. She was instrumental in developing the sport of triathlon 30 years ago, when only a handful were competing—and of that handful, precious few were female. She is also a member of the Triathlon Hall of Fame and a founder of USA Triathlon, the national governing body of triathlon. She is a prolific author with more than 22 books to her credit.

In addition to her achievements on the athletic and literary front, Sally has also carved out time to found a half-dozen companies. Her energies drive Heart Zones® USA (www.heartzones.com)—a training, education, and coaching company predicated on cardiovascular and emotional training using the heart and personal training tools. Sally is a pioneer in this field: In the early 1990s she developed the first books, seminars, and certifications on the subject. Get to know this remarkable woman better, and join her as she drives The Sally Edwards Company (www.TheSally EdwardsCompany.com) to get America fit one person at a time.

On a personal level, Sally has played an invaluable role in making fitness and adventure a remarkably fun and important part of my life. Until I met Sally, I never would have considered being an outdoor adventurer. Since then I have summitted mountains, both literally and figuratively. Sally has shown me how to use an ice ax, crampons, and snowshoes. She has taken me to the bottom of the Grand Canyon and across glaciers to the top of Mt. Whitney. We've hiked slot canyons in southeast Utah and trails around Mt. Rainier. You see, Sally helped to convert me. As a New Yorker having lived a lifetime in Manhattan, I would not have guessed that my life's passion and work would be triathlon. I'm honored to produce two of America's greatest all-women triathlon series.

Sally is now supporting me in my latest adventure: entrepreneurship. Following an extensive career in men's professional tennis and an equally extensive career in women's triathlon, I started my first business, The Xxtra Mile, LLC, owner and producer of the Trek Women Triathlon Series and the Danskin Women's Triathlon Series. Sally's gentle yet firm reminders—"Make yourself a priority," and "Fit people are happier and more productive people"—along with her support have allowed me to believe in myself and embrace my newest challenge.

Since our early days together, one of Sally's favorite questions has been "When was the last time you did something for the first time?" This book may lead to a first-time experience for you—to think of doing a triathlon or perhaps training to do even better at your next triathlon. So read this book, pass it along to a friend, or keep your copy and snag another one as a gift. It's one of the greatest gifts you can give to a girlfriend, believing in her just as Sally does, telling her that she can be a triathlete.

I say, go on, give it a "tri"—this is your time.

Maggie Sullivan is chief entrepreneurial officer of The Xxtra Mile, LLC, and series director of the Danskin Women's Triathlon Series and Trek Women Triathlon Series, www.danskintriathlon.net, www.trekwomenstriathlonseries.com.

Preface to the Fourth Edition

Women everywhere are becoming triathletes. We're winning races, better-ing our run times, swimming before work, and touring on our bikes rather than in our cars. There are more women in sports today than at any other time in histo-ry, and we are feeling the effects—enhanced self-esteem, feelings of accomplishment and happiness, and the joy of being more fit and healthy. What took us so long?

You can do it!

This book is for any woman who wants to say, or loves to say, "I am a triathlete." It is for any woman who is con-sidering the sport of triathlon or who wants to bring her training and performance to the next level. This book embraces the multisport lifestyle in the hope that more women will become part of this healthy, active way of life. It also takes on the obstacles that prevent a woman from reaching her full potential. My goal is to educate and inspire you, whether you are an experienced triathlete seeking to expand your horizons or a newcomer considering a triathlon and what it takes to embark on this lifestyle.

When I first wrote *Triathlons for Women* in 1992, I wanted to share my expertise as a coach, exercise physiologist, and professional triathlete as well as my experiences with women triathletes since the sport began. I was fortunate to be one of the first paid professional triathletes. I completed sixteen Ironman races, finishing second in the 1981 Hawaii Ironman®, and I'm a former Ironman masters record holder. In the years since, it's been my pleasure to be the official spokeswoman for the Danskin Women's Triathlon Series and the Trek™ Women Triathlon Series, led by Series Director Maggie Sullivan. These triathlons attract women of all abilities and backgrounds. As the official sweep athlete, I am the final finisher so that no other woman has to finish last, making the race more accessible and appealing to women from every level of fitness and experience. Through my journeys—from last to first place—I have learned a lot about this sport. My company, Heart Zones USA, trains triathlon coaches who go on to lead training programs for women. All of these experiences have allowed me to work with a broad spectrum of women athletes. I know that as women, we train and compete differently than men; in this book I will tell you how and why.

Equipment, training, nutritional needs, and racing are different for women than for men. Just as all the materials used in the making of a women-specific bike will be the same as those used for a men's bike but will be put together differently, so the various "components" of triathlon training and racing will be similar but also different for men and women. My book acknowledges the commonalities between the genders in triathlon while celebrating the differences. After all, what brings women to the starting line of triathlons is very different from what brings men to the same place, and the journey to the finish line is different as well. As women, we tend to be more caught up in misperceptions of our athleticism and mired in self-doubt. Although a race is a competitive event, I encourage every woman to "run her own race" and compete against her expectations.

Since 1990, when the Danskin Women's Triathlon Series—the first of its kind—began, I have traveled to cities across the United States to speak to women about the challenge of training for a triathlon. When I look out into the audience, I see women with strollers, women who have battled cancer, women who have climbed the corporate ladder, and women who are struggling with obesity. I reassure them, just as I will reassure you, that every one of them can be a triathlete. They have different circumstances but similar struggles. Training will look different for some of them, but the rush of crossing the finish line is the same. It's my hope that for every woman, the journey from self-doubt to the triumphant finish-line photos on race day is the beginning of a healthy, active lifestyle.

Ultimately there are four messages that run throughout this book, whether I'm discussing training goals, skill development, diet, or race day itself. These apply to any triathlete, but I have written about them specifically with women and newcomers in mind.

1. You *can* be a triathlete! There are at least two monkeys (some might consider them gorillas) that will be part of your first triathlon experience.

The first is Fear. This monkey asks, *How deep is the water? How steep is the hill? How will I run that far?* The second monkey is Self-Doubt: *I'm too big, too old, too young, too busy, too whatever* (fill in your fear here) *to succeed as a triathlete.* I've spoken to thousands of women who have faced these two monkeys. Throughout this book, you will learn how to shake them.

Almost any woman can complete a triathlon, regardless of age, weight, athletic background, or fitness level. (In the past I've found that even a lack of willingness to compete can be overcome, thanks to my persistence.) It's true that training for a triathlon requires physical and mental effort, but if you learn efficient biomechanics (how your body moves), get the proper equipment, and consistently train with a good plan, you will enjoy success.

2. You *can* change your lifestyle. This book contains training plans and tips that will help you keep it all together and not quit. It won't be easy to do what I ask, but believe me, you can do it. I know you aren't reading this book or training for triathlons because you are bored or because you have nothing else to do. You probably find yourself wanting more: more challenges, more information, more motivation, and yes, more energy. You've taken an important step by reading this book. My goal is to keep you motivated. This is your life, and this is your agenda—it's not like starting a diet. In the long run, diets typically fail because you change only what you eat, not what you do. If you do it right, the sport of triathlon is a lifetime fitness program and a serious and rewarding commitment of will. I can promise that if you train for triathlons, you will see your life improve.

3. You *can* find the time to train. You might look at your calendar and ask, "When can I find time for all of this training when I'm already busy?" If there is a place for fitness in your life, there is time for triathlon training. Triathlon is a natural fit for women who are accustomed to multitasking— many of us already juggle jobs, family, and home responsibilities. It won't be easy, and you may have to make some trade-offs. But when you make your health your first priority, and when you know that being physically fit is the foundation of your health, training takes on a new importance. When all else fails, be flexible and train when you can.

4. You *can* find other resources and triathletes to help you. This book will provide you with a solid foundation. Beyond it, there is a vibrant triathlete community awaiting you. Network through your local contacts. Most communities have bike, swim, run, and triathlon retail stores that can connect you with other triathletes. There are athletic clubs—such as the YMCA, the JCC, and private health clubs—that you can join. There are organizations like mine, Heart Zones USA, that can help prepare you for events, as well as online communities of triathletes where you can find encouragement, ask questions, and help support others in the sport. The network is already there—join it.

> **TIP** You can always contact me; I love to hear from readers. Drop me an e-mail at staff@heartzones.com.

If you go to a women-only event, you will see women giving their best while offering encouragement to those around them. These races are an opportunity for women to work together in support of common goals: individual performance, strength of will, and fun!

In putting together the fourth edition of *Triathlons for Women*, I wanted to capture that spirit of encouragement because I believe encouragement coupled with resolve can make a triathlete of any woman. Throughout this book you'll find stories from my career in the sport, stories about women like you, and plenty of advice for beginners. I've highlighted the accomplishments of professional women triathletes, not to intimidate you but to encourage you to take pride in other women's accomplishments. I've tried to remove the intimidation factor by explaining every detail you need to know about fitness and training.

The fourth edition of my book also includes all the latest research I think you'll need to know about, more instruction on technique that will allow you to compete in three sports for years to come with fewer injuries, more drills for improving technique, and more background on nutrition. I've also included an entirely new chapter on weight loss because, let's face it, this is a common motivation for training.

It all comes back to this: You don't have to be a good swimmer to be a triathlete. You don't have to know how to ride a bike with clipless pedals. You don't have to be able to run a mile. To start training for your first triathlon, you simply need to *want* to be a triathlete. That one desire is more powerful than you know. One thing I know for certain: You can do it.

Acknowledgments

When was the last time you did something for the first time? I ask that question whenever I speak at an event, and I can assure you that I understand the implications of a new challenge. I've written a number of books, but I always like to take the opportunity to reflect and appreciate everything and everyone who made it possible—friends, family, and enthusiasts—whether it's the first or the umpteenth time to thank them.

First, I appreciate every woman (and man) who has undertaken the challenge of doing a triathlon. For most that is a big step, and I've known many people who have undertaken the daunting task of training for a triathlon without a sports background.

Next, I am grateful for the great staff at VeloPress—Renee Jardine and her team of editors, including veteran Connie Oehring. Special thanks to Erin Striff, whose writing assistance helped to make this new edition possible.

I am grateful to the contributions and endurance talents of my dear friend and celebrity event producer Margaret "Maggie" Sullivan. For more than 20 years Maggie and I have worked together diligently to develop the sport of "women's triathlon," which is so different from the sport of Ironman triathlon or Olympic triathlon. It is a breed of its own, and when you experience one of the races owned or produced by Maggie Sullivan and her team at The Xxtra Mile, you will understand why the sport of women's triathlon has exploded. Maggie's women's triathlons epitomize support and acceptance, risk-taking, and personal achievement. Though I've been part of the sport from the beginning, it's still a powerful experience for me.

Whether you are a seasoned triathlete or a newcomer, whether you are male or female, young or old, little or big, orange or green, I sincerely thank you for accepting the responsibility of getting fit and staying fit. When was the last time you did something for the first time? *Now.*

Share this book and your training experience with your family and friends, and invite them to join you at the starting line. They will have you to thank for the invitation to a healthy, active lifestyle.

Introduction

Just as knowing the layout of the racecourse will improve your performance, knowing the course a book will take will help you get the most out of it. I hope the following outline will be especially helpful for experienced triathletes who are looking for the most useful advice to incorporate into their regular training. More advanced triathletes might want to skip chapters or sections that cover familiar ground and focus on the topics that most interest them. Newcomers to the sport can learn about every aspect of training and competing by reading cover to cover.

Chapter 1, "Women as Triathletes," and Chapter 2, "Get Inspired," are intended to do just what they say—inspire you, fire you up with the belief that you can do a triathlon—because you can. We'll tackle head-on the realities of life that might hold you back if you let them, because I'm certain that you do not have to let them. If you are already a triathlete, these chapters will remind you that you can improve your current performance and have even more fun! We'll take a look at the history of women's triathlon and consider what we can achieve if we set our minds to it.

To learn exactly what you need to do to set goals and plan for particular events and race distances, read Chapter 3, "The Fundamentals of Smart Training." This is the chapter to turn to if you want to begin working on a plan right away. It is here that I also explain the concept of heart rate zones.

This chapter introduces the theories that will make up the foundation of your training. Once you understand the basic structure of successful training and the principles of goal-setting, it will be time to get started: *Plan the work, work the plan, and the plan works.*

In Chapter 4, "Training Plans," I describe my approach to training in detail and show exactly how it translates into a beginner plan and an intermediate workout plan. What is a training load? What are the five essential parts of a cardiovascular workout? How much training do you need? All these questions are answered in Chapter 4. For more experienced athletes, I will help you develop a personal training plan.

In Chapters 5–7 we will look at the three sports of triathlon: swim, bike, and run. Each of these chapters includes an introduction to the sport, a description of proper form and the drills that will help you achieve it, and workouts to help you build your skills in that discipline. If you are an experienced multisport athlete, I recommend that you focus on the chapter that addresses your weakest sport because that is where you will be able to reap the greatest benefit.

You'll learn more about race transitions—much more—in Chapter 8, "The Art of the Transition." It is here that you will discover a wealth of information about how to prepare your transition area for the smoothest possible moves from one sport to the next.

Chapter 9, "Racing: You Go, Girlfriend!" describes what happens on race day in each of the disciplines as well as in the transition zone. We'll build on the skills you learned in Chapters 4–7 as you learn racing techniques and get tips on making quick transitions.

In Chapter 10, "Tools of the Triathlon Game," I describe all the equipment you will need to compete in the sport of triathlon. Because triathlon is a triple-fitness sport, equipment is an important consideration. Turn to this chapter for expert guidance before buying any gear, from clothing to heart rate monitors and other accessories.

To be successful in any sports endeavor, you need to fuel yourself with the right energy—the ingredients of the right diet. As a triathlete, you should be very careful about what you put into your body. Chapter 11, "Eating for Training and Racing," addresses the demands of everyday nutrition and hydration as well as what foods and drinks you should use on race day.

If losing weight is among your goals, you'll want to read Chapter 12, "Weight Loss for Triathletes." This chapter is new to the fourth edition. I want to empower you with a different approach to weight loss that takes into account how your training, your metabolism, and your emotions will affect your fitness. Ultimately I'd like you to shift your focus from losing weight to gaining fitness. However, if you adopt my approach and commit to training, better eating, and listening to your body rather than the world around you, I'm confident that the weight loss will come as a result of your healthy, active lifestyle.

Finally I describe my approach to health and wellness in Chapter 13, "Wellness and Triathlon." Physical problems can occur when you are active in such a demanding endeavor, but there is much you can do to remain healthy and strong as you train. When you put this commonsense approach into practice to take good care of yourself, you can protect your body and enjoy the benefits of fitness for a lifetime.

I can't wait another second to help you get started.

1

Women as Triathletes

Think about the powerful statement: "I am a triathlete." Say those words to yourself. If you've picked up this book because you're interested in triathlon, start by believing them. In this chapter we will look at some of the obstacles women have faced in realizing that dream—and how they have overcome them throughout the history of this sport. Deciding to train for triathlon begins with a transition, a shift in perspective: changing how you view yourself. There is a woman inside you who wants to have the chance to succeed: By engaging in the sport of triathlon you can give her that chance. In fact, you will become this new woman when you cross the finish line, because this is who you were born to be.

I am a triathlete.

Those considering a fitness program or bringing their training to the next level may not immediately think that the sport of triathlon is for them. Triathletes have been branded as pain-seeking athletes—the toughest of them all. I am always amazed that, when people ask me who I am, and I say I'm a triathlete, a look of reverence appears on their faces. That didn't even happen when I used to say I was an ultramarathoner who won 100-mile races—something I did prior to competing in triathlon.

It's just not true that all triathletes eat nails and only know how to talk to a bike, their running sneaks, or themselves as they float, coast, and shuffle. We are really simple folks. We train because we enjoy it, certainly not for the money or the fame, and usually not because of our egos. When I tell people that I have fun when I train, the look of awe turns into a look of incredulity. Nevertheless, for me, being a triathlete is a matter of being a kid again. I have fond memories of swimming, riding bikes, and running as a child, and triathlon lets me frolic in that playground again.

"Can it really be fun to train so much?" some might ask. For me it's the truth—training is the best part of my day. When I train, I can get away from my desk and the pressure of making business decisions. I set aside shopping lists and other errands. I can free my mind from the daily grind. As a result, I have some of my most creative moments when I am training. And although I do get tired, it's a "good tired." It's a time for me and my health and fitness. To be a triathlete is to have fun.

Now you know why I train. Here's a question for you: Why do you want to train? I ask a lot of women this question. Most often the answer is something like "I want to train in order to change my life," or "It's time to get healthy and fit." If your answer is similar, be assured that as you begin to train for triathlon, you will be taking those first few difficult steps toward fitness and changing your life. It isn't going to be easy, especially at first, but you can do it. You can find your inner athlete.

"I AM A TRIATHLETE"

If you pick up triathlon magazines you might conclude that this is a man's sport—more specifically, young, white, perfectly toned men. Don't buy into this myth. As you already know, the ranks of women triathletes are growing. And I'm not talking about the thin, muscular women you see in triathlon magazines (particularly not the swimsuit issues)! Triathletes can of course be people of color, they might inhabit a body you might not expect to see crossing the finish line, or they might be "of a certain age." Triathletes look like you.

With all the assumptions that go on about the sport, simply identifying yourself as a triathlete can be both challenging and empowering. When many people think of triathletes they think of the Ironman World Championship, with chiseled athletes battling it out on the lava fields of the Big Island. In fact, in interviews with experienced women triathletes, I found that many did not consider themselves to be triathletes if they had "only" competed in a sprint-distance triathlon (approximately 0.5-mile swim, 12-mile bike, 3-mile run). Some women thought they could not "be" triathletes until they had completed at least an international-distance triathlon (approximately 1-mile swim, 25-mile bike, 6-mile run).

Competing in a triathlon is about meeting and exceeding your goals, whatever the level, whatever your experience. And once you have completed a sprint triathlon, you are a triathlete. Consider Ruth Kaminski, who, in Susan L. Kane's book *Flying over the Finish Line: Women Triathletes' Stories of Life*, says, "I thought that my shining moments of epic events were past me . . . until at the age of 50 I became a triathlete." The idea of becoming and remaining a triathlete can be a significant boost to your self-esteem, enabling you to commit to a lifetime of healthy living.

Maybe you've finished several triathlons but still don't identify yourself as a bona fide triathlete. You can relate to Susan Farago, who in the same book talks about her journey from competing in sprint-distance competitions to the Ironman World Championship held in Kona, Hawaii. She says, "After five years of hard work and dedication, I found myself amongst the greatest triathletes in the world. I felt like such a poser." She explains that when she and her husband were in Kona people would ask Leary if he was excited about the race: "He would correct them and proudly declare that it was me, not him, doing the race." In Susan's experience these sexist assumptions came from spectators. Her fellow triathletes knew better, and through this she began to feel more comfortable as part of the triathlon community. She was well on her way to knowing she wasn't a "poser" after all. The more you say, "I am a triathlete," the more you will connect to your inner athlete and get comfortable with her. And before you know it, you'll find yourself reaching your triathlon goals more easily, because with that shift in identity comes a new confidence.

BEING A WOMAN, BEING AN ATHLETE

If you are reading this book, you want to be an athlete, too—or you already are one. Years ago, if a woman wanted a sports career, she became a physical education teacher. But now it is common to see professional and Olympic female athletes used as inspirational advertising images.

As women, most of us want to be feminine, too. Somewhere between being feminine and being athletic there still seems to be a problem: We feel we can't be both, because the two still seem like such opposites that one must suffer for the other. We want to be athletes, which requires that we be tough, aggressive, forceful, and even dominant. But we feel we must suppress our athletic side when we want to be feminine, a role that is understood to be supportive, passive, tender, and emotional. What's a woman athlete to do?

It's the same problem I have as an Ironwoman competing in the Iron-man. All of the t-shirts, award plaques, and prize-money checks that I've ever received have read "Ironman," and yet that's not me. There's a large amount of what sports psychologists call "role conflict" involved with being a woman and being called an Ironman.

As women we have internalized so much of what we have been taught about our roles. It's tough to break with tradition; some people never can. In my case, I was taught, as my mother was, to grow up, marry, have 2.2 children, and live happily ever after. However, thanks to my military-officer father, who raised my three older brothers to be athletes and sol-diers, I was also reared as an athlete. By the time I came along, my mom and dad just didn't know any other approach. It's not hard to understand why more of my athletic sisters aren't lining up at the starting line with me. In my age group, grand masters (age fifty and up), the majority of fe-males weren't given even the mixed support that I had as a child. I must thank each of the masters women who are there. I know what it takes to run against the tide, go against the peer-group pressure that requires conformity, and defy those inner doubts. I know how hard it is to arrive at a race and see all those larger and stronger males. But with each passing event, we are giving the world new ways to finish the saying "a woman's place is . . . " Now, more than ever, a woman's place is on the track, on the bike, and in the water on a triathlon racecourse.

Not all men are comfortable with these changes, or are willing to accept women biking down the road in front of them. In their discomfort, they might try to put you down. Even spouses and partners can feel intimi-dated by your interest in triathlon and try to discourage you. But don't allow yourself to be discouraged. As your partner sees how happy you are training and racing, he will most likely find your enthusiasm to be conta-gious. The men in your life have an opportunity to be spectators to your success. If you participate in a women's triathlon, you will be amazed by the number of men cheering on the sidelines, playing the all-important role of supporter.

Besides the barriers that come from within and the barriers that you may face from your partner, there are, sadly, barriers to women's success that come from within the sport itself. Do race promoters and the media take women as seriously as men? In most races, women start in waves behind the men. They frequently receive smaller and fewer trophies, and the winners on the awards stage who receive the loudest applause and the most attention are always the top finishers in the men's division. The photos in the newspaper the next day usually show the men's winner breaking the tape. If there is a picture of the women's winner, it is typically buried in the "continued on the back page" part of the article, just as women's results are. When reporters interview a female professional triathlete, they often highlight her marital status or how many children she has alongside her race results, the underlying implication being that even though she is an athlete, she is a wife and/or mother first. Not as often do I read of a male triathlete as "husband and father of three."

When I became one of triathlon's first professional triathletes, men in our sport were earning more than women in prize money and always, as is the case today, getting better sponsorship deals. I'll never forget when I finished third at the Nice Triathlon (France) in 1982, and John Howard, the third-place male, was handed a check for $7,000, while I was handed a check for $3,000. When I stated to the French race organizers that I had swum, biked, and run the same distances as my male counterpart but earned 57 percent less for the same effort, they said that there were not as many women in the race as men.

At that moment, I resolved to address gender discrimination and to inspire and enable more women to compete in the sport. As the then vice president of what is now the Olympic governing body, USA Triathlon (USAT), and as a member of the original rules committee, I helped to ensure there would be equal prize money for men and women as part of the sanctioning requirements. I expect that women will soon trump men in participation, though I wonder if women's prize money will ever consistently equal men's worldwide.

As the sport has evolved, women have become involved in triathlon in ever-increasing numbers. Currently, 37 percent of USAT members are female, and that number is growing. In addition, one-third of these women are in the age group for those between the ages of thirty-five and fifty. As of 2008, women made up 27 percent of the competitors in the Ford Ironman World Championship in Kona. What we see in the media doesn't reflect this rise in participation.

There are other signs of the upswing in women's participation in triathlon as well as sports in general. The Women's Sports Foundation shows that before Title IX (the 1972 federal law prohibiting discrimination on the basis of sex in educational programs, including athletics), 1 in 25 women played sports. Now, that number is a stunning 1 in 3.

GETTING OFF THE SIDELINES AND INTO THE SPORT

You might attend triathlons or athletic events regularly, but not as a participant. Maybe you've been sitting on the sidelines as a spectator. You've come to the races to support your man, helped to carry the gear, entertained the kids, taken pictures at the finish line, and brought the post-race food and drinks. You've given the massages, and in return you've received laurels of praise for your support. Maybe you've wondered about joining a race yourself, and then you saw this book and decided to explore the idea. And perhaps you are wondering whether your partner will be there to support you in return. Will he bring the kids and the camera and wait for you to finish? Why not give him the opportunity? You may just find that your partner is not only willing to support you, but thrilled to have your companionship on bike rides, swims, and runs.

CHALLENGES FOR WOMEN TRIATHLETES

Women are encouraged to believe that time spent on themselves is time lost, and few women want to live just for themselves. But with the added energy and fitness that a triathlon lifestyle can bring, how might you be inspired to achieve in other ways? What training can bring you, beyond a certain level of fitness, is the knowledge that if you can compete in a triathlon, you can achieve other goals that the people around you can benefit from.

> Not to have confidence in one's own body is to lose confidence in oneself. . . . It is precisely the female athletes, who, being positively interested in their own game, feel themselves less handicapped in comparison with the male.
> —Simone de Beauvoir, The Second Sex

Are you worried that the time you spend training will take time away from your kids or your partner? Read on to find out how the time you spend training can benefit them. Do you think all of this may be great for the young, but you are too old to start? Banish that thought: Plenty of women are still fit and still participating well into their seventies and early eighties.

Relationships

Being a triathlete takes time and energy, and some women fear their commitment to the sport will make it difficult to maintain their relationship with their "significant others." It's true that the time spent apart can lead to hardships if not handled carefully. The division of daily duties can become a source of conflict. Your life outside the relationship, and the camaraderie that develops with training buddies, can cause friction in the relationship or make partners feel more distant from each other.

TRAINING AND RELATIONSHIPS

Sports psychologist Charles Brown has given advice on how to nego-tiate a triathlon training schedule while maintaining a healthy relationship:

Exercise with your partner. That way, you can spend time together *and* do the training you need.

Develop a special supportive role for your partner. Partners who are in-volved in the triathlon process will feel more invested in that aspect of your life. Your partner might want to act as a race volunteer or photographer, for example.

Talk about the impact of training. Acknowledging the time training takes and the pressures that it can put on the relationship is one way of clearing the air if these issues become a problem.

Stay socially active as a couple. Get together with mutual friends, not just your training buddies. Otherwise, your partner could feel isolated and less a part of your life.

There are certainly aspects of triathlon that could contribute to the decay of personal relationships. Triathlon, like running, is often a solitary endeavor that can become both self-absorptive and narcissistic. Even if both partners participate in multisport, training together is not always practical. Training also leads to enhanced self-confidence. This new or increased self-esteem can lead to subtle and not-so-subtle changes in a relationship. A woman just becoming more serious about athletics may question her life choices, among them whether to proceed with a marriage or have children. And there's just no denying that training takes time. The time it takes to train is sometimes the same time that a triathlete would have spent with friends and family. Sadly, the competition for time can be such a fierce battle that when the dust settles, there may not be a relationship.

Training alone can't make or break a marriage—or any other relation-ship—or divide a family. However, if training becomes an obsession and dominates your life to the exclusion of all else, it's time to do some self-analysis in order to find out what has driven you to such an extreme. Sport should enhance your life, providing you with the riches of health and good experiences, but it is a monster if it controls you.

Although negative consequences are possible, they are not by any means common. There are also aspects of multisport that can have a positive effect on personal relationships. Training can lead to stability, commitment, discipline, and tenacity, and getting in shape often results in increased emotional stability, toughness, and flexibility. When both of the partners in a relationship are meeting personal goals, staying active, and fulfilling their potential in their areas of interest, the relationship is generally stronger, not weaker.

Couples can benefit from sharing a lifestyle that includes athletic participation. Being a triathlete may strain a healthy relationship, just as exercise can strain a healthy heart—but it can be for the good, strengthening the relationship over the long run!

Tri-Parents

After having children, parents often must redefine what "tri-fitness" means to them. Luckily, you're the one who gets to write that new definition, so you can either give up training and wallow in soap operas and chocolate or get with a program. Taking care of your physical self *is* taking care of your kids. After all, you must have energy to keep pace with the kids' shenanigans, energy that comes from good health and exercise. And while you are exercising, you'll be showing them that it's important to take care of your health and be fit. Your choices will enhance their lives, too. Sure, it's tough to be a fit mom, but it pales in comparison to giving birth. You've overcome plenty of obstacles and challenges as a mother, too. That's how tough you are. You will have to work out the logistics, but training will bring so many rewards that you won't want to turn back.

Age

When you participate in a triathlon, a race organizer will write your age on the back of your leg with a marker. If you are a masters level triathlete, you should consider that indelible ink a badge of honor. You've come a long way to earn that number. But what effect will your age have on triathlon performance? Should your expectations for your performance change as you age?

FIVE WAYS TO THRIVE AS A TRI-PARENT

Here are a few ideas about how you and your kids can thrive as you train for triathlon:

Get the right equipment. If your children are young, you may need to invest in a baby jogger for running, a backpack baby carrier for walking, or a bike trailer for cycling.

Find another parent to be your training "partner." We typically think of training partners as people who provide companionship for us while training. In this case, your training partner will be a support to you as a parent, and vice versa. While one parent is working out, the other watches the children. The children love it, because they can be outdoors, too (which equates with play to them). If both moms have children about the same age, then the children get the benefit of having a fun playdate. If you can't find a fellow parent to be your training partner, try local health clubs and triathlon clubs.

Join an athletic club that provides child care. Check before you join to make sure child care will be available when you need it, and ask other parents about their experiences with the club.

Enroll your children in sports programs. At the same time your kids are learning to swim or training with their soccer, basketball, or softball teams, you can train. I know one professional athlete who brings her bike and track stand to her kids' games.

Involve your kids in your pursuits. If you are concerned about the time you are "taking away" from your children to train for that all-consuming race, remember that you are being a role model, especially for your daughters. Encourage your kids to become race supporters. They can make "Go Mommy, Go!" signs or t-shirts. Your children will not only be inspired to be more healthy themselves, they will also take pride in your accomplishments.

The answers to these questions are mixed. It is true that as we age, athletic ability decreases, on average. However, that does not mean that your own individual athletic ability must decline as you age. If you sit at a desk for thirty years with minimal interest in fitness, and then begin to work out at fifty, you will grow stronger and more fit over time.

Historically and socially, there is a taboo in America—for women in particular—about disclosing one's age. The reason is that our culture heralds youth and the kind of beauty, sexiness, and vitality that it represents. And

SEE JANE TRI: WOMEN-ONLY EVENTS

If you are new to triathlons, you may be looking into trying a women-only race. Or you might wonder why women-only events exist, asking why we all don't just get on with racing without drawing attention to gender difference. Doesn't this just foster a sense that women are not good enough to "compete with the boys"?

Maggie Sullivan, who moved on to direct the Trek Women Triathlon Series after being the series director for the Danskin Women's Triathlon Series since 1992, says, "I do think there's a sense of safety when women are amongst their own. It's not that they feel unsafe with men or in dual-gender events but that they feel more safe and more supported when they're with each other."

Women-only events and training groups provide a support network, especially for those who lack confidence as athletes. Women traditionally have been encouraged to exercise mainly as a way to stay thin and attractive, not as a way to promote a healthy lifestyle or to excel at a particular sport. Women's events give women the opportunity to help each other address fear and self-doubt. In addition, many of these events offer the opportunity to train for the event as part of a women-only team, through organizations like my company, Heart Zones® USA, and that can be a very valuable experience.

yet, when I set the masters world record at the Ironman in the mid-1980s, it was a record that I cherished particularly because it meant that as I was getting older, I was getting better. Prevalent attitudes toward aging in this country haven't reflected my Ironman experience—it is more common to hear that as you get older you get worse. In fact, each year I get older, though my times are not better, my health, my fitness, and the joy I take in finishing a race become greater. It's more than an attitude about aging, it is a fact: It gets better as you get older if you stay fit.

If you are past your midpoint and considering starting a triathlon program, I urge you to begin training. Of course, like anyone else beginning a fitness program, regardless of age, you should check with your physician first. Once he or she gives you the go-ahead, set your goals and move forward, using the guidelines in this book. You will glean important psychological, physiological, and social benefits; the excitement of a new challenge in itself can make it worth your while to take the triathlon adventure ride. You're never too old to start something new. Some people might retire from life at age fifty and while away their time in a recliner, but that doesn't mean you have to do the same.

For me, aging is a secret athletic weapon, because each year I understand so much more about the sports experience—and learn so much more from the experiences I have as well. If you asked me why I did so well at the Ironman Japan Triathlon one year as a masters competitor, I would tell you it was because I knew what it would take to excel in a way I'd never known before. It wasn't my heart and lungs that made it possible; it was being the best at who I am—a triathlete and a woman.

WOMEN TRIATHLETES WHO CAME BEFORE YOU

From triathlon's beginnings, women have been in it for the duration—the long haul and even the hard crawl. Triathlon stands out in the history of sports, since from its inception female triathletes have been accepted as bona fide competitors, not as a sideshow to the main event. Compare this with track, where women were barred from competing in anything longer than 200 meters until the 1960 Olympic Games, because the International Olympic Committee decreed that greater distances were too strenuous for the female constitution. The women's 3,000-meter run wasn't even added to the Olympics until 1984, the same year the women's marathon was first included as an Olympic sport. Finally, triathlon is an Olympic event, and women's triathlon was the opening event for the 2000 Olympics in Sydney, Australia.

Julie Moss brought a new level of attention to the sport in 1982 by showing that you don't need to win a race to be remembered and respected. In that race, she collapsed, pulled herself up, stumbled again, and eventually crawled to the finish line even as Kathleen McCartney passed her. She showed human spirit and dedication in the face of ultimate challenge. Moss's bravery drew people to the sport for many reasons, but one prominent reason is that triathlon can be about reaching your personal best and not annihilating the field. ABC television captured the moment and televised it across the world as one of the most heroic finishes ever in the history of sports. (I didn't see Julie's finish at the time because I was still back on the course. I ended up tying for third with Lyn Brooks. See the next section for my story of that race.) Many current Ironpeople have said that watching Julie crawl those last yards so inspired them as they watched from their living rooms that they decided to take up the sport. In

1987 the scene was replayed as Jan Ripple crawled across the finish line, suffering in the same way, and an amazing moment of combined abasement and victory was again presented to the world.

According to European multitriathlon champion Sarah Springman, a professional triathlete with a doctoral degree in engineering, now a professor in Switzerland, "Triathlon arrived in Europe in 1982 with the first Nice

WOMEN IN TRIATHLON HISTORY

Women have been committed to the sport of triathlon at every level, from the first-timer doing a sprint, to elite athletes, to women who have helped develop the sport as race directors, or, like me, through involvement with its governing body, USA Triathlon. Here is a timeline of some highlights of women's participation.

1974: First modern-day triathlon takes place in Mission Bay, California, with women as competitors.

1979: In the second year of the Ironman competition, Lyn Lemaire places fifth and becomes the first Ironwoman.

1980: Valerie Silk becomes race director of the Ironman and remains as either race director or chair until 1989. The race is moved from Waikiki to the lava fields of Kona on the Big Island of Hawaii.

1982: Julie Moss, suffering from severe dehydration and exhaustion, crumples to the ground 15 yards from the finish line, moments before Kathleen McCartney passes her for the first-place victory. Moss crawls across the finish

ABOVE: JULIE MOSS
RIGHT: PAULA NEWBY-FRASER

line in an inspirational moment to take second place. (I tied for third with Lyn Brooks, coming in behind Julie Moss.)

The first computerized timing program, which produces split times (including transition times), is developed by Bonnie Miller (Joseph).

The first women-only triathlon is held at Marine World Africa USA, sponsored by Bonne Bell, the skin care and cosmetics company.

SUSAN WILLIAMS

The first European triathlon, the Nice Triathlon, is held.

1990: Danskin, the women's dancewear company, introduces a new line of women's athletic apparel and sponsors a three-city national triathlon series.

1992: Paula Newby-Fraser sets an Ironman course record with a time of 8:55:28, taking eleventh place overall.

1999: Lyn Brooks completes her twentieth and final consecutive Ironman World Championship.

2000: Triathlon becomes an Olympic Sport, and the women's event opens the Olympic Games in Sydney, Australia.

2004: American Susan Williams wins the bronze in the Olympic women's event in Athens—the first American triathlete to medal.

2008: American Laura Bennett places fourth in the women's event in the Olympics held in Beijing.

Yvonne van Vlerken beats Paula Newby-Fraser's 1994 time in the Quelle Challenge in Roth Germany, with a time of 8:45:48.

2009: British triathlete Chrissie Wellington claims a third world title when she wins the 2009 Ford Ironman World Championship in Kona, setting another new course record wtih a time of 8:54:02. The Trek Women Triathlon Series begins, led by Series Director Maggie Sullivan and me as the spokesperson.

CHRISSIE WELLINGTON

Triathlon." In 1984, Springman and her all-female team were competing in the London-to-Paris Triathlon (which consisted of a swim across the English Channel, individual 30-mile cycling time trials, a 50-mile team time trial to Paris, and a marathon run by a relay team of four). Her team finished in tenth place out of sixteen mostly male teams. The outcome "rearranged some male egos and impressions of triathlon women," Iron-woman Springman recalls.

When Paula Newby-Fraser broke the course record with a 9:01 in 1988, few ignored the fact that no man had broken 9:01 before 1983. Her 1988 Ironman finish (eleventh overall) has been called the "greatest performance in endurance sports history."

In triathlon, amateurs perhaps feel a stronger link to, and gain inspiration from, elite athletes, because an Olympic athlete and an age grouper can do the same sport on the same course, and in many events, compete in the same race. Elite women in this country have been tough competitors and provide inspiration for those women seeking to bring their involvement in this sport to the next level. The United States won its first and only (so far) Olympic triathlon medal in 2004, when Susan Williams placed third in the women's event in Athens. Another particularly inspiring athlete is Olympian Laura Bennett, who achieved fourth place in the 2008 Beijing Olympics at the age of thirty-three. She had narrowly missed out on the Olympics twice, having been the second alternate in Sydney in 2000 and the first alternate in Athens in 2004. Her continued commitment to the sport is an example to all women.

REFLECTIONS ON THE FINISH LINE

In my second Ironman competition, I shared a memorable finish-line experience. The year before, in 1981, I had finished second in what is now considered a slow 12 hours and 37 minutes, and a woman named Lyn Brooks had taken third place. In February 1982—the same year Julie Moss electrified viewers with her crawl to the finish line—I knew that Lyn was ahead of me as I started to run the marathon, and I knew that running was her first sport, as it was mine.

After 9 hours spent swimming 2.4 miles and cycling 112, at the 5-mile point in the marathon, I caught Lyn. We were both exhausted and reduced to running a fatigue-laden, 8.5-minute-per-mile pace, so we shuffled along, side by side. It was the first time we had met—we knew of each other only by reputation.

Neither of us had the energy left to compete, so I asked Lyn if she would like to run those last few miles together and tie. Without pause, she agreed, and a wave of relief passed over me. I'll never forget those last few miles together running, sweating, and frying under the Hawaiian sun that gave no mercy. That day Lyn and I shared something that is difficult to find in most places in life—the mutual respect, trust, and love that athletes experience when they have given their all in pursuit of self-accomplishment and the finish line.

We ended up tying for third, with a final time of 11 hours and 51 minutes, almost one hour faster than our times had been the year before. In fact, our 1982 time was fast enough to have won the 1981 race. Lyn and I were obviously not the only ones improving our times. Indeed, the toppling of finish-time records in women's triathlon has been a consistent phenomenon, and we have come a long way very quickly.

At the pre-race party several nights before the 1998 Ironman, the master of ceremonies honored all those who were seasoned triathletes, as is his tradition. He asked everyone who had finished the Hawaii event five times or more to stand. Hundreds of the 1,500 entrants stood. Then, slowly, he asked everyone to sit who had not finished the race six times. Dozens lowered themselves into their chairs. Next, he asked those who hadn't finished seven times, then eight, then nine, then ten times, and so on, to sit down, until he finally asked for those who had not finished the race eighteen times to take a seat.

Two individuals were left standing—1982 and 1985 Ironman champion Scott Tinley, and Lyn Brooks.

He then asked anyone who had not finished nineteen times to sit down.

Scott sat. Lyn stood. Lyn was the solitary figure left standing at the end of this rite, in an audience of thousands, in an event that draws competitors from around the entire globe, in a race that compares to no other. The woman who tied with me for third place was still racing what is considered one of the toughest races in the world. In 1999, she finished her twentieth and last consecutive Ironman.

2

Get Inspired

As I reached the turnaround point on the 112-mile bike leg of Iron-man Japan, I saw a banner stretched above the road, the only English banner among the hundreds the Japanese had placed along the route. On it were three short words that struck me with the force of a thousand. The power in the brevity of this statement has had a lasting impact on me: *Do your best!*

As a woman in triathlon, this is what I race for and this is what I want for you, regardless of your finish time or place.

Completing your first triathlon is a great goal, and one that can lead you to a whole new idea of yourself. I have seen thousands of women make their way to the finish line of a triathlon—an accomplishment they never would have considered possible before they started training. Finishing is winning, and along the way you will also gain fitness and pride in yourself and your achievement. Your goals will get you there.

Before we get to work on your personal goals, consider three questions that will begin to bring into focus what competing in this event will bring to you. Some common responses are also provided.

Why do you want to do a triathlon?
I want to get back into shape.
It gives me motivation to reach for a goal.
My friends are training for it.
I want to lose some fat/weight.

~~~~~

What obstacles do you expect to face?
I don't know how.
I am scared and I might not finish.
I've never done anything like this before.
I don't have time to add one more activity to my lifestyle.

~~~~~

What will motivate you to complete your first triathlon?
I love to be outdoors.
I find new challenges exciting.
I need to exercise because I know that it is good for me to do so.

THINKING WEIGHT LOSS?

Many women begin training for their first sprint-distance triathlon because they want to lose weight and get in shape. If you can identify with this goal, I would encourage you not to focus on the negative idea of losing weight, but on the positive one of gaining fitness. We all need to begin our training with a goal that holds meaning for us and connects our hearts to our performance. Losing weight is a goal, but isn't it better to set your sights on something you can gain, rather than on something you can lose?

If you are not training for your first triathlon—but your fifth, or your tenth—you may still share some of the sentiments mentioned above. You may have ambitions of improving your performance or tackling a longer triathlon for the first time. From your perspective as a more experienced triathlete, consider some possible responses to similar questions:

Why are you training for triathlons this season?
I am more motivated to train regularly with a race on the calendar.

I finished my last race thinking I could do more.
I want to build more strength.

~~~~~

What obstacles do you expect to face?
Training will be harder this time around.
I am worried that I might not make my goal time.
I've never finished a swim, bike, or run leg of this distance.
I don't have much free time in my schedule for more training.

~~~~~

What will motivate you to compete at a higher level than in your first triathlon?
I found a training partner or training group with similar goals.
I want to achieve a faster or longer race before my next birthday.
I purchased a plane ticket to a destination race.

TRAIN, DON'T EXERCISE

When you head out the door for a run or bike ride, do you think of it as exercise or training? There's a big difference between the two. It is the motivation behind the activity that separates those who train from those who exercise.

Someone who exercises does it usually for the purpose of getting or staying in shape. A person who trains has a greater goal in mind, a dream. Whether you want to enter a race, beat a nemesis, learn more about yourself, meet new friends, or expand your horizons, what counts is that you set goals and accomplish them. In my playbook, athletes define their goals and then train to achieve them.

A woman who is new to running might train with the goal of competing in her first 5-km race. An Ironwoman trains with the goal of testing everything she has in the most grueling one-day race around. Exercise is part of training, but it isn't the only part or even the most important part. If you identify your goals, you will have a greater purpose to drive you out the door to train even when you don't feel like it.

MAKING YOUR GOALS PERSONAL

The best goals are aligned with our values, those things on which we are willing to spend our resources—time, effort, money. You can identify values in all areas of your life, and these priorities change over time. They motivate you, direct your focus, and define how you feel when you are done. Start from the heart, taking responsibility for where you are right now. Take some time to identify, clarify, and prioritize your values. For example, for some women, family and relationships are at the top of the list. For others, work, appearance, or intellectual pursuits are important. What is important to you? What makes you feel good about yourself? Are there changes you need to make in your life to better align your choices (how you spend your time and resources) with your values?

Next, consider why you do what you do when it comes to your athletic pursuits. In short, why are you training? Maybe you have a family and little fitness, and you want to do something for yourself and your health. Or maybe you've hit a fitness plateau and really want to accomplish more. What is it that you hope to accomplish through multisport? Write down your top three goals when it comes to triathlon and what it means in the big picture for your life.

I encourage you to do this exercise now. Don't wait until later to identify the three things you hope to get from training. This is an important step in defining your goals.

Once your goal comes into focus, keep the big picture in mind. The things you are training for are large goals, and there are many smaller goals that will help you achieve them along the way. As we get into the training chapter, you'll find that the microcycles of training target these smaller goals.

Here are some examples of specific goals that you can set as markers en route to your larger goal:

To get back into shape and stay in shape so I can do my best.
To finish a run that is at least three-quarters of the race distance four weeks prior to the event.
To beat the clock—the time I have planned on finishing the race.
To help my friend get through training and finish the race.
To finish with a joyful smile on my face.

Although the smaller goals are important, I firmly believe the large goal is what you need to fix your thoughts on. It's like having an elephant in your garden, trampling your violets. You could work on completing a small goal—protecting your violets—by fencing the flowers off with chicken wire. However, since elephants aren't chickens, that probably won't work very well. What would work better is to focus on the bigger picture—getting rid of the elephant—by calling your local animal rescue program. Give your attention to the elephants in your life and your violets will grow beautifully.

OVERCOMING OBSTACLES

Because there's more at stake when you decide to train, not exercise, I can promise you that obstacles will happen. If there's anything to be learned from Chapter 1, it's this: Women are strong, and we've achieved athletic feats that our grandmothers never had the opportunity to dream of. If you need more convincing, let's take a look at what I know are the biggest obstacles most women face. In each case, there is motivation to be found, and a clarity of purpose that will prove very rewarding.

Available Time

If you think about it, you have this in common with a professional athlete: the same twenty-four hours in a day. The difference is that a professional has too much time for training and consequently faces the threat of over-training. For you, on the other hand, time is probably scarce. You might compensate by cutting corners (sleep or meals with family) to get in your workouts. But these sacrifices will come at a cost.

Think of it this way. If a workday consists of eight hours, this means you have the equivalent of three full eight-hour workdays in each twenty-four-hour period. If you spend one of these segments at work, and you sleep for another segment, you still have one bonus segment—the equivalent of one full workday—left to use as you wish—and this is where you can fit in your training and other activities.

Training for triathlons truly requires that you learn to deal with time. You will have to juggle the time demands of training schedules, sleep requirements, good nutrition, professional work, your family, and, finally, your own personal growth, in a day that contains only twenty-four hours. Perhaps you've come to the conclusion that you simply cannot accomplish as much as you would like to in one day. Ask yourself whether this conclusion is justified. Is it possible that there is some time in your day that is wasted? Are the things that you hope to accomplish in a day in line with your values and your goals? And are the things you actually spend your time on in line with these values and goals?

The reality is that if there's consistently a huge difference between the time you have and the demands you place on yourself, you will eventually crash and burn. Stay ignited, and find a new way to relate to time. It has been said that referees call time, prisoners serve time, musicians mark time, historians record time, slackers kill time, and statisticians keep time. As athletes, we race against time. The fact remains that we are all given the same amount of time. There are still 24 hours in a day, 168 hours in a week. Make it your goal to use them fully—live every moment.

Know-how

If you are new to triathlon, you undoubtedly have countless questions about how to approach your goals. Where you are today—in terms of fitness, endurance, and speed, for example—will be an important factor in how you shape your training. Fitness and endurance will be key to finishing your first race, while speed and intensity will be more important for experienced triathletes. Rest assured, you've come to the right place, and Chapter 3 will explain everything you need to know. Knowing how to train can be difficult even for experienced triathletes, and sometimes even more of an obstacle.

If you have a few triathlons under your race belt you may be finding it hard to know if you are still improving. When someone moves from doing no activity to doing some activity, the benefits are obvious and significant. As you approach the limit of your fitness, performance, muscle development, and stamina, it won't appear to be in proportion to the amount of training you invested. Rather, at this level you are putting in an increasing amount of effort for smaller returns. Each percentage point of fitness and skill improvement costs more than the previous point. You must be kind to yourself—and patient—because the improvements will probably be harder to detect. You can also look to Chapters 3 and 4 and the sport-specific chapters for ideas about how to refine your technique and do more quality workouts that can lead to the breakthroughs you're looking for.

Support

In Chapter 1, we talked about the challenges of maintaining your relationships as you train for triathlon. As women, we are accustomed to being the ones who give support rather than asking for it. When I travel from city to city to talk to triathletes about how to train, I look out in the audience and see mothers with young kids in strollers, professionals, and women who have years of experience written on their faces. All of these women have friends and family who count on them for support, just like you do. And yet they come because they are looking for something more. Something just for them.

You are the source of your performance. This is the accountability piece in training. You can't blame others, or your circumstances. Some people may obstruct you, and some may help you enthusiastically, but you are the one who either puts them off or invites them aboard. You will determine your own success and your own failure. You can ultimately achieve the best overall condition of your life.

It won't be easy. It won't happen quickly. It won't be without sacrifice. And it isn't based on luck. Rarely are the accomplishments that we strive for achieved without giving. When you get to that first finish line, or reach a new personal best, you will know that it hasn't been without direction, for you will have modeled yourself in pursuit of goals and good habits. Nor will it have been without tools, because triathlon requires the tools of the trade. Or without knowledge, for, if you follow the guidelines set out in this book, it will be with the help of a heart rate monitor and a few simple training principles that you will grow toward achieving your full potential.

There are times when you are so focused on what you have set for yourself as an achievement that once that level is obtained, you might lose perspective. The triathlon event is not everything in life, but it can be life changing. Being reminded of what you have already achieved by participating in a mentoring capacity creates a healthy appreciation for your abilities. Through a triathlon community composed of many performance levels, a dose of reality creates a balanced and compassionate look at yourself and other triathletes. We can all be victors in the challenges we set for ourselves, but to be superwinners, you must accept the additional challenge of lending your experience and knowledge to others. When the race is over, life still goes on, and the next day brings fresh opportunities. Lend your voice and experiences, share with others around you how and why you work out, and help build a network of women triathletes who are living the healthy, active lifestyle.

The human being is one of the most awesome athletic wonders to ever walk the planet. When we respond to the thrill of an event like the Olympics, we're not responding to whose training regime was the best or which country had the best nutritionist. Instead, we respond to people who grasp a small part of that potential in each one of us and reach out.

It is that reach—especially the reach toward others—that is important. I have been lucky enough to stand at the starting lines with great athletes, and I've been privileged to make whatever small marks I've made. But what I have come to learn is that the reach is more important than the grasp.

The Fundamentals of Smart Training

When I was training for the 1984 Olympic Marathon trials, after barely qualifying with a 2-hour, 50-minute finish at the Phoenix Marathon, I used a hard/easy training cycle. One day I would go hard, running either short or long intervals followed by rest intervals, and the next day I would run easy for long-distance training.

This is a simplified version of the training approach I now recommend. Many coaches refer to the progression as "periodization," and I think of my approach as a hybrid of this training method. I now use "progressive training," which is the sequencing and distribution of training load within a specific training time period. Each phase of training has a different goal or focus. The overall effect of the training sequence is best summarized as stress, response, adaptation. In Chapter 4 we'll take a closer look at the different phases of training and how they work together to help you achieve your ultimate goal.

Stress → Response → Adaptation

Your training will depend on many factors, but it all comes down to your capacity for training stress and how quickly you adapt to that stress. In triathlon, it's possible to make a little training go a long way. If you train

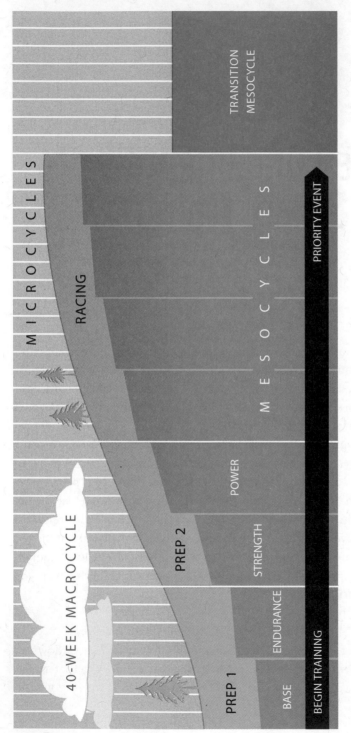

Note: A 40-week plan would be more appropriate for an intermediate or experienced athlete.

FIGURE 3.1: Progressive training

appropriately, you don't need to train hard or long. (Of course, if you're training for an Ironman-distance event, there is no way around long hours of training.) You can get to a new height of fitness, and get there fast, by using a smart training plan and a few training tools. First, let's review the fundamentals that make up smart training.

INTRO TO PROGRESSIVE TRAINING

The experience of training can be compared to climbing a mountain (see Figure 3.1). Your journey to the summit (the race or goal you are training for) is the *macrocycle*. Imagine yourself beginning your trek. At first, you are walking a gradual incline that is easy to moderate. As you reach the base of the climb you can see the changing terrain ahead. The different types of terrain you pass through represent *mesocycles* of training. Each mesocycle can be planned based on specific training objectives (base, endurance, strength, power) leading up to your goal race. In each mesocycle the focus of your workouts will change to meet those objectives.

Microcycles are like the inclines, twists, and turns that you encounter within each mesocycle of your training. My training plans will recommend a specific amount of time to be spent in each heart rate zone as a way of distributing intensity between the workouts. There will come a point when, as you climb up to the next mesocycle, workout intensity shifts from being mostly *aerobic* to being mostly *anaerobic*, or above threshold. You might think of this as getting to above treeline, where the air is thin and your lungs are working hard. This marks a significant increase in the intensity of your training. As the weeks go by, you will train in *progressively* higher training zones that have more weight and value in terms of your training load.

In this chapter, you will learn how to calculate your training load, which involves the frequency, duration, and intensity of your workout sessions. You will learn how to structure a workout so you can get the most out of every training session. You will also learn more about the different types of workouts—and why you need to incorporate all of them for successful training. If you are new to triathlon this is a good overview, but don't get too bogged down in the details. In Chapter 4 you'll find two complete training plans that will put all of this into practice and prepare you for your first event. Then you can return to this chapter and perhaps get more out of it.

TRAINING VOLUME

Your weekly training should be 20–25 percent swimming, 40–50 percent cycling, and 20–25 percent running, because this generally reflects the breakdown of distances on race day. Naturally, you will need to adjust your training volume to give more time to your weakest sport.

As a general rule, over the course of your training you need to work up to distances that are at least 70 percent of the swim, bike, and run mileage you will do on race day. Table 3.1 lists the common race distances for sprint, international, half-Ironman, and Ironman distances. You can most likely count on that extra 30 percent coming from race-day exhilaration and the joy of knowing that your long training is finally at a natural, expected conclusion. Let's consider some examples.

> **TIP** Your weekly training should be 20–25 percent swimming, 40–50 percent cycling, and 20–25 percent running.

To finish an international-distance triathlon (commonly referred to as an Olympic-distance triathlon), you want to be able to complete in a single workout approximately 70 percent of those distances: For the swim that's about 30 minutes (0.7 of a mile), on the bike it is a ride of about 90 minutes (18–20 miles), and for the run about 45 minutes (4–5 miles). The estimated durations will vary based on your typical pace, so focus on distance, rather than duration, as you build race-readiness.

In case the ultimate long-distance triathlon challenge is of interest to you (and I encourage you to imagine it), preparation for an Ironman-race distance would build to a 1.7-mile swim, an 80-mile bike ride, and an 18-mile run. Sprint triathlons are considerably shorter, but they are no walk in the park. Most professional sprint triathletes train long distances to condition themselves for race day.

TABLE 3.1 Common Triathlon Race Distances			
	SWIM	**BIKE**	**RUN**
Sprint	750 m / 0.5 mi.	20 km / 12.4 mi.	5 km / 3.1 mi.
International (Olympic)	1,500 m / 0.93 mi.	40 km / 24.8 mi.	10 km / 6.2 mi.
Half-Ironman	1.2 mi.	56 mi.	13.1 mi.
Ironman	2.4 mi.	112 mi.	26.2 mi.

INTENSITY

There is a time and place for training hard. Intensity is your measure of just how hard you trained. This is also where some training tools come into play. Before we get technical, let's review the most basic measure of intensity.

Rating of Perceived Exertion

Even if you've never heard of the Rate of Perceived Exertion (RPE), or the Borg scale, you've probably used it intuitively. The Borg scale, originally designed by Gunnar Borg, was intended to give you an approximation of your heart rate at different levels of exertion. The scale went from 6 to 20, estimating a resting heart rate of 60 bpm (beats per minute) and a maximum heart

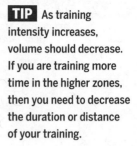

TIP As training intensity increases, volume should decrease. If you are training more time in the higher zones, then you need to decrease the duration or distance of your training.

rate of 200 bpm for the average person. Each rating was described by how an athlete felt while working out at different intensities—ranging from an easy effort to incredibly hard.

The Borg scale was later adapted by Carl Foster. I prefer his version because it can be tricky to consistently measure the subtle differences between a rating of, say, 13 and 14 on the Borg scale, both of which are moderate. Foster's scale, with 10 levels, leaves less room for interpretation—and, of course, we have countless tools to give us a clear picture of heart rate, which we'll look at next. See Table 3.2 for a comparison of Foster's revised RPE scale and heart rate training zones.

Researchers disagree on the extent to which RPE is an accurate measure of training intensity. Really, it depends on how well you know yourself. But even then, some days your training session will seem unreasonably easy or hard. How you feel when you train is important, but it is best considered in conjunction with heart rate or some other measure of intensity.

Heart Rate

When we look at heart rate and RPE together, we can have a more objective measure of intensity. While subjective methods may seem easier to grasp, they can also be misinterpreted. Have you ever been told by a fitness instructor or coach to "feel the burn" or to "go harder"? Training harder day after day is not likely to give you the results you're after. If you are looking for improvements in fitness, your training will have to entail more than just high intensity. It needs to be specific and it needs to allow for recovery. By using a heart rate monitor—and applying the information that it supplies in the specific ways described below—you can accomplish more in your training.

TABLE 3.2 Training Zones			
ZONE	PERCENT OF MAXIMUM HEART RATE	RATE OF PERCEIVED EXERTION (RPE)	DESCRIPTION
5	90–100	9–10	Extremely hard to maximum effort
4	80–89	7–8	Very, very hard
3	70–79	5–6	Hard
2	60–69	3–4	Moderate to somewhat hard
1	50–59	1–2	Very light, easy

There are five heart rate zones used to reflect exercise intensity. Each one promises different results. By training in each zone you can maximize your fitness. In order to identify your training zones you have to first identify your maximum heart rate or your threshold heart rate. By definition, a maximum heart rate is the fastest your body will let your heart contract within a 1-minute period. You only reach this heart rate in an all-out effort. You'll know you are there when your intensity increases and your heart rate does not increase. Please note that maximum heart rate is not age-dependent (as previously believed).

Your heart does have one true maximum heart rate—you're born with it. Your running maximum heart rate is the best approximation of your genetically determined maximum heart rate because there are more large muscle groups involved in running than in swimming or biking. Swimming is likely to produce a lower sport-specific maximum heart rate because of your body position (horizontal) and the water supporting your body weight. In testing, upper-body-intensive sports such as swimming tend to produce maximums around 10 bpm lower than running does, even for very fit people. There is some disagreement among elite cyclists and runners as to whether a maximum heart rate for the bike is likely to be lower than a running maximum heart rate. You may see very similar heart rate numbers for your cycling and running. All that matters is that you write down the number you see and retest at regular intervals.

While maximum heart rate is genetic, threshold heart rate is trainable. Threshold training anchors the five zones on the threshold heart rate number, or the intensity that is the crossover between aerobic and anaerobic (or above-aerobic) training. The maximum heart rate system anchors the zones on maximum heart rate, or the highest number that you can genetically achieve. I prefer maximum heart rate for its simplicity, so that is the method we'll use in this book. It will save you the trouble of continually testing your threshold heart rate and readjusting your training zones accordingly. (For more on threshold training, read *Heart Zones Cycling,* which I wrote with Sally Reed.) If you are new to training and or you've never used a heart rate monitor, so you don't know your maximum heart rate, you can use the test in Appendix A to arrive at a good estimate. For women beginning with less fitness, it is important to avoid pushing to total exhaustion in this test.

Ultimately, the goal (and the true definition of cardiovascular fitness) is to raise your threshold heart rate as close as possible to your maximum heart rate. So high-performance triathletes who are training to improve speed need to spend at least 25 percent of their weekly time near their threshold heart rate. Remember, threshold intensity is dynamic—it can move up or down based on daily factors. So don't get too discouraged if there are days when your threshold seems low.

ZONE 1: THE HEALTHY HEART ZONE
50–59 percent of your individual maximum heart rate (RPE 1–2)

This is the safest, most comfortable zone, reached by walking briskly, swimming easily, or doing any low-intensity activity, including mowing your lawn. Here you strengthen your heart and improve muscle mass while reducing body fat, cholesterol, blood pressure, and your risk for degenerative disease. You get healthier in this zone but not more aerobically fit—that is, it won't increase your endurance or strength, but it will improve your health.

ZONE 2: THE TEMPERATE ZONE
60–69 percent of your individual maximum heart rate (RPE 3–4)

Zone 2 is easily reached by going a little faster, such as increasing from a walk to a jog. Although still a relatively low level of effort, this zone starts training your body to increase the rate of fat released from the cells to the muscles for fuel. Some people have erroneously called this the "fat-burning zone" because up to 85 percent of the total calories burned in this zone are fat calories, but in truth we burn fat in all zones.

ZONE 3: THE AEROBIC ZONE
70—79 percent of your individual maximum heart rate (RPE 5—6)

In this zone—reached by running moderately, for example—you improve your functional capacity. The number and size of your blood vessels increase, your lung capacity and respiratory rate improve, and your heart increases in size and strength. The result is that you can exercise longer before becoming fatigued. You're still metabolizing fats and carbohydrates, but the ratio has changed to about 50—50, which means both are burning at the same rate.

> **TIP** You can do a zone 5 or upper zone 4 workout every 24 hours if each workout involves a different sport activity.
>
> The specific muscle recovery process requires 48 hours. After a red-line or upper zone 4 workout, you need to take a 48-hour break before you can train again in this specific sport activity.

ZONE 4: THE THRESHOLD ZONE
80—89 percent of your individual maximum heart rate (RPE 7—8)

This zone is reached by going hard—running faster. Here you get faster and fitter, increasing your heart rate as you cross from aerobic to anaerobic training. At this point, your heart cannot pump enough blood and oxygen to supply the exercising muscles fully, so they respond by continuing to contract anaerobically (without sufficient oxygen). This is where you "feel the burn." You can stay in this zone for a limited amount of time, usually not more than an hour. That's because the muscle just cannot sustain working anaerobically without fatiguing. The working muscles protect themselves from overwork by not being able to maintain the intensity level.

ZONE 5: THE RED-LINE ZONE
90—100 percent of your individual maximum heart rate (RPE 9—10)

This is the equivalent of running all-out and is used mostly as an "interval" training regimen—exertion done only in short- to intermediate-length bursts. Even world-class athletes can stay in this zone for only a few minutes at a time. It's not a zone most people will select for exercise, since working out here hurts and there is an increased potential for injury. You do burn lots of calories, mostly carbohydrates.

BALANCING VOLUME AND INTENSITY

Training load, or workload, is a measure of the physical stress placed on the body to achieve certain physical adaptations that result in increases in fitness. To measure your training load you need to consider the duration and frequency of your training (volume) and how hard you are working (intensity). For intermediate and advanced triathletes, training load is critical. Your daily, weekly, and monthly training should be planned to apply the appropriate amount of load in a sequential manner, with adequate time for both stress and recovery. This will optimize the training effect and result in a positive training adaptation. And this is what progressive training is all about.

> **TIPS** A single day's red-line (zone 5) workout should not exceed 10–15 percent of the total training time for the week.
>
> Total workout time in zones 4 and 5 should not exceed 25–35 percent of your total training time.

The ready-made training plans in Chapter 4 are based on a careful progression of training load leading up to race day. To be successful, you just need to follow each workout's instruction for volume and intensity. If you want to be able to adapt these training plans or create one of your own, it helps to know the logic behind the training progression. My training plans are mostly made up of four basic types of workouts that will help you balance volume and intensity from week to week:

Recovery workouts: These are zone 3 or easier—relaxed, fun, and low intensity to allow the body an opportunity for active rest.

Steady-state workouts: This is a workout where you stay at the same intensity continuously without periods of rest.

Interval workouts: This type of workout includes alternating between stress and recovery, hard and easy.

Combination workouts: This type of main set is a mix of any of the three listed above.

Table 3.3 shows how these workouts would fit into a busy week of training. If you are a beginner, start with three to six single-workout days

TABLE 3.3 Sample Training Grid			
	SWIM	**BIKE**	**RUN**
Monday	—	—	—
Tuesday	Interval	—	Steady-state
Wednesday	—	Interval	Recovery
Thursday	Steady-state	—	—
Friday	—	Steady-state	Interval
Saturday	Recovery	Combination	—
Sunday	Combination	Recovery	Combination

per week. We'll talk more about double and triple workouts later in this chapter.

If you don't know exactly what your objective is for a workout, you're not going to get as much out of it as you could have. Eliminate "junk" workouts—not only are they a waste of time, but they could ultimately hurt more than help.

When I coach athletes and train coaches using the Heart Zones Training system, every training session is designed to accomplish specific training outcomes that fit into a weekly, monthly, and annual plan. The focus of the workout, the intensity, and the duration must all contribute to meeting those objectives. We'll take a closer look at the goals of different phases of training in Chapter 4. As for the workout itself, here are five different components of successful cardiovascular training sessions, which are also summarized in Table 3.4:

Warm-up: The purpose of the warm-up is to slowly prepare the body for higher-intensity work and speed of movement. Warming up properly prevents injuries and stimulates you mentally. If you have training partners, you may still be chatting with them. Physiologically, however, changes are beginning to take place. Your core temperature and heart rate are slowly rising, and your muscles are becoming more supple. This is a time of low intensity.

Skills and drills: In this phase you will hone in on sport-specific movement patterns at an easy pace and typically moderate intensity. Games may be incorporated at this stage to make skill training more fun. Drills should focus on improving the techniques required for the specific sport. (See drills for swimming, cycling, and running in Chapters 5–7.)

TABLE 3.4 Components of a Focused Workout			
	PURPOSE	**DURATION**	**INTENSITY**
Warm-up	Gradually increases heart rate and circulates blood to working muscles	5–10%	Zones 1 & 2
Skills & drills	Focuses on biomechanics, improves sport-specific techniques, and develops balance and coordination	5–10%	Zones 2 & 3
Main set	Improves cardiovascular health, endurance and aerobic capacity, builds strength, and improves max fat-burning heart rate	60–80%	Depends on the type of workout (see Table 3.5)
Cooldown	Gradually decreases heart rate and helps blood circulate from the muscles to other parts of the body	5–10%	Zones 1 & 2
Stretching	Improves range of motion, prevents onset of muscle soreness, and helps prevent injuries	5–10%	Zones 1 & 2

Main set: The main set is the primary focus of the workout. There are typically four different types of main sets, as mentioned above: recovery, intervals, steady-state, and combinations.

Cooldown: This is the end of the workout, providing you with a much-deserved opportunity to slowly recover rather than abruptly stopping. By slowing down the intensity and pace at the end of the workout, you prevent fast drops in blood pressure and blood pooling.

Stretching: If you don't incorporate stretching into your training, you are more likely to experience tightness, which can pull on your joints, causing pain and sometimes injury. Yoga is a good supplement to your training and will help you stretch safely. (See Sage Rountree's *The Athlete's Guide to Yoga* and the supplemental flexibility workouts in *The Athlete's Pocket Guide to Yoga* for more instruction on stretching.)

Training Points

When heart rate monitors were first introduced, I developed a method of quantifying training load (training points) based on the amount of time spent in each heart rate zone. If you vary your workouts and watch your training load progression from week to week, you will be far less likely to get injured, overtrain, or burn out.

TABLE 3.5 Training Load for Four Basic Workouts		
WORKOUT DESCRIPTION	**TRAINING LOAD**	**TOTAL TIME**

RECOVERY
Warm-up
  5 min. zone 1
Main set
  Increase to 60–65% of max HR
  Hold for 30 min.
Cooldown
  5 min. zone 1
	70 points:
	10 x 1 = 10
	30 x 2 = 60
		~ 40 min.

STEADY-STATE
Warm-up
  5 min. zone 1
  5 min. zone 2
Main set
  20 min. at 75% of max HR
Cooldown
  5 min. zone 2
  5 min. zone 1
	90 points:
	10 x 1 = 10
	10 x 2 = 20
	20 x 3 = 60
		40 min.

INTERVAL
Warm-up
  5 min. zone 1
  5 min. zone 2
Main set
  2 min. at 80% of max HR
  2 min. at 70% of max HR
  Repeat 5 times.
Cooldown
  5 min. zone 1
  5 min. zone 2
	100 points:
	10 x 1 = 10
	10 x 2 = 20
	10 x 3 = 30
	10 x 4 = 40
		40 min.

COMBINATION
Warm-up
  5 min. zone 1
  5 min. zone 2
Main set
  5 min. at 70% of max HR
  Increase HR gradually (~3%) every 5 min. to
  80% of max HR, hold for 5 min., use resistance
Cooldown
  10 min. zone 2
	100–115 points:
	5 x 1 = 5
	15 x 2 = 30
	15–20 x 3 = 45–60
	5 x 4 = 20
		40–45 min.

Note: Skill or Drill sessions (5–10 min.) should follow the main set, and they will vary depending on your individual needs. Please see Chapters 5–7 for specific examples. Stretching (5–10 min.) should follow every workout.

Heart Zones Training points are the product of the intensity of the effort and the duration of the effort. Intensity is quantified by the heart rate zone, 1–5. Duration is measured in minutes. To calculate your training load, you will multiply the minutes spent training in a particular zone by the number of that zone. Table 3.5 illustrates four different 40-minute workouts. If you do the steady-state workout, you will ultimately spend 10 minutes in zone 1, 10 minutes in zone 2, and 20 minutes in zone 3. In the training load column, you can see how these values add up to a total of 90 training points. Looking at the different workouts, you can see how training load varies based on the different intensities and goals for each workout.

If you train with a heart rate monitor, it is possible to access your minutes spent in each heart rate zone for a given workout, day, or week, making training points even easier to implement. To learn how to calculate your training load for the week, see the sidebar "Weekly Training Load Goals."

WEEKLY TRAINING LOAD GOALS

Calculating the training load of a single workout is simple (the procedure is demonstrated in Table 3.5). If you do two workouts in a day, you simply add the points from the first workout to the points from the second one to derive your daily training load. Weekly training load takes a bit more time to figure out, but it's not difficult. It's simply the sum of the daily training loads that you accumulated throughout the week.

When you use this method, you'll be determining what your weekly training load should be by following the principles of progressive training, the gradual increase of training load over time. Here are some ranges that you can use for guidelines when setting training loads based on your fitness level and activity goals.

- Beginners, general fitness: 400–500 points
- Weight maintenance: 600–800 points
- Weight loss: More than 800 points
- Sprint triathlon: 800–1,000 points
- Cycle 50–75 miles or run 10 km: 1,000–1,200 points
- Olympic-distance triathlon or half-marathon: 1,200–1,500 points
- Marathon or half-Ironman-distance triathlon: 1,500–1,700 points
- Ironman-distance triathlon: 2,000–3,000 points

Work-to-Rest Ratio

Work-to-rest ratios are most useful in conjunction with your interval training. If you are swimming and the workout calls for 5 x 200 easy and 10 x 100 hard intervals, the total workload is 2,000 yards, with 50 percent easy and 50 percent hard. This is a 1:1 work-to-rest ratio. If the next day you run 5 repeat miles at a fast 7 minutes per mile, with a 2-minute rest between each mile, your run will be 45 minutes—35 minutes at a hard pace (5 repeats of 7-minute miles) and 10 minutes at an easy pace (5 repeats of 2-minute recoveries). Your work-to-rest ratio will be 3.5 to 1.

> **TIP** Increase either distance or intensity in a workout week but not both in the same week and never more than 10 percent per week at a time. To assess workload, you can look at the ratios, training points, or total workout minutes, whichever works for you.

Training Race Pace

Think of your race pace as the highest heart rate or exertion that you can sustain over the entire event. It marks the borderline that could either push you to better performance or cause you to blow up. As you become a more experienced triathlete, these high-intensity workouts will become a bigger part of your race preparation. Time trials and intervals are the key to improving your race pace. For races longer than 20 minutes, your race-pace heart rate is most likely below your threshold heart rate, unless weather or other factors force it to be higher.

Unforeseen or uncontrollable variables are proof of how helpful heart rate can be. What happens to your pace when the temperature increases 15 degrees, when you hit the hills on the course, when there is shade, when you missed the aid station, or when your blood glucose (sugar) levels drop? Your heart rate monitor will reflect your body's physiological responses to the various racing stresses, whereas all the best the race clock can do is give you a historical perspective. That time they call out is the elapsed time from your last mile, your after-the-fact pace. What about now and in the next mile? I have been using my heart rate monitor for the past twenty-five years, and I am still surprised by the difference between what I perceive about my pace or rate and the heart rate monitor data. I recommend that you train using tools that provide biofeedback: time (chronograph), speed and distance (miles per hour), power (watts), and heart rate (beats per minute). Chapter 10 will offer more help in finding the right tools.

Adding Double or Triple Workouts

In the beginning, you'll want to be training three to six times weekly, with no more than one workout each day and at least one full day of total rest within each week. Later, after the lifestyle changes start to sink in, an aspiring triathlete can add to her training volume by increasing both her training distance and the number of training sessions. You'll still want to take one day of rest per week, but you might choose to go from six workouts per week to ten by adding multiple workouts to one or more days. Competitive age groupers and professional athletes usually average between 1.5 and 2.5 workouts per day, adding up to a week that consists of between nine and fourteen training sessions.

In determining which sports to combine on double-workout days, consider your daily schedule so that training fits into your home and professional lifestyle. Since running and cycling both require lower body stress, triathletes specifically train in both sports in a "brick" workout. This term is derived from the name of the person who first advocated using this type of training, New Zealander Mathew Brick, but it also describes how your legs feel after you master this combination workout—heavy as bricks!

Progressively increase from one double workout per week to several, eventually adding your first triple workout to your week's schedule. Start with six single-workout days per week and gradually add workouts until you reach your goal. See Table 3.3 for a sample training grid that shows how you can eventually include twelve workouts per week.

Adding triple-workout days requires planning, especially since few of us are full-time triathletes. Triple days are usually part of your day off from work or school because they demand so much time. Back-to-back triples (performing all three workouts with no rest between them) resemble a triathlon time trial and are recommended only if you want to train for the transition. Otherwise, it is best to rest between each workout on double- or triple-workout days to allow your metabolic reserves to rebuild and to enhance each individual workload session.

OVERTRAINING INDICATORS

We all worry about not training enough, but you should also be wary of training too much. High-intensity training—that is, training in zones 4 and 5—is very stressful on every system in your body. If you spend too much time in these zones, you could find yourself overtrained. This is just one reason to balance your training in the upper and lower zones. You also need to be aware of the impact of work, family, and other commitments. Regardless of whether you progress to double- or triple-workout days, you must tune in to your body and its signals.

Resting Heart Rate

Your resting heart rate is a good indicator of how your body is adapting to the stress of training and managing the stress of life. If your morning resting heart rate (before you get out of bed) is five beats above your normal average on a particular morning, drop your training for the day by at least one zone or take a complete rest day. An incrementally increased resting heart rate signals that your body's energy systems are overstressed and it is time to back off. There are different ways to track your resting heart rate. What's most important is that you are consistent.

Delta Heart Rate

Some athletes prefer to track their delta heart rate, which is an indicator of an individual's current health and stress condition. If your delta number varies by more than five beats per day or test, this is a sign that you should be aware of the stress or other adverse conditions in your life. European athletes commonly perform the delta test described below and use change in delta heart rate to determine their daily training workload. American athletes tend to use high daily variation in resting heart rate as their indicator of overtraining. Either way, you'll want to monitor and record your delta rate using the following test:

1. Put on your heart rate monitor and lie down for 2 minutes. Relax completely.
2. Look at your monitor and record the number. This is your resting heart rate.
3. Stand up and watch your heart rate increase to a high point and then drop.
4. Remain stationary for 2 minutes and record the number on your monitor.
5. Calculate your delta heart rate by subtracting your resting heart rate from your standing heart rate.

Table 3.6 demonstrates how you might use your heart rate data to make subtle changes in your exercise workload throughout your training.

Mindful Recovery

Mindful recovery refers to a way of using your mind and the emotional and mental regulatory power it has to reduce heart rate, especially recovery heart rate. Though it has not always received much attention in modern Western cultures, it is related to practices that have been important for thousands of years in the East. Mindful recovery involves visualization, deep breathing exercises, relaxed body positioning, and other relaxation and meditation techniques to intentionally, purposefully lower your heart

TABLE 3.6 How to Read Training Indicators

RESTING HR DELTA HR	HR WHILE TRAINING	SPEED	DESCRIPTION/DIAGNOSIS
Normal	Normal	Normal	Everything is fine. Train as planned.
Normal	High	Low	Commonly occurs during base training. Indication that training intensity is too high.
Normal	Low	High	Commonly occurs after a high-intensity interval workout. Do a recovery workout or take the day off.
High	High	Low	Indication of fatigue setting in. Be aware that your immune system is more vulnerable.
Normal	High	Normal	Symptomatic of dehydration. (Training speed might be low.)
Normal	High	Low	Indication of fatigue.
Normal	Normal	Low	Indication of tired or "dead" legs.
High	Normal	Normal	Indication of minor stress, worry, mental anxiety, or concern.
Normal	Low	Low	Indication of a chronic, seriously fatigued state.
High	Low	Normal	Commonly occurs when you are unable to maintain training HR. Symptomatic of overtraining.

rate and your stress response. It is an excellent tool for the analysis and interpretation of stress, whether the source of that stress is emotional, physical, or metabolic. Using mindful recovery for stress reduction makes your heart rate monitor into a "stress monitor." When your "stress monitor" number rises, you can use mindful recovery to lower it. Doing this successfully takes practice.

Throughout your training, refer back to the tips highlighted in this chapter. They summarize important concepts of smart training, and they will guard you against overtraining.

THE TRAINING LOG

Every triathlete should keep a training log. Next to your training plan, it is the most important planning tool you will have. Why? Because it is only by having the ability to see how things went in past training that you can figure out how to plan the next stage of training. Use the triathlon log to keep a record of the training you have completed and to note any details about how things went that might be helpful in the future. Consider it a private training diary—you can admit to your problems and your revelations, workouts missed, difficulties encountered, and personal records set.

You can purchase a triathlon log (available at www.heartzones.com), but your log does not need to be fancy; it could be a blank spiral notebook, as long as you remember to record essential details. Research shows that athletes who log their workouts stay on a training program longer and with more success than those who don't keep a log. Keep a log. Be more successful.

FINDING THE SWEET SPOT

You can plan your training progression and time your intensity and recovery carefully, and there is still an element of the unpredictable in every race. This is why your personal goals and values are so important—they will ground you when things don't go as planned.

The day before the 1998 Ironman World Championships, I was in serious pre-race rest preparation sitting on the beaches of Kona, Hawaii, when I received an e-mail from a couple of business friends. Teresa and Mary have finished the Ironman nine times. They know what it's about. Their e-mail was brief and to the point: "Take no prisoners."

They knew that, for me, that race was the big one, and that my goal was to set the grand masters record. They knew that in every race I came from behind and passed all of the other grand masters women. I knew that I would again have to catch my competition during the marathon leg of this race.

The next day, at the start of the marathon, my nemesis had a 28-minute lead, and I knew that her strength was running. I went after her knowing her lead was substantial. There came a moment during the marathon when I had reached the point of absolute exhaustion—the high heat and winds had taken their toll. I knew I had to shake the weariness. Slowly, I felt a strange rush of sensation, one difficult to explain. I call it the "sweet spot."

It was as if everything were coming together and the exhaustion was being let go; it was a feeling of possibility, blended with a sense of hope. I started to feel better—I picked up the pace, and I was joyfully conscious that what was happening was a rare phenomenon.

One of my close friends and training partners rode by on a moped—she was working as a spotter that day. When I asked her for an update she told me my competitor was about to finish. I was still miles from the finish line—it hurt to hear that.

Still, I took strength from my previous taste of possibility and decided that I would give it my best, because in sports no one knows the outcome until the last competitor crosses the finish line. I happen to also believe that in sports your competition is ultimately with yourself, a finishing clock, and a course, not the people around you.

The woman ahead of me beat me by 9 minutes in 11 hours of racing. Yet I took that moment—the sweet spot—as mine. Both the victory and the defeat would be what I made of them, and I left the experience with hope for the future.

The sweet spot is about the indomitable human spirit. For women, our collective spirit grows stronger with the mounting acceptance of women as athletes and fully capable and equal human beings. To find your sweet spot, you must be connected to the truths and desires of the human spirit. And, conversely, following the calling you feel in these moments can help you find your own internal, life-affirming spirit. I encourage you to find it and live it—you will take very good care of yourself in the process.

4

Training Plans

Allez! Allez! Allez! The French fans along the course of the Nice Triathlon shouted these words at the top of their voices as I raced over the Alps and down the cobblestone streets.

These words are burned into my memory. I use them frequently in training. *Allez* means "let's go." But it's not just "let's go" the way we might say it in English—simply meaning that it is time to go somewhere. It also conveys attitude and urgency: For the French, it is a single word that combines "go" and "power."

Now I use *allez* whenever I need a boost of energy. You can also use these words of encouragement to keep going as your triathlon training becomes more difficult. In the beginning, we are easily motivated by better

health: weight loss, toned muscles, increased stamina, and cardiovascular improvements. But after settling into a routine, you may forget why you began triathlon training and wonder why you are putting yourself through so much trouble. In those moments, shout out an *allez*. Let's go!

MEASURING YOUR FITNESS

Some people are naturally more responsive to training than others, and how fit you are to begin with is certainly relevant. Fit or not, training pays off. But to get the biggest payoff, you have to be honest about where you are starting from.

Here's why. Fit and unfit people burn fat differently. The key is to burn the greatest amount of fat in the least amount of time. As your fitness improves, your body is adapting to more effectively use fat as a source of calories during exercise. This means that the more fit you become, the more total calories you can burn at a given heart rate.

Fit people are fat-burning machines. Because oxygen must be present for fat to burn in the muscles during exercise, unfit people need to exercise in lower intensities to maximize fat burning. This has led to the common misunderstanding that there is a "fat-burning zone"—you've probably noticed it on the cardio equipment at your local gym. Once you establish a baseline of fitness, you'll burn fat in every zone. If your triathlon goals include the challenges of weight management and increasing your activity level significantly, you can find other helpful resources written by me and others in the Appendix.

TABLE 4.1 Fitness Scorecard

Conduct a benchmark test in each sport at the start of the season and periodically throughout your training.

	SCORE	TIME		
		Swim (400 yd.)	Bike (3 mi.)	Run (1.5 mi.)
	20.0	5:00	5:53	7:35
	19.5	5:05	6:00	7:40
	19.0	5:10	6:08	7:45
	18.5	5:15	6:17	7:55
	18.0	5:23	6:26	8:05
	17.5	5:31	6:35	8:20
Advanced	17.0	5:40	6:45	8:35
	16.5	5:49	6:55	8:50
	16.0	5:58	7:05	9:10
	15.5	6:07	7:17	9:30
	15.0	6:16	7:29	9:50
	14.5	6:25	7:41	10:10

CONTINUED →

	SCORE	TIME		
		Swim (400 yd.)	Bike (3 mi.)	Run (1.5 mi.)
Fit athlete	14.0	6:35	7:54	10:35
	13.5	6:45	8:08	11:00
	13.0	6:55	8:23	11:30
	12.5	7:05	8:56	12:00
	12.0	7:15	9:14	12:35
	11.5	7:27	9:33	13:10
	11.0	7:39	9:54	13:50
	10.5	7:53	10:16	14:30
	10.0	8:07	10:40	15:15
	9.5	8:22	11:05	16:10
	9.0	8:37	11:35	17:00
Beginner	8.5	8:52	12:10	17:50
	8.0	9:12	12:50	18:40
	7.5	9:32	13:30	19:40
	7.0	9:57	14:10	20:40
	6.5	10:22	14:55	22:55
	6.0	10:52	15:40	24:10
	5.5	11:22	16:30	25:30
	5.0	11:55	17:20	26:50
	4.5	12:30	18:10	28:20
	4.0	13:05	19:00	30:00

TABLE 4.1 (continued)

Note: Times are in min.:sec.

You will start with a benchmark test in each sport. Take the swim, bike, and run benchmark tests on different days and allow adequate rest between tests so you can perform at your best. You will swim 400 meters, ride 3 miles, and run 1.5 miles, making an all-out speed effort at each. Make sure you include an easy warm-up and cool-down elsewhere with your test.

Then, using the fitness scorecard (see Table 4.1), determine where you currently fall according to your performance in each sport. You can repeat these tests on a regular basis to measure improvements in performance. Don't be discouraged if your first round of tests doesn't turn up the scores you hoped for. You will enjoy seeing your ranking improve as you become more fit and accomplish your goals. Everyone has to start somewhere.

If you are already a fit, accomplished athlete, you will probably score in the upper tiers of each benchmark test. You should review the intermediate training plan and focus more of your training on the sports you are less familiar with.

GETTING STARTED

In Chapter 3 we explored the progression of training. If you are training for your first triathlon, common sense will tell you that first you have to get fit. If you are an experienced triathlete or athlete, it's likely that you already have a fitness base to build upon, and while the specifics of your training might be different from those of a beginner's plan, you will follow a similar progression through the training phases.

Plain, old-fashioned, nothing-fancy discipline is a big part of a winning plan that gets you to go faster. By planning the workouts and working out according to plan, you are practicing what sports psychologists call "patterning." Patterning is repeating an action until it is so ingrained that your brain doesn't have to make a decision: Your brain (and your heart) just follows a natural course, and the action becomes routine.

To use a down-to-earth metaphor, training for triathlons is like preparing, ingesting, and recovering from a major meal. It involves a recipe, ingredients, preparation time, equipment, planning time, labor, measurements, the actual event (eating the meal), cleanup, and rest afterward. Throughout the training program, as in cooking a meal, there are multiple activities occurring—different pans on the stove at the same time. Triathlon training is pleasurable because of the variety of courses and the way they complement each other. Finally, everything works together for a spectacular finish! Welcome to the gourmet training experience.

With that in mind, in this chapter I offer up two "menus"—a beginner plan and an intermediate plan. With these training plans—already laid out in detailed instructions like a recipe—you can get started right away. But as time goes on, you will want to develop your own recipes for success. As you gain experience and get to know your strengths and weaknesses better, you will need to design an individualized plan. Using the detailed guidelines later in this chapter, you will be able to do just that.

The beginner and intermediate plans presented here apply the theories we explored in Chapter 3. However, your contribution to the equation depends on your unique circumstances and needs. I hope that by now you will understand why I laid the plan out in this particular way, but use your intuition and creativity, too, so that the plan will meet your personal needs. If you scored higher than 9 on your benchmark test in all three sports you can choose between the beginner and intermediate training plans. When deciding between these plans, take your goals and time constraints into account as well as your fitness level.

THE BEGINNER'S TRAINING PLAN

In this plan you will prepare for a sprint triathlon in eight weeks. Over the course of training for your goal or summit, you'll get fitter. As you become more fit, the workouts will become easier, your performance will improve, and you'll find that your heart rate is lower than it was in the first few weeks of training. You will be working harder or going greater distances at a lower heart rate. When this happens, you need to change your training so you can continue to see improvement. The plan I've provided accounts for these changes, but you might need to make changes of your own.

Adjust this sample beginner's triathlon training program to fit your individual situation. Your current fitness level, your motivation, and your time constraints are all factors. The level of training will vary from sport to sport. If you are good at running, but qualify as a beginner in swimming and cycling, you might incorporate some of the run workouts from the Intermediate Training Plan into the beginner's program.

As you progress through the Beginner Training Plan, you will include different types of workouts. Table 4.2 details how the four basic workouts will shape up. For the skills section you can incorporate drills from the sport-specific chapters that follow this one (Chapters 5–7). For now, let's take a closer look at the plan in Table 4.3 to find out exactly how you will achieve your triathlon goals.

BEGINNER, PREPARATION I: BASE	WEEKS 1–2

Frequency: 3 workouts/week: 1 swim, 1 bike, and 1 run
Intensity: zones 1–3
Time: 20–30-min. workouts

The training base will emphasize just what you would expect: getting to the basics—swim, bike, and run technique and cardio fitness. The workouts are short and easy. You'll stay at a low intensity (zones 1–3) and only go short distances. The workouts are fun and aerobic. This phase of training will last two weeks. Each week you will be building your cardiovascular aerobic system. Work on improving your biomechanics or technique in

TABLE 4.2 Beginner Workouts

STEADY-STATE WORKOUT

	Zones	% Total Workout	Sample Run Workout
Warm-up	1	10	Easy to very fast walk (5 min.)
Skill set	2	10	Biomechanics: Work on running tall (5 min.)
Main set	3	70	Run 2–4 mi. at 75–80% of run max HR (15–30 min.)
Cooldown	1	10	Easy walk or jog (5 min.)

INTERVAL WORKOUT

	Zones	% Total Workout	Sample Swim Workout
Warm-up	1	10	Easy swim and stretch (5 min.)
Skill set	2	10	Stroke mechanic drills (5 min.)
Main set	2–3	70	Swim 500–1000m (15–30 min.): 50m fast, 80% run max HR 25m recovery, 60% max HR
Cooldown	1–2	10	Easy swim and stretch (5 min.)

RECOVERY WORKOUT

	Zones	% Total Workout	Sample Bike Workout
Warm-up	1	10	Ride easy, 1–2 mi. (5 min.)
Skill set	2	10	Cadence drill: 100 rpm, 1–2 mi. (5 min.)
Main set	3	70	Ride comfortably holding HR steady, 3–6 mi. (15–30 min.)
Cooldown	1	10	Ride easy, 1–2 mi. (5 min.)

COMBINATION WORKOUT

	Zones	% Total Workout	Sample Bike-to-Run Workout
Warm-up	1	10	Ride easy, 1–2 mi. (5 min.)
Skill set	2	10	Stroke mechanic drills (5 min.)
Main set	top of 3	70	Ride 6 mi. at 75–80% of max HR. (25–30 min.) Transition to run. Run 1.5 mi. at max sustainable HR (12–20 min.)
Cooldown	1	10	Easy walk, 0.5 mi. (5 min.)

Note: RPM = revolutions per minute

TABLE 4.3 Beginner Plan for a Sprint Triathlon, 8 Weeks

WEEKS	WORKOUT	TRAINING TYPE	ZONES	WEEKLY TOTAL (hr.:min.)
1–2	Swim 20–30 min.	Steady-state	1–3	1:00–1:30
	Bike 20–30 min.	Steady-state	1–3	
	Run 20–30 min.	Steady-state	1–3	
3–4	Swim 20–30 min.	Steady-state	1–3	1:30–2:15
	Run 20–40 min.	Steady-state	1–3	
	Bike 30–35 min.	Steady-state	1–3	
	Run 20–30 min.	Recovery	1–2	
5	Swim 20–30 min.	Steady-state	1–3	2:15–3:10
	Choice 25–30 min.	Steady-state	1–2	
	Bike 30–60 min.	Steady-state	1–3	
	Choice 40–50 min. (optional)	Combination	2–4	
	Run 20–40 min.	Steady-state	1–3	
6	Swim 20–30 min.	Interval	2–4	2:15–3:40
	Bike 30–60 min.	Recovery	1–2	
	Run 20–30 min.	Interval	2–3	
	Bike 20–40 min.	Steady-state	2–3	
	Choice 45–60 min.	Combination	2–4	
7	Swim race distance	Steady-state	1-4	2:30–2:50
	Run 25–35 min.	Recovery	1–2	
	Bike race distance	Steady-state	2–3	
	Swim 20 min.	Recovery	1–2	
	Run race distance	Steady-state	2–4	
8	Swim 20 min.	Recovery	2–3	1:00–1:10
	Bike 20–30 min.	Recovery	2–3	
	Run 20 min.	Recovery	2–3	
	RACE	Steady-state	2–4	

Note: "Choice" means you can decide which sport to train. Be careful to spend adequate time training the sports that are most challenging. If you want to add workouts, you can repeat a workout or make a workout slightly longer or more challenging.

BEGINNER PLAN

each sport. Ask a knowledgeable friend to observe and make suggestions so you can become more efficient, or check with a local health club to see if a personal trainer might be available for one or two sessions. It's a good idea to make sure you are not starting out with bad habits in the way you carry out the movements of each sport.

BEGINNER, PREPARATION I: ENDURANCE   WEEKS 3–4

Frequency: 3–4 workouts/week: 1 swim, 1 bike, and 1–2 runs
Intensity: zones 1–3
Time: 20–40-min. workouts

Your goal is to develop muscular and cardiorespiratory endurance during this training period. Introduce one endurance workout to your routine. To do this, pick one of the three sports and do one workout that is longer than you have ever trained before. Make that a session of 35 minutes or more in a low heart rate zone. This marks the start of building your capacity for endurance. Now that you have started to develop your aerobic base, it's time to push up the level of intensity. This means spending more time in zone 3.

BEGINNER, PREPARATION II: STRENGTH   WEEK 5

Frequency: 4–5 workouts: 1 swim, 1 bike, and 1 run, plus 1–2 workouts
  in your weaker sport
Intensity: zones 1–3
Time: 20–60-min. workouts

Keep the once-a-week endurance workout and extend it to 40 minutes or more. In Table 4.3 the run and bike workouts could serve as this endurance workout. If you already have some running and cycling endurance, you can adjust the steady-state swim workout to be your endurance workout.

In Week 5 you will also add a workout to your schedule to build strength in one sport. Strength, or the ability of your muscles to generate force against resistance, will help you develop power. The best way to build strength in the specific muscles where you need it the most for triathlon is to train with resistance: on hills, into the wind, with an overload of weight, using swimming aids in the pool, on a treadmill with elevation, and the like. Choose your weakest sport for this additional workout (described as "choice" in Table 4.3).

If your fitness is progressing well, you can add a combination workout this week. Combination workouts are any two sports done in succession, described in more detail in Chapter 3. You can try different combinations, but the most common combination workout in triathlon is the bike-to-run workout, commonly called a "brick." Bricks and other combinations are fun workouts. Invite a training partner to join you. Run or bike to the pool and back. Be creative with these.

BEGINNER, PREPARATION II: POWER (INTERVALS)   WEEK 6

Frequency: 5 workouts: 1 swim, 2 bike, 1 run, and 1 choice, adding an interval workout
Intensity: zones 1–3 or 1–4
Time: 20–60-min. workouts

Keep one endurance and one strength workout, and now add one interval workout. The fourth workout can be a steady-state training session in the sport that needs the most improvement.

One of the best ways to improve speed is to train using repeats, or short sets, where you go faster than normal. This is called interval training. Interval training is one of the most important times to use your heart rate monitor because you will be riding, running, or swimming in higher heart zones. Higher-intensity training improves your recovery ability and your ability to sustain the higher heart rates that you might experience during a triathlon.

BEGINNER, PREPARATION II: POWER   WEEK 7

Frequency: 5–6 workouts per week: 1–2 swims, 1–2 bike, and 1–2 runs
Intensity: zones 1–4
Time: 15–60-min. workouts

This week you will do time trials in each sport. The purpose of the time trial is to practice the race distances of each individual sport at the intensity you plan to sustain on race day. For a typical sprint-distance race: Swim 1 kilometer (1,090 yards) on your swim day; bike 12 miles on your bike day; and run 5 kilometers (3.1 miles) on your run day. Pace yourself, keeping your heart rate at a sustainable level (upper zone 3 to lower zone 4), even if you have to slow down a little to control it.

Time these workouts so you can get a ballpark estimate of your finish time—don't forget to add the two transitions into your calculations. If any one of the time trial workouts feels too demanding this week, you can attempt 70 percent of the race-day distance. Adrenaline can usually carry you the additional 30 percent on race day. Your training has prepared you for the triathlon, but these two or three race-distance workouts will make you even more confident.

BEGINNER, COMPETITION: TAPER	WEEK 8

Frequency: 2–3 workouts: 1 swim, 1 bike, and 1 run

Intensity: zones 2–3

Time: 20–45-min. workouts

This week might be your favorite. You have the excitement of the triathlon now just days away, and in order to do your best, you'll need extra rest this week. Your training load will be roughly half of what it was last week. The biggest difference is the intensity of your workouts. All of these workouts should be recovery workouts, where your heart rate remains in zones 1 and 2. Use your extra time to prepare emotionally and mentally for race day. Take the time to check out the race expo when you pick up your race-day packet, and sit in on a first-timers pep talk if you get the opportunity.

~~~~~

The process of change as you become a triathlete may seem minimal at times. Every step of the way, there are some things that will be the same. One constant is that you should continually be adding to your knowledge of the sport and how your body works. Start that learning process now. Read, ask questions, keep a training log, ask for help, join a training group, get a personal trainer or tri-coach, or sign up for an e-coach. Get help from someone who specializes in *you*—a woman, and, at this stage, a first-timer. Every step also requires determination, accountability, and conviction. If you set a goal that is from the heart, based on your values, you will be more motivated to stick with the plan. Every step requires action: Train. Your knowledge and determination will do you little good if you are not moving. And finally, every step takes effort. Knowledge, determination, action, and effort will take you all the way to the starting line, and, perhaps more importantly, the finish line.

And if you ever need support, know that there is a whole community of women triathletes who are rooting for you, including me. When you get onto the racecourse, you'll find us encouraging you every step of the way.

THE INTERMEDIATE ATHLETE'S TRAINING PLAN

Welcome to the union of fit women who have passed the first hurdle of lifetime athleticism—the novice, or beginner, stage. You have promoted yourself to the class of women who have made a commitment to the sport and who are taking their level of experience to new heights.

If you've already finished your first triathlon, you are in the middle of an evolutionary process: from the excitement of your first race, to being inspired to make triathlon a part of your life. As you approach each new level, you will add new parameters to your training. You will also need to understand more of the training principles and have a higher level of appreciation for the intricacies of performance training.

As a beginner, you may have been approaching training gingerly, working out for the purpose of gaining fitness and managing weight, and looking to comfortably finish a first-timer event. You have now hit the point where you've realized that training has a deeper purpose. Whether it is your intention to improve your endurance or speed or participate in more events, your intermediate workout plan uses the concept of training in heart zones (see Chapter 3) in greater depth. You will notice that the training plan that follows specifies the distance for each workout (with an estimated time), whereas the beginner plan was simply based on duration. Consequently, weekly training volume will vary based on your speed.

The intermediate plan also assumes that you are beginning training with some solid cardiovascular fitness. This is what allows you to begin the plan with workouts focused on building sport-specific muscular strength. You should have a decent base of endurance to start this plan. You can train for either a sprint or international-distance race with the intermediate plan; to train for a longer event, use the guidelines for building your own plan that appear later in this chapter.

INTERMEDIATE, PREPARATION I: ENDURANCE   WEEKS 1–3

Frequency: 4–6 workouts/week

Intensity: zones 1–4

Time: 30–90-min. workouts

In the first few weeks you will work on getting sport-specific strength with swim drills and hill running (see Table 4.4). If you are concerned about your endurance, you can keep the workouts in the first two weeks mostly in zones 2 and 3 to allow your cardiovascular fitness to build. In week 3 you can pick up the intensity and focus on building sport-specific strength.

As you train with this plan, you can adjust the workouts as needed. There could be weekdays when you can't fit in longer workouts—just shuffle the days around to suit your schedule. When you do this, try to maintain a pattern of workouts that will give you adequate recovery following consecutive challenging workouts.

The combination workouts start right away with this plan. I've specified some different combinations in the plan, but you can change them to build strength in the sports where you need it most. Many women like to bike to the pool, swim, and bike back home. The combinations can be fun and convenient. These are also great workouts to do with a training partner if you want to push yourself a little harder.

TABLE 4.4 Intermediate Plan, Weeks 1–3

	WORKOUT	TIME (min.)	1 23%	2 16%	3 45%	4 16%	5 0%	TRAINING POINTS
			TIME IN ZONES (min.)					
Mon.	Rest day	—	0	0	0	0	0	0
Tues.	Swim 800–1,200m (Interval)	30	5	0	20	5	0	85
Wed.	Weights/flexibility	20	5	15	0	0	0	35
Thurs.	Bike 10–20 mi. (Steady-state)	40–60	15	15	30	0	0	135
Fri.	Weights/flexibility	15	15	0	0	0	0	15
Sat.	Bike 6–10 mi., run 3–4 mi. (Combination)	55–80	5	5	25	25	0	190
Sun.	Swim 900–1,500m (Interval)	35	5	0	25	5	0	100
Totals	Swim 1,700–2,700m Bike 16–30 mi. Run 3–4 mi.	3 hr. 5 min.–4 hr.	50	35	100	35	0	560

INTERMEDIATE, PREPARATION II: STRENGTH   WEEKS 4–5

Frequency: 6 workouts per week

Intensity: zones 2–5

Time: 30–90-min. workouts

The purpose of this period is to increase sport-specific speed by training faster (see Table 4.5). You can see that intensity will reach zone 5 and the duration will also be challenging. Over the course of these two weeks you should repeat the benchmark tests you did at the start of the season. Make sure you are rested going into the tests, and test each sport on a different day. I hope you will see the rewards of your training.

TABLE 4.5 Intermediate Plan, Weeks 4–5

	WORKOUT	TIME (min.)	1 9%	2 45%	3 22%	4 17%	5 8%	TRAINING POINTS
			TIME IN ZONES (min.)					
Mon.	Swim 1,000–1,300m (Interval)	25–40	0	20	0	5	5	85
Tues.	Bike 15–18 mi. (Steady-state)	60	10	15	35	0	0	145
Wed.	Run 3–4 mi. (Interval)	30–45	0	25	0	10	10	140
Thurs.	Swim 1,000m, run 3 mi. (Combination)	55–60	0	35	15	20	0	195
Fri.	Rest	—	0	0	0	0	0	0
Sat.	Bike 14–20 mi. (Interval)	60	0	30	0	20	10	190
Sun.	Run 5–7 mi. (Recovery)	60	20	20	20	0	0	210
Totals	Swim 2,200–3,300m Bike 29–38 mi. Run 11–14 mi.	4 hr. 50 min.– 6 hr. 40 min.	30	145	70	55	25	875

INTERMEDIATE, PREPARATION II: POWER   WEEKS 6–7

Frequency: 7 workouts/week

Intensity: zones 2–5

Time: 30–90 min. workouts

The focus of this period is power, meaning you will make it your goal to be as strong and fast as you can be. Intensity remains high, with training in zones 4 and 5. Volume remains steady so you can have as much endurance as possible for your coming race.

In one of these two weeks I encourage you to do a time trial in each sport that matches the distances of your event. If you are doing a sprint-triathlon, swim 1 kilometer, bike 12 miles, and run 5 kilometers. If you are training for an international-distance race, swim 1.5 kilometers, bike 25 miles, and run 10 kilometers. The time trials should be done on separate days. If you look at the workouts in Table 4.6, there are steady-state days for swimming, cycling, and running.

Allow ample time for an adequate warm-up and cool-down. In week 7 you may want to repeat your benchmark tests and check your progress on the fitness scorecard (Table 4.1). You should only do this if you feel adequately recovered.

TABLE 4.6 Intermediate Plan, Weeks 6–7

	WORKOUT	EST. TIME	TIME IN ZONES (min.)					TRAINING POINTS
			1 0%	**2** 13%	**3** 58%	**4** 21%	**5** 7%	
Mon.	Swim 1,500–1,600m (Steady-state)	45	0	10	35	0	0	125
Tues.	Bike 15–17 mi. (Interval)	60	0	10	15	20	15	220
Wed.	Run 4–6 mi. (Steady-state)	45	0	5	5	25	10	175
Thurs.	Swim 1,000–1,500m (Recovery)	30	10	10	10	0	0	60
Fri.	Bike 12 mi., run 5 mi. (Combination)	75	0	5	60	10	0	230
Sat.	Rest	—	0	0	0	0	0	0
Sun.	Bike 15–25 mi. (Steady-state)	90	0	5	70	15	0	280
Totals	Swim 2,500–3,100m Bike 42–54 mi. Run 9–11 mi.	5 hr. 45 min.	10	45	195	70	25	1,090

INTERMEDIATE, COMPETITION: TAPER   WEEK 8

Frequency: 4 workouts

Intensity: zones 2–3

Time: 30–60 min. workouts

Your race is fast approaching, so it's time to taper. Your week will consist of recovery workouts with some short intervals to maintain your fitness for race day (see Table 4.7). The overall volume of your training will feel considerably shorter, but you've done this before. You know how important it is to be patient and save your energy for race day. Seven weeks of challenging training could be for nothing if you choose not to take this week to rest tired muscles. Keep your sights on that goal. I know you will accomplish what you set out to do.

	WORKOUT	EST. TIME	TIME IN ZONES (min.)					TRAINING POINTS
			1 0%	2 48%	3 52%	4 0%	5 0%	
Mon.	Swim 1,000m (Recovery)	30	5	15	10	0	0	65
Tues.	Bike 10 mi. (Recovery)	40	5	15	20	0	0	95
Wed.	Run 3 mi. (Recovery)	25	5	10	10	0	0	55
Thurs.	Swim 1,000m (Recovery)	30	5	10	15	0	0	70
Fri.	Rest	—	0	0	0	0	0	0
Sat.	Race expo	—	0	0	0	0	0	0
Sun.	RACE (Steady-state)	*tbd*	0	0	0	0	0	*tbd*
Totals	Swim 2,000m Bike 10 mi. Run 3 mi. + event	2 hr. 25 min. + event	20	50	55	0	0	285

TABLE 4.7 Intermediate Plan, Week 8

INTERMEDIATE PLAN

Note: Weekly totals will include your event, to be determined (tbd).

DESIGNING YOUR WORKOUT PLAN

By now you understand a lot of important training concepts. These concepts will become more clear as you design your own plan. The plan you put together will be based on mesocycles and microcycles, workout types, heart rate zones, and training load calculations. I've given you some sample plans so that you can get started with your training quickly. But ultimately, you will need to design your own workout plan. In this section, you will learn how. Based on your goals, you will determine what your training load will be, then figure out how to divide that up into weekly and daily workouts that will target specific objectives.

Remember, goals account for the difference between exercising and training. The goals you set for yourself in Chapter 2 will help you set up the framework of your macrocycles. But there are also small goals, sometimes called objectives, that represent the steps you must take to accomplish the large goals. These small steps will be the focus of your microcycles. Although it's the microcycles that determine what you do day to day and week to week, keep your eyes on the prize—that is, the macrocycle goals. That is how you will stay motivated to do your best in those day-to-day workouts.

To simplify it further, I like to think of a plan as being made up of four practical cycles: annual, seasonal, monthly, and weekly.

Annual Cycle

The annual cycle is probably the most difficult to formulate because it requires you to look into the future. Still, I believe if you've done your interior work on clarifying your values and goals, the exterior planning will be much easier. To design an annual cycle, you need to answer this question: In terms of my health, fitness, and athletic dreams or goals, what would I like to accomplish this year and next year?

An annual cycle gives you the opportunity to plan your training over the long term. An example of an annual cycle goal is: "I will set my first year of training as a learning experience, one in which I will finish one triathlon and afterward plan for another." In your second annual cycle, you might want to train for and enter five triathlons of both sprint and international distances and complete a metric century bike ride (62 miles). In year three, you might want to finish a long-course triathlon and attempt your first 26.2-mile marathon.

Jot down a few annual goals that may have occurred to you as you read this chapter. Be ambitious. Put your heart on your sleeve and spark your imagination. You can look them over later and analyze their appropriateness.

Seasonal Cycles

Seasonal cycles are usually two to eight months long. Some triathletes draw a training map based on seasons of the year: spring, summer, fall, and winter, making four seasonal cycles. This is a good place to start, but as you become more experienced, you may prefer to divide the year into as many as seven seasonal cycles, based on your racing schedule.

My year is typically made up of two seasons. For eight months of the year I race in triathlons, and for four months I run in road races or adventure races. Seasonal cycles can be individually tailored to your athletic goals and interests in this way.

One way to plan your seasonal cycles is to get a big year-at-a-glance wall calendar. Put everything on it—your birthday, anniversary, mammogram appointment, car pool days, school vacations—all the things that are already scheduled, important or otherwise. For example, you should note the dates that you will be traveling, the date that school starts or the week you'll be taking final exams, and, of course, specific races you plan to enter. All of this should begin to give you an idea of how to set up your year-long seasonal cycle plan.

Monthly Cycles (Mesocycles)

Mesocycles are generally periods of four to ten weeks within each seasonal cycle. Each mesocycle is dedicated to improving one major factor of your performance—for example, speed. A series of mesocycles will form a progression, from base training to post-race recovery, for each seasonal cycle.

In March 1992, for example, I started my season with a goal of training for four Ironmans. I aspired to set the masters world record in all four. I accomplished that goal, thanks to a solid training program based on these principles. After the Ironman World Championship in October, I needed a rest mesocycle, so I gave myself 11 weeks to rest, until January 1.

The Training Progression

Training is a progression—a series of steps that lead you to the completion of your goals. Whatever your seasonal training goal, the little steps needed to get there will take you through the six different mesocycles: base, endurance, strength, power, competition (racing), and recovery (transition). Refer back to Figure 3.1 for a visual of the training progression.

BASE MESOCYCLE: 2 WEEKS–2 MONTHS

This is a cycle of low intensity and low training volume, when you lay the foundation of your training program. Exercise physiologists call it the "aerobic buildup phase," because you are training for the aerobic, not the threshold or above threshold, component of fitness. The cycle consists of workouts that are easy and continuous and that lead to strength and stamina, not necessarily speed, although you will need to introduce some speed work into the later mesocycle weeks. This is also a stage of developing strength, so include weight workouts with machines or free weights as well as sport-specific strength workouts, such as running and cycling hills.

ENDURANCE MESOCYCLE: 2–4 WEEKS

The endurance mesocycle focuses on sport-specific training and improving technique. It is a time to fine-tune your swim, bike, and run biomechanics—to concentrate on developing the movement skills more than the endurance skills. You might want to enlist the aid of a local expert or tri-coach at this point, because it is difficult to see the flaws in your own technique and movement patterns. You don't have to commit to an ongoing coaching program; just a few sessions can help you to eliminate any bad patterns that may be developing and ensure that you are off to a good start. Approximately 80 percent of your training volume during this cycle will still be aerobic and endurance training.

STRENGTH MESOCYCLE: 2–4 MONTHS

This is a demanding and vigorous cycle. Here, you take the base and skills you've developed over the prior two mesocycles and add intensity training. This period will usually include the highest training volume of any mesocycle. Approximately 50–60 percent of your training volume will still be long, slow, distance training, aerobic training, and aerobic time trials. The balance needs to be in interval training, such as time trials, resistance repeats, and threshold and above-threshold intervals. You can also do "fartleks" (Swedish for "speed play"). Fartleks involve doing an easy pace interspersed with speed work; see the sidebar "Fartleks" for ideas on how to incorporate fartleks in your training. This is a good time to enter an individual sport race such as a 5 km road race or a bike time trial.

POWER MESOCYCLE: 2–4 WEEKS

This is a short mesocycle characterized by training at higher intensity for shorter distances. Physiologically, you are stressing your energy systems at high speeds in order to gain speed overall. You also work on refining your technique during this cycle. Triathletes use two different terms to refer to this cycle. It is called peaking because of the decrease in training volume, which allows you to put together the three components (endurance, strength, and speed) in all three disciplines (swim, bike, run) in preparation for a big race. But it is also called sharpening because of the skills refinement component.

EVENT MESOCYCLE: 1–4 MONTHS

This is the cycle when you are capable of racing at your best. I think of it as the dessert of training, because it is such a delicious stage for a competitive athlete. Over half the training during this cycle will be in zone 3, the aerobic zone. This is a time to train actively while in the midst of a racing schedule and all that it entails (travel, diet changes, psychological stress). Maintaining your aerobic base should be central to your planning. Interval training should represent approximately 10–15 percent of the training volume.

FARTLEKS

A fartlek is a specific type of interval training. You are familiar with intervals—interspersing a faster pace or harder set for a particular distance or time, with a period of recovery at a slower pace or easier set. Fartleks open the door to more creativity. Stop signs, telephone poles, billboards, or any other marker you encounter on your ride or run can trigger a faster effort. When I'm riding in Sacramento we begin fartleks when we pass cows in the field. This usually means a 2–3-minute push (there are a lot of cows where we ride). The spontaneity is refreshing and challenging. Do fartleks on your running route, running faster on alternating city blocks. What does a fartlek look like in your neighborhood? While we don't commonly think of fartleks in the pool (and there are fewer objects to choose from), you could begin a faster effort every time you pass a swimmer in a nearby lane, and finish the effort after you've touched the wall twice. Be creative—that's what makes fartleks fun.

To maintain a long event mesocycle, up to four months, you would need to have a high level of fitness, most likely developed over several years or seasons of training. Be careful that you don't extend this period too long or you could end up injured or overtrained. You can revisit some of the tips for preventing an undesirable end to your season in Chapter 3.

RECOVERY MESOCYCLE: 1–4 MONTHS

This is the rest or recovery phase of training, when you can slow down. Training in this cycle is of very low intensity and moderate to low volume. It is a stage when sport-specific training is unimportant. You may take up new activities such as cross-country skiing, in-line skating, or dancing. It is an active restoration period—you might enjoy playing team sports like volleyball or softball and work on your team-playing skills. Enjoy the recovery mesocycle but stay active. This isn't a time for the couch and candy bars.

Once you are past the beginning stages of triathlon training, no one else can really map out a plan for you. There are no generic triathlon plans that are one-size-fits-all. Think of it this way: Say a swim coach writes a workout for all the members of her team to perform. On the team of thirty swimmers, three are stars, and the remainder perform adequately but not as well. Why? There are a number of reasons, but probably the most prominent is that the coach has designed a training program that is working for only those three swimmers. The other twenty-seven need a different program—one that works for them.

For you to create your training plan, you will need to write it down: a sample format, a worksheet, a template, or an outline. You already have most of the information that you need to fill in the blanks; what you are missing is the swim-bike-run workout for each individual training day.

I know that writing your weekly training plan can be daunting. You might be hesitating, not putting pen to paper for fear of overcommitting or underachieving. Start somewhere. I guarantee that a systematic training plan will help you achieve two major goals: You will get the most out of each individual workout session, and you will do it in the least amount of time. If you dedicate adequate time to planning your schedule, the returns will be enormous. Isn't it better to wake up in the morning and know what you are planning to do for the day's workout? Part of your plan is to have fun, so don't stress out by wondering what to do every time you head out to train.

I suggest starting with the annual cycle. If you know what you want to achieve this year, you can then determine what your seasonal goals should be in each season of the year. Then, focus in on the first season, the one you will start out in tomorrow. Let's look at my sample season planner in Table 4.8. I've allowed space for twelve months, but you might be planning a shorter season. Divide the season into mesocycles. Start with the base mesocycle and fill in the other training mesocycles. This will help shape the focus of your training when you sit down to map out the daily workouts.

You'll want to plan at least a week's worth of workouts in advance. You can refer to Table 4.9 to see how this is done. You can see that I started with my goal and then figured out the objectives or steps that will help me reach it.

Training Volume

Your total annual training volume will depend on what you want to accomplish and what your goals are. It also depends on how much time you have available and how well you are able to manage the time you have. Answer this question: On average, how much time do you have each day

TABLE 4.8 Sample Annual Training Planner

MONTH	AVERAGE WEEKLY VOLUME			GOALS
	Distance (mi.)	Time (hr.)	Training Load (points)	
March	S 2–3 B 30–40 R 8–10	6	1,000	Base sport-specific training with emphasis on getting cardio fit.
April	S 3–4 B 40–50 R 10–12	8	1,400	Get fitter by increasing my training load and keeping current on my training log.
May	S 3–5 B 40–60 R 8–12	10	1,800	First spring distance race with speed improvement.*
June	S 2–4 B 50–70 R 6–10	10	1,900	Focus on my bike split—it is my most challenging sport.
July	S 2–4 B 40–60 R 8–12	10	2,000	Increase training load and speed. More intervals, less junk.
August	S 3–5 B 50–80 R 9–15	12	2,400	Big training month. No races—increase distance, intensity, and frequency.
September	S 2–3 B 30–40 R 6–10	10	1,800	Racing month with big tapers.
October	S 2–3 B 30–50 R 10–12	8	1,500	Last tier training month. Eager to peak.
November	R/IC	tbd		Back off training and go into the "off-season."
December	R/IC	tbd		Try not to gain weight with low training load.
January	SS XC R IC	tbd		Try my first snowshoe race.
February	SS XC R IC	tbd		Last off-season month. Get eager.

*I live in California, where the tri season begins in May.

Note: B = bike, IC = indoor cycling, R = run, s = swim, SS = snowshoe, TBD = to be determined, XC = cross-country ski.

to train? Make a realistic appraisal here; it doesn't help to overestimate through wishful thinking. Then multiply that number by the number of days per week that you will train. I recommend that you schedule one rest day. For example, if you could work out for about 1 hour a day, 6 days each week, that would mean you had 6 hours a week for training. Multiply this number by the number of weeks per year that you are going to train. In our example, let's say you were planning to train consistently every week.

TABLE 4.9 Weekly Training Planner

WEEK: 6, POWER TRAINING

Date	Workout	Actual Dist.	Actual Time (min.)	Time in Zone (min.)				
				1	2	3	4	5
Mon.	Swim (SS)	1,500m	35	3	3	29		
Tues.	Bike (Interval)	25 mi.	90	20		35	25	10
Wed.	Run (Recovery)	5 mi.	50	20	15	15		
Thurs.	Swim (Fitness Test)	400m	44	10	10		24	
Fri.	Day off							
Sat.	Swim (SS) Run (SS)	1,000m 6 mi.	25 50	5 5	0 0	20 45		
Sun.	Bike (SS)	40 mi.	160		80	60	20	
Weekly Summary	Swim Bike Run	3,700m 65 mi. 11 mi.	104 250 100	83 83 10	105 210 20	214 642 50	69 276 18	10 59 2
Year-to-Date Summary	Swim Bike Run	18,000m 300 mi. 88 mi.						

Multiply 6 by 52, which equals 312. Thus, you could train for 312 hours this year. This is your annual training volume.

The number of weeks per year does not have to be 52. If you are planning to do a major triathlon in the fall and then take a few weeks off, don't count those recovery weeks in your volume calculation.

In Table 4.10, you can see how your annual training volume compares to that of other athletes at different levels.

| Training Points | Rating | Daily Health Check | | Notes |
		Resting HR	Weight	
81	5	68	140	
275	4	65	140	
95	4	72	138	
126	3	65	139	
65 170	4 5	69	139	
320	4	65	139	
454 min. 1,132 points	Training Load			

TABLE 4.10 Typical Annual Training Volume (hours) for Different Sports				
PROFICIENCY	TRIATHLON	RUNNING	SWIMMING	CYCLING
Professional	800–1,400	500–700	400–600	700–1,200
Competitor	400–800	300–500	300–400	350–700
Intermediate	300–400	200–300	200–300	200–350
Beginner	<300	<200	<200	<200

SCHEDULING YOUR VOLUME

How far should you swim, bike, or run in your workouts? This is not necessarily an easy question to answer, because there are many factors that could be taken into account. Nevertheless, there is one straightforward, easy way to tackle it: Take the lengths of each segment of the event in which you wish to compete and make your training distances a multiple of these distances.

For example, the Trek Women Triathlon Series has the following distances: 1 km for the swim, 20 km for the bike, and 5 km for the run, which are the standard lengths for a sprint triathlon. If this was your target race, you would simply take a multiplying factor and apply it to those distances. I've used 3 as the multiplier in this example, the level of an experienced beginner. To determine your weekly training volume, multiply the sprint distances by 3, and that will equal your weekly training distance.

Multiple	×	Distances	=	Total Distance to Train per Week
3	×	1 km swim	=	3 km swim per week
3	×	20 km bike	=	60 km bike per week
3	×	5 km run	=	15 km run per week

This approach to training is called the "power of the distance." Using the power of the distance, on the third level, your total weekly volume for a sprint triathlon would be 3 kilometers (just under 2 miles) of swimming, 60 kilometers (37 miles) on your bike, and 15 kilometers (9 miles) of running. For an international-distance triathlon, your weekly volume would tally to 4,500 meters (2.75 miles) for swimming, 120 kilometers (75 miles) for cycling, and 30 kilometers (18.6 miles) for running.

APPLYING THE POWER OF DISTANCE

How much time would it take you to train at the power of three for a sprint triathlon? Here we'll do some more math. It wouldn't do for you to think you were doing power-of-three distances only to discover that it was impossible to meet that goal within the parameters of your annual training volume. Calculate the time it would take to go these distances each week at reasonable speeds for your ability, then see if you can fit power-of-three distances into the amount of time you have available.

The easiest way to calculate the time needed is to break the distances into parts, time the parts, and then multiply the result by the total distance. For example, we found earlier that using the multiplier of 3, you would need to swim 3 kilometers per week if you wanted to compete in a sprint triathlon. If you can swim 100 meters in 2 minutes, then swimming 3 kilometers (3,000 meters) per week would take you 60 minutes a week (30 times as long). You would do a similar calculation based on your running and cycling times. Add them up, and you have it.

Let's look at an example to see just how this method works. Let's say that a novice triathlete, Ann, wants to do the Trek race. She can swim 100 meters in 2 minutes, so, as we know from the example above, she will need to swim for an hour each week. Next, let's say she can bike at a speed of about 20 kilometers per hour. So the 60 kilometers a week required by the power-of-three method would take her 3 hours. Finally, if Ann can run a kilometer in 5 minutes, then 15 kilometers will take her 1 hour and 15 minutes. Add it all up, and Ann needs at least 5 hours and 15 minutes to train each week (not counting warm-ups, stretches, and the like).

If she had less than 5 hours and 15 minutes available for swim, bike, and run workouts, she could go down to a power of two; if she had more time, she could go up to a power of four. Either way, this principle would keep her workouts well balanced.

As you become more dedicated to tri-training and your fitness level increases, you should increase your multiplier to 4 or 5. This is preferable to increasing your intensity or training in higher training zones. Your average speed will vary depending on your experience and your ability, but you can use Table 4.11 as a rough guide. When you are just getting started you select the power that most closely resembles your last consistent week of training. When the workouts seem easier and your performance plateaus, you can step up to the next level. Of course the duration and intensity of your workouts will vary throughout the week.

Maybe you are under the impression—or have even read—that there is a secret formula that triathlon greats have used to compete effectively and stay healthy. In fact, no such formula exists. Training is specific and

TABLE 4.11 Estimating Training Schedules Using Power of Distance

EXPERIENCE	POWER	MINIMUM WEEKLY DISTANCES (km)			AVG. DAILY WORKOUT (hr.: min.)	EST. WEEKLY TRAINING (hr.: min.)
		Swim	Bike	Run		
Novice *Train at this level 2–4 weeks.*	1	1	20	5	0:15–0:30	1:30–3:00
New to triathlon *Train at this level 4–8 weeks.*	2	2	40	10	0:35–0:45	1:50–4:30
Beginner *Train at this level until you are ready to move to the intermediate stage.*	3	3	60	15	0:35–0:55	3:30–5:30
Intermediate *Train at this level 4–12 weeks.*	4	4	80	20	0:50–1:10	5:00–7:00
Advanced	5	5	100	25	0:55–1:15	5:30–7:30
Competitor	6	6	120	30	1:10–1:20	7:00–8:00
Elite or pro	7	7	140	35	1:20–1:30	8:00–9:00
	8	8	160	40	1:30–1:40	9:00–10:00
	9	9	180	45	1:40–2:00	10:00–12:00
Ironwoman	10	10	200	50	over 2:00	>12:00

individual to you. I've entered my sixth decade and my third decade as a professional athlete, and still I follow a training program, write my plan around my goals, log every key indicator, and review my plan. If you want to improve in the future, record the present and review the past.

~~~~~

Faido! Faido! Faido! Japanese chanted this rhythmically as I raced on roads lined with rice paddies and over the narrow macadam streets of Ironman Japan. As I approached the finish line they continued applauding, yelling "Faido!" I thought the word meant "second," since that was my position in the field. When I asked an English-speaking Japanese triathlete for the meaning she told me *faido* means "to fight."

I was startled to hear this, since "fighting" in my mind meant causing harm to others, and while I am competitive by nature, I don't think of fighting my opponents. She saw my confusion and ex-

Faido! Faido! Faido!

plained that to the Japanese *faido* is fighting against the internal obstacles or inner self that prevents you from doing your best.

Once you've done the training, this kind of doubt is the only obstacle that remains in your path. I'm confident that you will overcome it.

5

Basic Moves for Swimming

S ome triathletes seem to feel more comfortable in the water than on land. Their favorite workouts are the swim sessions. Others still feel a little reluctant to get their feet wet—that first plunge just never seems easy. Whichever category you are in, if you want to do well in triathlon, focusing on the swim is extremely important.

If you are already a strong swimmer, focusing on your form and working on drills will improve your overall performance. Plenty of swimmers put in time at the pool but are still missing out on reaching their optimum performance because they are not making the distinctions in their form that will bring their swimming to the next level. If you are not a strong swimmer, this chapter will offer you plenty of tips and help you feel more comfortable in the water. The emphasis here is how to train more effectively, race faster, and enjoy the entire process more. This chapter covers correct swimming form as well as swimming distances and swim drills that will be useful in training for a triathlon. For tips on how to swim in a racing situation, see Chapter 9, "Racing: You Go, Girlfriend." To plan what to buy for swimming, see Chapter 10, "Tools of the Triathlon Game."

For many people the swim is the most challenging of the three sports. I have met countless people who said they might try a triathlon if it weren't for the swimming. But the more you train in the pool, the more you will enjoy the swim. If swimming is a strong sport for you, it sets you up for a great race. If you find swimming a challenge, be encouraged by the fact that it is the shortest leg of a triathlon, both in terms of time and distance, so once you are done you can move on to the rest of the race, feeling proud of all you have accomplished to get to T1 (the first transition of the race). Having the experience and skills to get yourself into a good rhythm is an important goal. If you feel strong and confident in the water, you will be relaxed and more prepared, both physically and mentally, to complete the race.

The first decision you'll need to make when it comes to swimming is where to swim. Finding access to water can be a challenge, since many gyms do not have pools. If you can join a YMCA, JCC, or other community recreation center with a pool, you're in luck. Colleges and universities often offer community memberships for their athletic centers. But even training in a backyard pool has its benefits, and some people who swim regularly even install lap pools on their property or in their basements. Some hotels will allow members of a community to pay a fee to use the pool, too. The other option, of course, is a private swimming club membership. Check out the options in your community, and compare the hours for lap swimming to make sure you'll be able to work out without having to dodge people who are there just to relax and play. (For more information on choosing a pool, see Chapter 10.)

Some women avoid swimming because they dislike wearing a bathing suit. Once you get in the water, though, no one can tell how you look in your suit anyway, so get in that water and start to swim! If you lack confidence in the water, starting swim training sooner rather than later will give you a chance to feel more confident.

FREESTYLE TECHNIQUE

For practical reasons, the stroke used in triathlons is the freestyle (also known as the "crawl"). The breaststroke, the backstroke, the butterfly, and others simply are not as efficient or as quick as the freestyle. Chapter 9 explains the importance of having a backup stroke that you have practiced and feel comfortable with in case of unexpected situations on race day, but use the majority of your training to develop your best freestyle stroke. As you work on your swimming, an efficient stroke that relies first and foremost on correct body positioning is the key. Without proper form, you can exert tremendous energy and find that you are lagging behind your goal times and fellow competitors. Form takes practice, but you can make tremendous gains if you enlist a knowledgeable swimming instructor to watch your technique. You can't just power through the swim—even very subtle errors will create drag that will add seconds or minutes.

First we'll cover some basics about body positioning, breathing, stroking, and kicking. Then I'll explain how to approach your swim training and give you specific drills to help you improve your technique.

> **TIP** Form is what gives you economy of movement and allows you to glide through the water as efficiently as possible. By rotating your body, you swim on your side instead of flat in the water, and this streamlines your body position so that you are creating as little drag as possible. With proper hand positioning, you maximize efficiency and forward velocity.

Body Positioning

The more streamlined your body is, the less resistance you will cause and the faster you will move. Compared with fish, humans aren't very streamlined creatures, but we can compensate a great deal by positioning our limbs to reduce the amount of drag our bodies create against the water. It used to be that swimmers would try to lie as flat as possible, with the body parallel to the surface of the water. The assumption was that this was the most hydrodynamic position. The more recent thinking on swimming is to spend more time at an angle to the water by being on your sides, with each hand extended above your head in turn and your head positioned so that you're looking straight down at the bottom of the pool. This makes you longer in proportion to your width, with a silhouette more like a fish; therefore you have less resistance and can go faster for less energy expense. Once you get the hang of this, you will feel yourself slipping through the water with long, powerful strokes (see Figure 5.1).

When you swim, you are really slicing through the water with each hand extended to your full reach, not pushing through the water with your shoulders. Don't hang your head, and don't look forward, except to see the pool wall. Keep your spine straight, from your head down to your hips—don't swivel at the waist. Core strength, meaning the strength of your chest, abs, and back, is very important in swimming. Use that core to power your arms and keep your legs up. Count the number of strokes that you take for one length of the pool. The fewer strokes the better. Extend your body fully with each stroke, focus on swimming tall, and try to glide between strokes, making each glide long and smooth. Try not to make bubbles, as they create drag. You want to eliminate as much drag or resistance in the water as possible.

Check your freestyle form for these essential placements:

FIGURE 5.1: Proper freestyle position

- The body is rotated to a balanced position on the side, creating a frontal area that can be imagined as a body-width tube.
- The hand and lead arm are anchored as the catch is initiated.
- The head is aligned with the body and remains in this position through the full stroke cycle.
- Underwater exhalation is continuous between inhalations. No nose plugs are needed if you can learn to exhale this way!

CHECK FORM AS YOU SWIM

As you are swimming, keep returning to your body positioning and check your overall form. It is all too easy to get into bad habits, so run a mental check now and then to make sure you are addressing these three important issues:

Question 1: Is Your Body Level in the Water?

Make sure that your lower body is not sinking. Trying to lift the head too high or not kicking efficiently can both cause the lower body to drop down too low in the water.

Question 2: Is Your Body Moving Sideways (Laterally)?

Make sure you're not wasting energy by moving sideways instead of forward. Sideways movement can be caused by moving your head out of alignment; also, lateral (rather than vertical) movement of the arms tends to produce lateral movement of the body.

Question 3: Is Your Body Rolling Enough?

Make sure your torso and legs are rolling from side to side so much that your shoulders alternately point toward the pool bottom. Roll is necessary to give you that streamlined glide.

Stroking

THE CATCH

The catch position (as the reaching hand enters the water) initiates the body rotation (see Figures 5.2a and 5.2b). Under the water, the palm is facing you; your arm is slightly rounded as if you were reaching around a barrel. With the catch hand anchored by the rotated body, a high elbow position, and a straight line from the elbow to the finger-tips, the body is pulled through the imag-ined frontal area tube. The elbow remains high as the hips pass the anchored hand, so the body must have rotated to the other side by that time. The other hand will have entered the water as the body rotated. Try this in a mirror!

THE PULL

The direction of the pull is straight back, but in reality, it slips a little bit at an angle due to the physics of motion in water. Press down with your shoulder, using your body strength, to add power to the stroke (see Figure 5.3).

When your arm enters the water, it stretches forward as your body rolls. While one arm is extended completely forward, pause briefly while the other arm is finishing the stroke. The other arm should finish the stroke almost against the side of your body. This makes you longer in the water, which helps you move faster. The goal is to move farther with fewer strokes.

FIGURE 5.2a: The catch, part 1

FIGURE 5.2b: The catch, part 2

FIGURE 5.3: The pull

Breathing

Correct breathing technique in swimming takes work and practice. As you rotate in the balanced freestyle position, your head should cause a wake that creates a water-free trough (or bow-wave), perfectly located for you

> **TIP** "Thumb by thigh, elbow high": Keep this mantra in mind while you swim the freestyle. It's a phrase I learned from Josh Davis, five-time Olympic medalist. What he means is, as you pull your arm out of the water, keep your thumb close to your thigh (and the whole side of your body), so that the elbow is the first thing to come out. Try it: It really works!

to make a quick inhalation (see Figure 5.4). If you lift your head, or fail to rotate properly, you will end up craning your neck to gasp for air, thus losing the balanced swimmer position. If this sounds familiar, let's work on your breathing, one step at a time. To get good breathing technique,

FIGURE 5.4: Breathing

first try and relax! Try breathing with your ear in the water—resting on the water like a pillow. Do not lift the head to breathe, but rather, roll. The rotation comes from your body, not from turning your head. When you lift your head, your feet sink, causing you to break the horizontal alignment and requiring a harder kick to maintain body position. Your head and neck position remains the same throughout the rotating/breathing sequence. Your face turns sideways, as if you were looking across the horizon or across the water. One eye should be in the water, and you should try to open one side of your mouth, like Popeye, to inhale. As you breathe through your mouth, roll partway to the side and twist your neck hinge on its axis, just enough to get air, without lifting your head.

The foundational skill for swimming is learning to balance and rotate. Breathing and propulsion follow naturally. Once you have the basics of breathing down, you can work on skills such as bilateral breathing (alternating breathing on each side), which is useful in triathlons for sighting.

Kicking

Kicking is not a major part of distance swimming (i.e., distances over 200 meters). Generally, aim for a two-beat kick (each leg kicks once with each arm rotation). Since the two directions in a kick—up and down—are perpendicular to your direction of travel, it may seem almost counterproductive to kick. It's not. The flutter kick is a very important aspect of the crawl. The primary purposes of the flutter kick are to give you stability first and forward motion second, since the legs offer minimal propulsive force while you are swimming long distances.

It is vital to note that the up-and-down leg movement must not be rigid, or it will cancel itself out. This is one reason swimmers are flexible—they must have a large range of motion, particularly of the feet and ankles, to allow for forward propulsion, because the feet serve as flippers. The legs contribute to streamlining and body positioning (alignment) and help to keep the body from weaving laterally. To be stable, you must flex

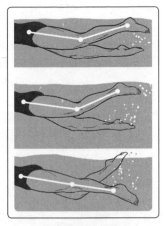

FIGURE 5.5: Two-beat
flutter kick

your hip and push downward with your thigh as you begin the downbeat and point your toes upward and backward. Because the body rolls as you kick, there is a slight kick outward as well. Your downbeat is finished when the leg is completely straight and just below your body (see Figure 5.5).

Do not kick too forcefully or it will cause your legs and feet to drop. And kicking too strenuously will leave you too little energy for the bike and run to follow! Your kick should not make a big splash, but rather just "churn" the water. Keep your legs straight, but not rigid, with your toes pointed out, and kick up and down. Continue kicking the entire time.

TIP The leg action is loose and whiplike, especially in the ankles, during a flutter kick. The downbeat is a more powerful action than the upbeat. Pay attention to the details until good kicking form feels natural to you:

- Pointing your toes is essential to get power from the flutter kick.
- Don't kick too hard—instead use your kick as a rudder.
- Kick only the minimum amount necessary to maintain body positioning.
- The legs should hesitate between kicks.

Getting the Whole Picture

The problem with arranging your body into the correct alignment is that it is very difficult to visualize yourself as you swim. Ask someone knowledgeable, such as a coach or fellow swimmer, to check your body position-

FREESTYLE POINTERS

The illustrations that follow highlight the most important aspects of good freestyle technique. This builds on what we've covered: breathing and the catch and pull.

DURING THE FIRST PART OF THE STROKE THE ELBOW IS HIGHER THAN THE HAND.

AFTER THE ARM IS EXTENDED FORWARD, PAUSE BRIEFLY WHILE THE OTHER ARM CONTINUES TO STROKE.

THE PULL SHOULD FEEL LIKE REACHING OVER A BARREL.

THE HAND STAYS BELOW THE BODY IN THE WATER.

ing in the water regularly. Find out if there is a masters swim organization near you. Masters swimmers clubs organize workouts, clinics, and even local competitions for adults, which can be both motivating and social. It would also be to your benefit as a swimmer to train for a triathlon with a Heart Zones USA certified coach or to take some private swimming lessons. Total Immersion offers triathlon-specific classes. Find a swim coach to videotape you swimming so that you can see your form for yourself. This is an invaluable training tool. Get as much expert advice as you can regardless of your experience or skill level. You might think that only advanced triathletes should get help from a coach to refine their swimming. But it is equally important for beginners to get advice so that they do not develop incorrect habits right from the start.

SWIM TRAINING

Now that you have the information you need to perfect your form, it's time to consider the importance of swim workouts and drills. When you are at your training pool, find a lane that matches your speed. There may be signs at the ends of the lanes indicating whether they are for slow, medium, or fast swimmers. Familiarize yourself with the way pool etiquette operates before getting into a lane. For example, ask what the "pool protocol" is when you have to share a lane. In many pools, two swimmers will split a lane. If a third enters the lane you will swim in a counterclockwise fashion, and if someone taps you on the foot they are indicating that they want to overtake you. It is usually expected that you ask before you share a lane.

Swim training entails the use of vocabulary that might be new to you. You should also begin to understand the metric system of measuring distances if you do not have a basic grasp of it already. Although most U.S. pools are still measured in yards, some are measured in meters, which is how competitive swimming is measured. Once you've found a pool to train in, find out its length. Sometimes the pools are advertised as Olympic distance when they are really 25 yards, not 50 meters, so ask the lifeguard what the actual length is. Since triathlon race distances are generally in meters for the swim (and kilometers for the run and bike legs), you'll need to know how to make the conversion from yards to meters and vice versa to make sure your workouts are for the correct distances. For example, 1 yard is equivalent to 0.91 meters, and 1 meter is the same as 1.09 yards. The typical sprint triathlon has a swim segment of 750 meters, or 820 yards. Therefore, the swim portion of a sprint triathlon is roughly equivalent to 33 lengths of a 25-yard pool, and the swim portion of an Olympic-distance race is approximately 66 lengths. Usually a "lap" means up and back (one round trip, in other words), and a "length" means from one end to the other (a one-way trip), but this terminology can vary from person to person.

Swimming uses a training system based on high volume and intensity. This is because competitive swimming events tend to be short. Swim training is thus different from training for running and biking, both of which require more endurance. While endurance will be a challenge for some beginners, most of a triathlon swimmer's workout time is spent training for speed and technique rather than simply swimming long distances.

Triathlon swimmers should follow an interval training system, a method of using multiple, timed, repeat swims in a combination of rest and intensity. An example of the interval training system is to swim five 100-meter swim repeats at 80 percent of max heart rate, with 30 seconds of rest between each effort. An acronym for this format, and a way to help trigger your memory of the four parts to a set, is "RIND," which stands for rest, intensity, number, and distance. In the same way that a rind such as that of an orange or apple is the shell that encases the fruit, a RIND is the shell that encases the interval training system. All sets contain a RIND:

R = the rest interval between each repeat (in our example, 30 seconds)

I = the intensity of each repeat (in this example, 80 percent of max heart rate. Some swim coaches like to express intensity in other terms, such as:

Heart rate, such as 150–160 beats per minute

Departure time from the wall, such as at every 1 minute

Rate of perceived exertion, such as 7 on a scale of 10

N = the number of repeats in the set (in above example, five repeats)

D = the distance of each of the repeats (in our example, 100 meters)

TABLE 5.1 Optimal Rest Intervals		
DISTANCE (m/yd.)	REST INTERVAL	
	Beginner	Intermediate
25	5–10 sec.	5 sec.
50	10–20 sec.	10–15 sec.
75–100	10–45 sec.	10–30 sec.
150–200	20–60 sec.	20–45 sec.
200–400	45 sec.–2 min.	30–60 sec.
400+	1–3 min.	1–2 min.

Rest Interval

The rest intervals are usually described as a ratio between the amount of time spent swimming and the amount of time spent resting. Hence, a 5:1 ratio means 5 minutes of swimming and 1 minute of resting. The rule of thumb is to keep the rest interval less than one-half the time of the swim, or no more than a 2:1 ratio. The most common ratios in swimming are 3:1 or 4:1. If you swim a repeat of 50 meters in 45 seconds, a 3:1 ratio will entail a 15-second rest. Typically, you improve your aerobic fitness more effectively with short rest periods than with long ones. As your swimming improves, your swimming interval will be a harder effort, and you'll welcome the rest. If you are doing a steady-state workout (to train endurance), effort will be more moderate so your rest interval might be shorter. For an intermediate swimmer, the pace for 25 meters will be significantly different from the pace for 200 meters. Suggested rest intervals based on repeat distances are supplied in Table 5.1.

Intensity

The best way to gauge your intensity is to use a heart rate monitor. Taking your pulse after each interval simply isn't practical; a heart rate monitor designed for swimming is waterproof and easy to check. Many swimmers rely on their subjective perceptions of how hard they are swimming and periodically check their heart rate manually, but this method is just not as precise.

Number of Repeats

A group of interval repeats is called a *set*. Each set should last no less and not much more than 10 minutes in total swim and rest time. Ten minutes is about the minimum amount of time for a set because it takes 3 or 4 minutes for your body to warm up to training intensity. The balance of the time is then devoted to stressing the body's cardiorespiratory system so that the training effect can occur. The training effect is the improvement to the specific physiological system that occurs as a result of exercise, which enhances your overall athletic performance.

Distance

The training effect is not as dependent on the distance of each repeat as it is on the length of time of the entire set. So, to offset boredom or monotony, vary your repeats using distances from 25 meters up to several hundred. In a short-course pool—that is, one that is 25 meters in length—a 50-meter repeat will obviously require you to swim continuously for two lengths, whereas in a long-course (50-meter) pool, a 50-meter repeat will only require you to swim one length.

~~~~~

Keep in mind that using rest intervals usually doesn't work well with groups, because with group training there are generally multiple swimmers in a lane, and some are ready to start while others are resting. Therefore, in this situation swimmers generally use "departure time" rather than rest intervals.

A departure time is the sum of the length of the rest interval and the length of the swim interval. In our example, the departure time would equal the rest interval, 30 seconds, plus the length of time it takes you to swim 50 yards at the desired intensity—let's say 45 seconds. So, you would add 30 seconds and 45 seconds, and your departure time would equal 1 minute and 15 seconds. You would then depart from the wall for each repeat at the 1 minute and 15 second (1:15) point, as indicated by the pace clock. Some coaches would write this set as follows: 5 × 50 yards @ 1:15.

As your conditioning improves, your departure times will drop. After several weeks it may surprise you, because for the same perceived effort or heart rate number, you will be able to use a 1 minute and 10 second departure time and feel that the workload is the same. This is called positive training effect—you'll become stronger, fitter, and faster.

Let's take a look at some sample workouts to see the intervals at work. You'll remember that any workout, regardless of your skill level, should consist of three parts: a warm-up period, the main set, and a cooldown, as outlined in Chapter 3. (The swim drills specified in the workouts that follow are detailed later in the chapter.)

INTERVAL WORKOUT FOR BEGINNERS

Warm-up: Swim 100m (four lengths of a 25m pool). Swim continuously if you can; if you can't, rest at the end of each length until you're ready to go again.

Main set: Swim 4 × 25m, with a rest of 15–30 seconds between each effort. Use each repeat to work on your stroke mechanics (swim drills).

Cooldown: Swim 50m at a slow pace to cool down.

This workout is only 250 meters, or 10 lengths of the pool, but it's a great start. As you improve, you can increase the number of repeats. You want to work up to swimming at least 33 lengths, or 750 meters, continuously, since that's what you'll be doing in a sprint triathlon. Remember, it's not important to swim as fast as you can; rather, you need to be able to swim continuously for 750 meters. You don't want to try to race this, since you'll have to bike and run afterward.

INTERMEDIATE INTERVAL WORKOUT

Warm-up: Swim at an easy pace for 250m.

Drill: Swim 4 × 25m doing the Finger Drag Drill.

Main set: First, swim 4 × 50m, with a 15-second rest between each effort. Focus on your technique. Then either kick or pull for 200m, depending on whether you want to work your arms or legs. Finally, swim 2 × 100m with a rest of 20–30 seconds between each effort.

Cooldown: Swim for 50m at an easy pace.

This intermediate-level workout will give you a tbotal swim length of 1,000–1,050m. You can modify this workout by going shorter or longer distances or doing more repeats. Tailor it to your ability and comfort level, and vary the intensity to keep it interesting. Doing the same thing repeatedly is not only boring but can lead to injury, so be creative. Use the RIND concept to work on different aspects of swim training.

Building Endurance

In training for a triathlon, it's a good idea to swim the distance of the race at least once during your training, perhaps several weeks to a month before the race. If you are a reasonably strong swimmer, you might want to swim farther than the race distance to better prepare for race day. Since most pools are measured in yards and the race is measured in meters, you need to know how far to go. Use the multiplier of 1.09 yards for each meter. Here's how it works:

$$750 \text{ meters} \times 1.09 = 817.5 \text{ yards}$$

For an endurance swim a sprint triathlete should swim 1,000 yards (910 meters). First try it in sets, then try the distance continuously.

You can also use a steady-state heart rate test to see how you've improved. Time yourself swimming a set distance, such as 400 or 500m, keeping your heart rate steady in your aerobic zone (70–80 percent of your maximum heart rate). Repeat this test once every month or so. With training, you should take less and less time to swim the same distance at the same heart rate. This is a great way to gauge your progress in the water.

DRILLS TO IMPROVE TECHNIQUE

One important way to work on your stroke mechanics is to use drills. Drills train your muscle memory to have the proper body positioning, giving you more efficiency in the water. Always do drills at a slow pace, and keep yourself focused on your form instead of your speed. Drills are also good to do as part of your cooldown.

Balance Drills

There are a number of skills you can work on to improve your balance and become more comfortable in the water.

Basic Breathing Drill

If you are a beginner, this drill will help you become more comfortable with basic breathing technique. Head position is an important part of balance, and ultimately, body rotation. Most beginners crane their necks to breathe, creating drag.

FIGURE 5.6:
Breathing drill

1. *Stand in the water with your hands on the wall. Put your face in the water with your arms extended in front of you.*
2. *Blow air out slowly with your face in the water (make an "ahhh" sound with your mouth open).*
3. *Rotate your shoulders with your head and neck in a fixed position. Just before your mouth exits the water, do a big exhale out both your mouth and nose.*
4. *Inhale with your mouth shaped like Popeye's. When you breathe your head should lay on the water, as if it is on a pillow, with your ear in the water. Try to keep one goggle under the water.*
5. *If you naturally rotate your hips with your shoulders slightly, that is fine; you may even drop an elbow for better rotation. Make sure you are not rotating your head with your shoulders fixed; that could develop into a bad habit.*
6. *Turn so your face enters the water again and repeat this exercise on the other side.*

Dead Man's Float

This drill will help you find your pivot point, which can vary depending on how your body mass is distributed. A full-figured woman typically has a slightly different pivot point than a woman with a slighter build. When you hold your body in a relaxed position for this drill, you can identify this fulcrum and develop an awareness of it when you are swimming.

FIGURE 5.7:
Dead man's float

1. *In the deep end of the pool, get into a "dead man's float" position. That is, you should have your face in the water and your arms and legs dangling in the water.*
2. *When you need a breath, gently lift your head and experience the effect on your body in the water (do not use your arms at this point). Your hips may drop and you may start to sink.*
3. *Once you take a big breath and put your face back in the water, your hips will come back up to the surface.*

Rotation Drills

Single Arm Lead

This drill will develop balance, but it also introduces body rotation. You will learn to stabilize your head position, which will support proper hip position.

1. *Push off from the wall on your front, with your right arm extended, and begin to kick down the length of the pool.*
2. *Use the rotation of the hips to turn your body so that you can breathe. Do not rotate your head to get a breath of air; instead, rotate from your hips. You can rotate all the way to your back if you choose.*
3. *Lead with your left arm on the way back.*

FIGURE 5.8:
Single arm lead

Single Switch Drill

In this drill you will be doing the single arm lead while switching your arms. This exercise will help you develop correct hip rotation.

1. *Start in single arm lead drill (as described above).*
2. *Rotate your hips to get a breath, then take a freestyle stroke while rotating your hips back to center.*
3. *When the rotation is complete, your opposite arm is leading. In other words, keep one arm out in front as long as you can until you need a breath, then rotate and breathe. When you bring your head back into the water, your forward arm will finish the stroke and you will do the same thing on the opposite side.*
4. *Repeat for the length of the pool.*

Double and Triple Switch Drill

These drills build on the single switch drill to further develop your body rotation and bilateral breathing.

1. *Start with single switch drill as described above. Swim one length.*
2. *For the double switch drill, start on your right side, rotate to your left side, then rotate back to your right side and breathe. Repeat for a full length of the pool.*
3. *Finally, the triple switch: Start on right side, swim three freestyle strokes (rotating to the left, right, and back to left) and pause with your left arm leading and your body rotated to the left side. Breathe on the left side, rotate for three freestyle strokes, and breathe again.*

Stroke Mechanics Drills

Fingertip Drag Drill

Many new swimmers lift their hands out of the water first, rather than their elbows, in the recovery portion of the freestyle stroke. This drill will prevent you from forming that habit or help you to correct it.

FIGURE 5.9: Fingertip drag drill

1. *Swim the freestyle normally down the length of the pool, but drag your fingers on the top of the water as you recover.*
2. *Your elbow should be high and slightly in front of the hand. This can only happen if your hips and core have rotated so that you are on your side.*
3. *If you are swimming flat on your stomach without rotation, your arm will be flat and extended out in order to clear the water. If you notice that this is the case, work on getting the proper rotation as you repeat the drill.*

Catch-up Drill

This drill keeps the arms out in front of the swimmer and the body balanced optimally with perfect head position. Keep your body and spine straight, not twisting, and hold your extended arm straight for this drill. This will help you learn proper rolling technique and enable you to stretch out and go farther with each stroke.

FIGURE 5.10: Catch-up drill

1. *Start the freestyle stroke but leave your lead arm anchored in front until the pulling arm enters the water (having completed one full revolution or stroke) so that both arms are extended. (Be careful that you do not "cross over" center when your pulling arm enters the water. To prevent this, hold a kickboard in front of you, grabbing the back corners of the kickboard each time you finish a stroke.)*
2. *Then, pull with the opposite arm, leaving the other arm anchored in front.*
3. *Repeat this drill for the length of the pool, leaving the lead arm extended until the stroking arm catches up with it.*

The "catch" will happen in the middle of the pull. However, notice that the recovery arm had already entered the water just as the anchored arm began the pull sequence.

OPEN-WATER SWIMS

It is a good idea to practice swimming in open water as often as possible, especially as race day approaches. You need to get used to the conditions of open water, as it is often colder than a swimming pool and may be choppy. You may not be able to see the bottom the way you can in a pool, and there will be no walls to hang onto if you get tired. In a lake or pond there is generally some type of vegetation; if the swim is in the ocean, there are waves and salt water. The more you can practice in open water the more prepared you will feel. There will be lifeguards on paddleboards and in boats during the race to help you if you need it.

If you can, try to swim the actual racecourse as part of your training; it can make a tremendous difference to your confidence level, since you'll know on race day that you can do it. It will also make you aware of difficulties you didn't know you would have—for example, swimming in waves can be somewhat disorienting. With practice you will master these conditions. However, never swim in open water by yourself. Take along a training partner, swim with a group, or have a friend in a canoe or kayak to come to your aid if you get tired. Swimming through duckweed and waves is a very different experience from doing laps in a pool, and for your own safety you need to have someone on hand to help you out of difficulties.

Open-water swims are also the perfect time to work on your sighting. During the triathlon, swimmers need to lift their heads every few strokes to make sure they're heading in the right direction. You simply bring your head up out of the water and look ahead for the buoy or the finish, while you continue to stroke with your arms. Practice this regularly, so it's a comfortable part of your stroke. Without sighting, you can end up swimming from one side of the course to the other, especially if it's a wide swim course, and thus swim a lot farther than you need to.

Sighting Drill

One of the challenges of swimming in open water is poor visibility due to the number of swimmers and the cloudy water that is characteristic of most reservoirs and lakes. Since most people are unable to swim in open water frequently, it is important to practice sighting in a pool as if it were open water. If you can practice in open water, even better.

FIGURE 5.11: Sighting drill

1. *During an exhale, right before taking a breath but when your mouth is still under water bring your eyes up just above the surface of the water.*
2. *Don't bring your whole head up out of the water like a prairie dog popping his head out of his hole.*
3. *Glance for the buoy. If you don't see it, just look again next time. If you are practicing indoors, choose a stationary object at the end of the pool to substitute for the buoy.*

~~~~~

On race day, you'll be starting in the water with a wave of other women, up to about 100 people. (At the Ironman in Hawaii, all 1,700-plus people start together!) If you train with a group, plan to get together and practice this start. At some races, people will be in such a hurry to get going that they can swim right over you or accidentally kick or hit you while they're swimming. I recommend that people who aren't strong swimmers start toward the back or off to the side to avoid this risk. You can also simply take a breath and wait for the water to open up enough for you to feel comfortable before you begin.

No matter what your level of proficiency in swimming, it is extremely important that you focus on the details of your stroke and other aspects of your swim technique. Make sure every workout contains a significant set of drills as well as speed and interval work. With good technique comes a fast, yet comfortable swim. Races are unpredictable, so starting with a relaxed and practiced swim will leave you energized, not exhausted, for the bike leg of the race.

6

Basic Moves for Cycling

In a triathlon you spend more time on the bike than in any other leg. You are also more dependent on your equipment and your handling of that equipment than at any other point in the race. In this chapter we will be discussing bike-handling skills, drills, and training. To consider the additional skills you will need in racing situations, see Chapter 9, "Racing: You Go, Girlfriend!" If you are just starting out in triathlon training, you'll want to get the right bike at the outset; if you've been cycling for a while, you may be wondering if your current bike is right for triathlon. To make sure you're getting and using the proper equipment, see Chapter 10, "Tools of the Triathlon Game," which will also explain how to check for proper bike fit. If you have more than one bike (such as a road bike, a mountain bike, and a hybrid), and like to train on all of them, you should know bike-handling skills are affected by the type of bike you are riding and your position while riding it. The cycling drills in this chapter are best done on a road bike. Nevertheless, it is possible to ride different kinds of bikes for triathlon.

Some women feel intimidated by the idea of maintaining their bicycles. I would encourage you not only to learn how to do emergency maintenance on the road but also to do some of your own routine bike maintenance. You will find an introduction to basic bike maintenance in Appendix B.

You know you can rely on your bike to take you where you want to go when you understand what makes it run (and stop) smoothly and keep it in good shape yourself.

CYCLING TECHNIQUE FOR BEGINNERS

Becoming a truly good cyclist requires years of time in the saddle. It also requires falling in love with your bike—which becomes a continuing love affair that seems endless in miles and hours. However, at any level of cycling, there is a lot than can be done to make your cycling more enjoyable and more efficient. Once you've become acquainted with your bike (your second self), it's time to introduce the handling skills. These are the biomechanical riding techniques that enable you to control a bike effectively and efficiently in a range of situations. If this is your first time out on a bike in a long time, it would be a good idea for you to find a quiet street or parking lot in which to practice (church lots are good during the week, and school lots on the weekend). It is important for you to gain confidence in a controlled environment before you head out on the roads and into racing situations.

Mounting

If you are relatively new to cycling, you are using clipless pedals for the first time, or you haven't been on a bike for a long time, here are some tips on mounting your bike safely and efficiently.

Your bike should be in a small, easy gear before you mount. It's best not to have to exert too much force when you are just starting to ride, because that puts an unnecessary strain on your knee joint—often before you are warmed up—and could eventually lead to an injury. Once you get started, you can shift into the appropriate gear. This means that you should be in the habit of shifting to an easy gear before you stop your bike and dismount.

The exact way that you mount will depend to some extent on the type of pedals that you have on your bike. There are two basic kinds of pedals: clipless and toe clips. If you are just starting out in cycling, your bike probably has toe clips (cages attached to the pedal) because they work with most shoes. Clipless pedals require special bike shoes with a plate on the bottom to secure them "cliplessly" to the pedals.

If you have toe clips, start out with the right pedal in the two o'clock position so that you can start riding with a downstroke. To mount, straddle the bike and bring the pedal around to two o'clock, without sitting on the saddle yet. Your left foot should be on the ground about 4 inches to the left of the bike and slightly in front of the pedal. Tap the back edge of the right pedal with your right toe, turning the pedal to the upright position, and slide your foot into the cage without putting weight on the pedal.

The position may seem awkward at first, but once you are in and have tightened the toe strap, you will be snugly joined to your bike. Next, press forward on the handlebars, push off with your left leg while starting to pedal with your right, and with a smooth motion, slide your bottom back onto the saddle.

You will eventually be putting your left foot into the other pedal cage, of course, but for now leave that foot loose for emergency stops, especially if this is a brand new bike for you or a new toe clip. Practice riding around a parking lot or on a quiet street until you get a feel for the bike. Be sure to practice stopping so you can get some experience pulling your right foot back out of the cage. If your shoestrings tend to get caught in the cages, try tucking the shoestrings into your shoes before you mount the bike. Once you gain confidence and you want to get your left foot secured, just twirl the left cage by tapping it with your left foot as you ride until it is in the upright position, and then insert your foot. You'll need to learn how to reach down and tighten your left strap (with the pedal in the twelve o'clock position) while maintaining balance.

If you have clipless pedals, the process will be almost the same. You'll just need to get some practice "clipping in." To start, place the right pedal in the lowest position (six o'clock), step into the clip with your heel high and your toe pointed down, then push down firmly and listen for the "snick" as you snap yourself in. Then bring your foot up to the two o'clock position so that you can begin with a downstroke. The first few times you are trying out a new bike or pedal system, keep your left foot unclipped for emergency stops by resting your foot on the "wrong" side of the pedal. To release a foot from the pedal, kick your heel out a bit with your foot parallel to the road, using the toe as a pivot point. Practice clipping and unclipping on a quiet road until you get the hang of it. While you are learning, release your left foot well in advance of situations in which you know you will be stopping (or where you may be stopping, such as at an upcoming traffic light). And always click in with your right foot first.

Getting your foot onto the pedal must become second nature so that you are not looking down at your feet as you begin to ride. Look straight ahead so you can watch where you are going. All of this takes some practice, but you *will* get it. Once you do, it's going to seem so easy that you do it without thinking.

Dismounting

To get ready to stop, slow to a moderate speed by braking, but maintain enough momentum to keep your balance. Lean slightly forward, shifting your body weight to the right pedal and the handlebars, with your right foot and pedal at the bottom of the downstroke (six o'clock position). Unclip your left foot from the pedal (at the twelve o'clock position), apply the rear brake to stop the bike while leaning the bike slightly to the right, and step to the ground with the left foot. Slide off the saddle just as you come to a complete stop.

With some luck, you will always dismount on purpose. Once in a while, a rider dismounts without intending to (which is usually called "falling"). It's important to release the left foot from the pedal first because that way, if you do start to fall, you can simply put your left foot down on the ground to get your balance back, avoiding a fall in the direction of traffic. To further minimize your chances of going down, here are some tips on how to ride efficiently and safely with a variety of conditions.

Riding in a Straight Line

Once you feel comfortable with getting your feet in and out of the pedals, the first thing you will need to learn is how to ride in a straight line. If there's one skill that will keep you from crashing, whether on the road or during a race, this is it.

There's a rule of the road in cycling called "hold your line" that is particularly important to know when you are riding with other cyclists. Your riding partners or race competitors assume that once you've started riding, you will continue to ride in a straight line without changing direction by even a few inches. If you are going to change direction, you must let the riders around you know (see "Group Riding" later in this chapter).

You need to know how to ride in a straight line even if you are not in danger of hitting anyone. You wouldn't dream of running a 5K in an "S" pattern, right? Extra steps are involved, and that wastes energy. It's the same idea on your bike.

Practice the technique of riding in a straight line by actually riding on a line that is painted on pavement. Start out in an empty parking lot with long painted lines, then, if you have access to a quiet street with a line painted on the shoulder, practice there. If you weave like most first-timers, you might just need more practice. Relax and spend more time in the saddle. But if it seems difficult to get the hang of this skill, check to see if your bike fits you and make sure your saddle is positioned appropriately; it could be that you have to stretch your legs too far on the downstrokes. You might also be gripping the handlebars too tightly or have a bent frame or fork.

Once you have the basic technique, try holding your line when you shift gears, when you reach for your water bottle and take a big gulp, and when you encounter bumps. Next, find a curved line (or draw one with sidewalk chalk) and hold your line through a turn.

Braking

Understanding how your braking system works can help you brake safely. There are different types of braking systems, but in this book I will assume that you have the standard configuration, with the right-hand lever connected to the rear-wheel brake and the left-hand lever connected to the front-wheel brake. When slowing, use the right-hand lever, and when stopping, use both levers, but start with the one on the right. This ensures that your rear wheel slows the bike down slightly before the front brake engages.

> **TIP** To brake safely, you should always depress the brake lever for your rear wheel first (which should be the lever on the right-hand side; check to make sure your brakes are set up that way). Here's a handy way to remember which lever applies pressure to the back brake: The letter "r" is the first letter of "right" and also the first letter of "rear."

Try not to brake when you are going downhill, but if you must, use the right (rear) brake predominantly. It's better to "feather" your brake by squeezing the brake lever slightly and releasing than to jam the lever down abruptly. In addition, when you brake you should always have your left foot unclipped in advance so you will be ready to step down onto the ground. Before heading out to a road, practice braking in an empty parking lot, first while riding at a slow pace, then at gradually faster speeds.

CYCLING TECHNIQUE FOR EVERYONE
Pedaling

To pedal efficiently, you must develop a smooth stroke. It's easy for anyone, even experienced riders, to fall into the habit of simply pushing down on the pedals (also known as "mashing the pedals") instead of pedaling in a circular motion (see Figure 6.1). Instead, apply force on the downstroke and through the bottom of the stroke (well past six o'clock). On the recovery (upstroke), you should "unweight" the pedal, anticipating the forward force at the top of the stroke (eleven o'clock). When you make a habit of smooth cycling, you add power to your cycling. As for the angle of the foot

FIGURE 6.1: Mashing and circles

and the ankle, try to keep your foot parallel to the ground, with your heel at the same level as the toe, throughout the entire revolution. Don't be a toe pointer—pointing the toe down during the downstroke is less efficient than keeping the foot level.

Pedal continuously—don't stop pedaling when you're headed downhill. Instead, spin in a high gear (and cadence) on the downhills. Generally, you will want to spin at a cadence of 70 to 90 rpm (revolutions per minute) on flats or when going down a hill. Your cadence slows to between 50 and 75 rpm on the uphills, depending on the percentage of incline.

How do you estimate your cadence if you don't have a cadence function on your computer? Set your computer display to show seconds, and using your right foot, count how many times your foot is at the bottom of the stroke during a 15- or 30-second interval. Then multiply by 4 (for the 15-second interval) or 2 (for the 30-second interval). If you don't have a bike computer, you can use a watch that shows seconds (and I recommend that you use a heart rate monitor watch with a chronograph stopwatch).

With time, proper cadence becomes instinctual. You may have heard the term "high cadence" in reference to cyclist Jeannie Longo—her high pedal cadence certainly helped her win the women's Tour de France! The technique of pedaling rapidly is called "spinning."

Spinning

In "spinning," you pedal at a high cadence in a lower gear. The low gears are the easy ones to pedal; the high gears are more difficult. Spinning allows you work more efficiently by increasing your speed while decreasing the workload. It keeps you from exhausting your leg muscles before your ride is over. For long-distance riding, most cyclists spin at a cadence of 75–85 rpm, although there are some who prefer to spin at a cadence of up to 100-plus rpm.

To learn to spin, start by using extremely low gears and low resistance (ride on a flat course). If you train in low gears on the flats for a practice session, you may be embarrassed at how slowly you are traveling, but you'll get the technique right. Spinning is one of those techniques that takes as little as an hour to learn, especially if you are a beginner. If you already know how to ride, it may actually take you much longer to get the spinning technique, since breaking old habits can be difficult.

Some gyms have spin classes where you can try out the technique on a stationary bike, and this can be a useful introduction to spinning. My book *Heart Zones Cycling* includes indoor cycling workouts.

Shifting and Gearing

Shifting gears smoothly takes a little practice; understanding which gears you should be in for different types of terrain takes a little more practice. Again, understanding how your bike works will help you learn how to shift gears and why. When you look at your bike:

- You will notice that you have gears in the front (attached to the right crank arm), called chainrings, and gears in the back (attached to the rear wheel), called a "cassette." Each chainring and cog will have a different number of teeth on it. Figure 6.2 illustrates the chainrings and rear cogs.

FIGURE 6.2: Chainrings and cassette

- The shift lever on the left moves the chain onto a different gear on the front set of chainrings.
- The shift lever on the right moves the chain onto a different gear on the rear set. (Remember, "r" is for right and rear.)

- Higher gears produce lower cadences (fewer rpms) and make the bike go further for each revolution of the pedals. They feel great when climbing.
- Lower gears produce higher cadences (more rpms) and make the bike go a shorter distance for each revolution of the pedals. They feel fast and powerful on the flats and help keep you spinning on descents.
- Remember that you can only shift gears while pedaling. If you shift without pedaling, you will hear a loud noise and the chain may fall off when you begin pedaling again. If this happens, stop pedaling, or you may jam the chain. Practice shifting gears in an empty parking lot or on a quiet street while you are getting the hang of it. To begin, pedal smoothly at an even, easy pace and shift slowly, one gear at a time. Try out a variety of gears until you get a feel for them. You should avoid putting a lot of pressure on the pedals when shifting. (For information on shifting while climbing a hill, see the section on that topic later in this chapter.)

Try to hold a cadence of 70–90 rpm. As your cadence drops below 70 rpm (due to headwinds or a slight hill), shift the right shifter once or twice to move to an easier gear (inside, closer to the wheel), and your cadence will increase. As your cadence increases above 95 rpm, and especially above 100, shift the right shifter once or twice to move the chain to a gear further to the right (outside, away from the wheel), and your cadence will decrease. If you start to hear a rubbing or clicking noise that does not go away, it means the chain is rubbing against metal, the front derailleur. This is a signal to move the chain to a different front chainring.

One warning: If you have more than ten gears, avoid using the gear combination that stretches the chain from the inside chainring to the smallest or outside cog on the rear cassette, or from the outside chainring to the biggest cog on the rear cassette. The stretch can cause the chain to pop off.

Hill Climbing

This may seem hard to believe, but experienced cyclists have a passion for climbing hills. Hills are a measure of a cyclist's resolve; they present a personalized challenge and they allow group riders to break up into smaller packs. Hills are your friends, in one sense. If you can develop a passion for them, you will definitely get strong faster. Practice riding hills. Find one that is challenging and work it—do repeat rides up the hill until you master it. As you gain strength and confidence, you can try steeper and longer hills. The following guidelines will help you improve your climbing technique. Hills will make you a better cyclist so it stands to reason that hills are our friends!

- As you climb a hill, slide back slightly on the seat for more power, sit up high, and concentrate on applying power to the pedals (see Figure 6.3). If you stay seated, you are actually stronger than if you are out of the saddle. While you might be tempted to stand to maintain your pace, this forces the body to work harder, increases the heart rate, and causes you to expend too much energy. If you feel the need to stand, it will provide some relief to the muscles you use most (see Figure 6.4).

FIGURE 6.3: Climbing
in the saddle

FIGURE 6.4: Climbing
out of the saddle

- Climb with your hands on top of the bars—either next to the stem or resting on the brake levers. This position allows for more upper-body power and better breathing.
- Use your upper body to help you climb. Whether climbing in the saddle or out, pulling with resolve on the bars in rhythm with using your legs will help you keep momentum on the climb. Avoid excessive movement from side to side for optimal efficiency.
- Pace yourself. The goal when climbing is to reach the top of the hill feeling as strong as when you started it. Start at a comfortable, relaxed pace, and increase your effort when you are within the last third of the hill. Pedal over the top and enjoy the ride down!

On longer ascents, don't let your breathing get out of control so that you're gasping and panting. Control your speed, effort, and gearing so that you can keep breathing in a steady rhythm. During my first year of racing triathlons in Europe, a Frenchman rode up next to me and tried to start a conversation. My high-school French just didn't make casual chitchat possible, and I really didn't want to carry on a conversation during a race. I was using all my oxygen for more important matters. Curiously, he started breathing slower and deeper and gestured as if to demonstrate this to me. I realized then that I was breathing quickly and from the top of my lungs; he was trying to teach me the correct way to breathe. So I tried it—taking deep breaths, with my stomach cavity pushing out as I breathed in. Try this technique the next time you are climbing a hill—it works.

If the length of the hill seems daunting, try thinking of it in sections, such as thirds. Approach the hill in a gear that is comfortable and that allows you to spin at a good cadence. As you work into the middle section, try a slightly different gear or get out of the saddle occasionally to keep the momentum up. During the last third, you can try pushing the pace a bit.

Dealing with gears on a hill involves a relatively complex set of skills. As you approach a hill, do not anticipate it by shifting to the gear you think you will need. If you shift prematurely, you will lose momentum and make the hill that much more difficult to climb. However, you should shift to an easier gear before the grade becomes steeper. Shift to hold your cadence between 50 and 75 rpm (depending upon the incline). Find a "rhythm," and hold it up the hill. Another good rule of thumb is to watch your heart rate: Downshift as soon as your heart rate goes up by 5–10 beats per minute.

When you do shift, take the tension off the chain by pedaling as lightly as possible just before you move the lever, and don't move the lever too quickly—you don't want to get your chain jammed into the freewheel. First, shift the rear derailleur (using the right shifter) to an easier gear on the rear cassette (to the left, closer to the rear wheel). Then shift the front derailleur (with the left shifter) to the chainring closer to the bike. This method will allow you to shift gears while keeping a relatively constant cadence throughout.

As you reach the summit of the hill, the pedaling will get easier, and as you descend, you will want to shift your gears to increase resistance. First, shift the rear derailleur twice (using the right shifter) to reach a higher gear on the rear cassette (to the right away from the rear wheel). Then shift the front derailleur (with the left shifter) to the chainring to the right (further away from the bike). Continue to shift as you descend, and maintain your cadence on the downhill until you hit the point where you can gain more speed by holding a tightly tucked position than by pedaling.

Pedal on the descents with a cadence between 85 and 95 rpm. Do not brake excessively down the hill, and be sure to stay alert. As you approach the bottom of the hill and begin to slow down, shift your gears to make the pedaling easier and find a good rhythm that you can hold on the flat terrain. If another hill is coming up, shift back to a lower gear; be sure to take advantage of your downhill momentum to power up the next hill.

Descending Hills

Some triathletes find the downhills to be daunting, but they become less so with practice. I love the downhills; the wind flying by me, the speed, and the chance to close in on the competition are all exhilarating. On descents, position your weight back slightly (more on your seat than on your handlebars. Try not to squeeze the brake on the way down, but if you have to, then feather the right brake only (your back brake) to avoid flipping the bike. You can also slow yourself down by sitting up to increase drag and wind resistance.

Don't forget to pedal down the hill in a high gear; this will help you feel more stable. However, if you must coast down, squeeze your knees on the top bar for added stability. Find a hill you are comfortable with and practice. Lower yourself into the tucked position early on the downhill for better aerodynamics. In the tucked position, your chest is lowered to the handlebars, your knees firmly clutch the top tube, and your elbows are pointed in, with your head lowered.

Cornering

When cornering, adjust your speed and brakes before the turn for best traction. If you feel uncomfortable about your speed heading into the turn, then brake before the turn—do not wait to brake during the turn.

Your body weight should be centered between the wheels. Your upper body is relaxed, with flexed elbows. The pedal to the inside of the turn should be positioned between twelve and three o'clock. You may pedal through a turn, but time your pedaling motion to avoid hitting the inside pedal to the pavement. Put your weight on the outside pedal or press on the outside pedal as a counterbalance. Your shoulders and hips remain squared relative to the handlebars.

Unless you are going extremely slowly, all your turns will be based on leaning into the turn, not turning the handlebars. Survey your turn in advance, and pick a line (the path you will take) in the turn. Hold your line throughout the turn. To practice your cornering skills, see the cornering drill in the final "Drills" section of this chapter. Remember, in cycling, the rule is to hold your line, and here's another time when it's important to do so.

ROAD SAFETY

The number one safety rule in cycling is well known, but it bears repeating: *Always wear a helmet!* Your brain is basically like Jell-O. There are more ways than you want to know that even a relatively minor fall can cause brain injury, and a serious fall or a collision could cause a traumatic brain injury, which can be permanently disabling. You will find more important information about purchasing bicycling safety equipment in Chapter 10, "Tools of the Triathlon Game." Your helmet should be one of the types that meet the standards of the U.S. Consumer Product Safety Commission (CPSC) or one or more of the voluntary bicycle helmet certification organizations such as the American Society of Testing Materials (ASTM) or Snell.

Manufacturers also advise that you throw your old helmet away after five years and purchase a new one. In addition, once you have had an accident in a bike helmet, dispose of it, even if it doesn't appear to be cracked, as it may well have been internally compromised.

Here are some other essential safety precautions to take. I said above that wearing a helmet is the number one rule, and that is true. But staying alive and avoiding injury are the number one goals, and every one of these "tips" may be the one thing that saves your life in a given situation:

Equipment

- Buy and utilize a rearview mirror. Different styles are available; try them out to see whether you prefer the ones that clip onto your handlebars or the ones that attach to your helmet or even your sunglasses.
- Make sure you are visible at all times. Wear brightly colored clothing every time you ride. When riding at dusk, dawn, or dark, wear reflective clothing. Put reflectors and reflective tape on your bike.
- Use a white front light and a red rear light in low-light conditions. In many states it's a law that you do so at dusk and nighttime, but even if it's not a law in your state, it's essential.

Riding in Traffic

- Bicycles share the road with cars. When you bike, obey the road and traffic signals as you would in a car.

- Ride as far to the right side of the road as practicable, with the flow of traffic (in the same direction). Never, ever in a million zillion years ride against the flow of traffic. If you are going the wrong way, the driver of that 4,000-pound vehicle won't be looking for you there.
- Always anticipate what is ahead—and ride predictably. Anticipate hazards in advance so that you can adjust your position accordingly. These hazards may be anything from intersections to imperfections in the road that can throw you off balance. Hold a straight line when you ride and don't swerve in the road or between parked cars.
- Parked cars are another major hazard. If you are riding on a street with cars parked along the side, look for taillights that are on, which may indicate that the driver is about to pull into traffic. If the taillights are not on, look for people in the cars on the driver's side who may be about to open the door. Getting "doored" is common and often serious. Ride at least 3 feet from parked cars to avoid it.
- Before entering a street or intersection, check for traffic by looking both ways as well as in front of you and behind you. If you are waiting at a red light and it turns green, look before you enter the intersection to avoid cars that run red lights.
- Plan to stop for yellow lights.
- Always use hand signals to indicate your intentions to turn or brake. Remember to start making the signals in advance of whatever maneuver you would like to make. Signals are made with your left hand. Putting your arm straight out, parallel to the ground, means you are turning left. Turn your forearm to a 90-degree angle with your fingers toward the sky if you are making a right turn. Place your arm out to the side but pointing down at about a 45-degree angle if you are stopping or abruptly slowing.

Other Tips to Remember

- Pedestrians have the right of way when you are on the bike. Avoid using the sidewalk, but if there are parts of your route that make it necessary for you to do so, please use it as a guest and reenter the roadway as soon as possible.
- Slow down and use caution on wet or damp pavement.
- Use your left hand to drink from your water bottle. Practice drinking while riding when you are on a quiet street until it's easy for you.
- Never ride with headphones, not even on a trail set aside for non-motorized traffic. Not only is it unsafe, you are missing the sounds of

the outside world. You can't wear headphones in a race, so why become accustomed to it while you train?

- Don't even think about talking on the phone or a wireless device. You should have your cell phone for emergencies, but if you want to chat, stop and get off the bike first.
- Dogs like things with wheels. Dogs like to chase things with wheels. Dogs don't like water squirted in their faces from water bottles. Now you know why you have two water bottle cages.
- Why be a purist? Drive to the good spots for biking and avoid riding through the traffic. If you want to practice a favorite hill, try it before the daily commute gets going.

GROUP RIDING

Riding with a pack of cyclists requires fine-tuned handling skills. If you weave to miss a hole or dodge an object, you may veer into other cyclists and pay the price. When you attend your first group ride, hang back and learn, because when you are ready to ride in front, you will be responsible for letting the others know what is ahead. Some groups rely on hand signals for turns, potholes, slowing, stopping, and announcing an approaching car; other groups are more vocal; and some use both voice and hand signals. Find out what your group prefers.

Drafting

When you ride in packs and ride closely behind another cyclist in her slipstream, it's called "drafting." This technique allows the person in back to ride more easily, because the rider in front is reducing the wind resistance. Riding the draft can save you 15–20 percent of the energy requirements of riding compared to cycling solo.

Drafting, for that obvious reason, is not allowed in most triathlons. You will see drafting only in the Olympics, international races, and some pro races. However, when you ride with a group (and you should, to get used to other riders being nearby), you'll need to know how to draft, because this is a common practice in group rides. First, make sure that it's all right for you to draft—some riders don't want you "on their wheel," so some groups actually don't allow it or require you to ask. The way to ask is to say, "May I sit in?" If you don't ask, you can create a lot of angst or be considered rude.

TIPS FOR GROUP RIDES

Riding with a group safely takes a bit of practice, but it's an essential skill for you to learn if you plan to race in triathlon. With these tips, you will be starting that learning process; the next step will be to find a group, learn which rules it has adopted, and start out on an easy ride. Stay near the back of the pack until you gain confidence.

- Ride single file.
- Always let other cyclists know when you are passing them from behind— call out "passing on your left!" before you pass as you are coming up behind them. The rider you are passing may not know you are so close and cannot read your mind; you must communicate your position to avoid surprising her.
- If a car is coming from behind and you are at the back of the group, yell loudly "Car back," to let everyone know of the car's position. Likewise, if you are in the front and a car is approaching, yell "Car up."
- If you see broken glass or some other hazard in the street, point at the hazard or verbally communicate its presence to other riders to help them avoid it. Most cycling clubs have preferred methods of conveying such information.

As you ride in a draft position, you must be extremely focused, because you need intense concentration and skill to stay on the rear wheel of another cyclist. Finding the correct position will take practice, and it can vary depending on the wind conditions and terrain (see Figure 6.5). You will know you found the right spot when the effort required to maintain the pace becomes easier. Now that you are drafting you should shift your focus to keeping a safe distance from the wheel in front of you. When there are several riders drafting, the line of riders is called a "paceline" or "echelon," and the rider in front then pulls those behind. After her pull, she safely rolls off the

FIGURE 6.5:
Drafting

front of the paceline, rotates to the back, and tucks in behind the last rider to rest while the next rider in the pack takes the front position and pulls.

When it's your turn to pull, if you can't hold the speed of the paceline, drop back to the back of the line—it's okay to sit in the pack when you are new. All riders have experienced this at one time. Just explain that you are a novice; the others will appreciate the information and encourage you to sit in.

DRAFTING DIFFICULTIES

Drafting can be dangerous. One summer when I was riding with a group, we had a strong side wind coming from our right. An experienced and powerful rider was in the lead, taking us out at about 23 mph. After taking her 2-minute pull, she dropped off to the left. Due to the strong wind, the proper drafting position was about one foot back and two feet to the left, directly in the path of her retreat. As she slowed, we "crossed wheels," which means her rear wheel struck my front wheel.

The rider in the back always goes down in these instances, and I was no exception. I went down hard, hit my head, rolled onto my face, then my shoulder, then my hip. The next two riders dodged me and stayed upright. Knocked unconscious, I awoke to find an ambulance crew loading me into the rescue vehicle and dashing me off to the nearest hospital. A concussion, contusions, and a separated shoulder set my training back a few months, but it was a lesson I won't need to repeat—and one I don't want you to experience. Use extreme caution when drafting.

DRILLS TO IMPROVE TECHNIQUE

Bicycling drills will tighten up your skills and shape up your workout. Once you've mastered the basic skills described earlier in this chapter, advance to the ones that follow.

Cadence Drills

Here are two drills that may help you increase your cadence and maintain a smooth spin. If you don't have a meter with a cadence function, just count how many times your right foot is at the bottom of the stroke for 15 or 30 seconds to figure out your cadence. (If you count for 15 seconds, multiply by 4; if you count for 30 seconds, multiply by 2.)

Cadence Drill 1

Relaxation is the key to pedaling at a high cadence without bouncing. Keep your elbows, shoulders, and hips loose.

1. *Spin in a small gear, then gradually increase your cadence until your pelvis begins bouncing on the saddle.*
2. *Back off by about 5 rpm so that the bouncing stops.*
3. *Hold that cadence and concentrate on achieving a smooth pedal stroke for one minute.*
4. *Recover and repeat the drill.*

Cadence Drill 2

1. *Shift into a moderate gear and gradually increase your cadence until you're at 100–110 rpm.*
2. *Hold this cadence for 30 seconds.*
3. *Gradually ease back to 80 rpm. Repeat several times.*

Cornering Skills and Drills

One key to good cornering technique is to lean into the turn with your weight on the outside leg/pedal. Straighten the leg, and look in the direction of the turn. Your bike will tend to follow where you are looking. This is called "target fixation." The flip side of target fixation is that if you are looking at an upcoming pothole, you will tend to ride right into it. So be careful about what you are looking at; you might get there! With the following exercises, you can work on perfecting your cornering skills.

Cornering Drill 1

First, set up cones, sponges, or chalk markings in an empty parking lot. Make sure the cones are far enough apart so that you can accelerate to the cone and hold momentum through the curve. Then try the following turns. Experiment until you master each one:

1. *Attempt a serpentine course as you alternate which side of the cones you pass.*
2. *Try some U-turns as you ride up to a cone, circle around it, and ride back in the opposite direction.*
3. *Complete some figure eights around two cones.*

Cornering Drill 2

For this drill, mark off a straight riding course that is 20 meters long and 1 meter wide with sponges or chalk. Mark mount and dismount lines at the start and finish.

1. *Look straight ahead and ride down the course between the lines.*
2. *Your goal is to ride a straight line without touching the chalk lines or sponges.*

CYCLING WORKOUTS

What follows are some specific workouts you can incorporate into your training. If you are using either the beginner or intermediate training plan from Chapter 4, you can adjust the workouts to fit the duration and purpose of the plan.

For every workout, warm up for 5–10 minutes in zones 1 and 2 before beginning the main set, and cool down afterward. You may choose to combine two or more of these workouts in one training session.

> **TIP** Power meters, which measure your power output in watts, are useful for threshold rides. I encourage advanced riders to consider riding with a power meter.

Steady-State Training

Steady-state workouts are relaxed endurance rides done at 65–75 percent of your maximum heart rate (zones 2 and 3) for as long as you want or need to ride (typically over 30 minutes). Your effort is aerobic, and the pace is relatively easy. Steady-state training improves your stamina and builds a base of fitness.

STEADY-STATE WORKOUT FOR BEGINNERS

For a steady-state workout, cycle at the midpoint of zone 3 for 15–20 minutes. Improve your speed, endurance, and strength by increasing the total time over a number of weeks.

THRESHOLD WORKOUT FOR INTERMEDIATE CYCLISTS

Threshold training is a sustained effort done at a moderate to hard level of intensity, typically over 30 minutes. Set a continuous speed (using your bike computer) or a fixed heart rate number that is difficult but not impossible to maintain for the duration of the workout. Let's say you typically ride long intervals of 2–4 minutes at 19 mph. For a threshold workout, you would back down to a speed of 16–17 mph. Threshold training will improve your race pace and average speed.

Interval Training

Interval workouts consist of a maximum effort for short bursts, followed by easy spinning or rest intervals. On the bike, interval training teaches your legs to pedal faster and harder—that is, to produce more power—which results in speed and fitness gains.

Longer intervals (2–4 minutes in duration) will push your heart rate close to your maximum, sometimes pushing you to a more anaerobic effort. Long intervals improve your fitness and your tolerance for higher intensity training, ultimately making you faster. You will also burn more calories and have a greater training load by the end of these rides.

BEGINNER INTERVAL WORKOUT

Interval workouts can be simple, whether you use time or distance to mark your intervals. One simple workout idea is to use telephone poles as markers. Sprint for two poles and rest for three poles. (We talked about this as an inspiration for fartleks, which are a type of interval, in Chapter 4.) In the beginning, do three to five sets per workout; later increase both the number of sets and the distance (the number of poles).

Here's another interval workout based on time: Ride hard for 2 minutes into the bottom of zone 4 (80–85 percent of your maximum heart rate), then recover for 2 minutes to the midpoint of zone 2 (60–65 percent of your maximum heart rate). Repeat seven to ten times (28–40 minutes total).

INTERMEDIATE INTERVAL WORKOUTS

Workout 1. Ride hard for 2 minutes to the top of zone 4 (85–90 percent of your maximum heart rate), then recover for 1 minute to lower zone 3 (65–70 percent of your maximum heart rate). Repeat 12–15 times (36–45 minutes total).

Workout 2. Do a "ladder" of progressively longer intervals with 1:1 rest ratios. The first step up the ladder is 2 minutes "on" (riding as hard as you can in heart rate zone 4) followed by 2 minutes "off" (easy spinning for recovery in zone 3). The next step is 3 minutes on and 3 minutes off. The final step up the ladder is 4 minutes of hard riding followed by 4 minutes of rest riding. Next, go down the ladder, reversing the order of the intervals.

Recovery

These workouts will vary depending on your regular training load. Intermediate cyclists will be able to ride longer recovery rides without significant fatigue. That's key to the recovery workout. You are still developing your aerobic fitness, but it should leave you ready for more challenging rides, not exhausted.

BEGINNER RECOVERY WORKOUT

Ride at the easiest heart rate zone you can sustain for 20–60 minutes. Focus on biomechanics. Train your brain to think about cadence, technique, and hydration, and just enjoy a relaxed training session.

Fitness Assessments

AEROBIC INTERVAL WORKOUT

For this workout, you will find out how many times you can crisscross the aerobic zone. The fitter you are, the better you will recover from each effort.

After you warm up, start the main set by accelerating until you hit 80 percent of your maximum heart rate. When you kiss that number, back off and do an "active recovery" to the floor of zone 3, or 70 percent of maximum. When you hit the floor, quickly pick it up and go back to 80 percent. Continue this process, kissing the ceiling and recovering to the floor, for 15 minutes, counting the number of times you hit the top of the zone.

This is a cycling fitness assessment—the higher the number of crisscrosses, the fitter you are. Record all of this information in your log. But next time, try the workout differently: Zigzag from 65 percent to 85 percent of your maximum and count the number of times you hit that ceiling.

THREE-MILE PERFORMANCE TEST

On a 3-mile course, maintain the highest effort you can for the entire distance and record your time, average heart rate, and rating of perceived exertion.

This test established your cycling fitness benchmark in Chapter 4, and it's a useful measure of your fitness changes throughout the season. Refer back to the fitness scorecard in Table 4.1 to see your progression. If you do the test with other riders, do not follow too closely and gain a draft advantage, because this will skew your results.

~~~~~

Cycling is unique among triathlon events in that it does not take weeks for someone who has recently returned to fitness to become involved in regular workouts. Anyone can start an exercise plan immediately after getting a good bike.

It's a good idea to invest in an indoor trainer, or "wind trainer," that you can attach your bike to (see Chapter 10 for more details on this device). Using an indoor trainer, you can work out even when the weather precludes riding outdoors. Besides, there are some training exercises you can do on the indoor trainer that you can't do as well when you have the distractions of road conditions, handling skills, and weather. You'll be on your own bike, you'll be able to maintain your normal road riding positions, and, what the heck, turn on the sounds and the tube. Each time a food commercial comes on the tube, do a faster pedal cadence or switch to a higher gear until the commercial is over. Unless it's an infomercial, commercials last 30 to 120 seconds—the perfect length for an interval. I call this indoor training workout "the McJack," and my recently-returned-to-fitness friends report they are less motivated to stop at fast-food restaurants after they start doing this workout.

If you live in an area with indoor cycling classes at a gym, try one out. A 50-minute cycle class is a good approximation of the energy required to finish a 12-mile bike portion of a sprint triathlon. Try to find a club that uses heart rate monitors in the class so the instructor is providing you with verbal instructions that you can adjust to your own fitness level. "Take it up" could mean all sorts of effort levels, but "Zone 3 for the next 3 minutes" helps keep the group workout individualized for each participant. The extra motivation that cycling classes can provide can boost your morale in the early weeks of training. The bike mileage you need to put in to prepare for a triathlon will vary depending on your biking experience. As a minimum, for a sprint distance of 12 miles, aim for 12–25 miles of continuous riding or intervals in zone 3, the aerobic zone.

Hundreds of other bike-training workouts are available that you can use in your systematic training schedule (see "Other Resources" for my recommendations). You can also design workouts yourself—it's part of the fun. Or you can join bike-training groups or even a team (I recommend joining a women-only team). When you ride with other cyclists, you discover what they find most beneficial, and these same techniques may work for you, too.

7

Basic Moves
for Running

When it comes right down to it, the triathlon is a runner's race. You can be ahead in the bike and the swim, but to finish strong, you have to work on your running. Running is also the most convenient sport—you don't need a bike or a pool. Once you have the right shoes, something comfortable and functional to wear, and a few training tools, you can start running!

RUNNING BIOMECHANICS

Efficient running requires economy of motion. When you run economically, you will, like a car, get more miles per gallon of energy, and your engine will run with fewer breakdowns and with less wear and tear. I am going to show you how to improve your running economy so you can run more efficiently and faster.

It all begins with running biomechanics, or proper technique, which uses the structure, functions, and capability of movement to propel you forward in the most efficient way. It is also known as "running form." Small changes to running form can dramatically reduce rates of injury and increase economy. It has been shown that even a tiny improvement in efficiency can shave seconds and even minutes off of your time in a race.

GOOD FORM FOR BETTER RUNNING

Good form will not only make you a faster runner, it will also make you more comfortable. Best of all, when you are comfortable, running is bound to be more fun. When we repeatedly perform an action, we develop "motor memory." This means that improving your running form will require you to work against the habits you have formed over the years. The good news is that you can retrain motor memory. What follows are some things to think about to ensure proper biomechanics.

CORRECT RUNNING FORM

Head and Neck

- Jaw and face are relaxed.
- Eyes are up, looking 30 feet ahead.
- Head is up and neck is long.
- The crown of the head is the highest point.

Upper Body

- Shoulder blades are relaxed.
- Elbows are bent at close to a 90-degree angle.
- Arms swing low and relaxed, close to the torso and waist.
- Hands are loosely cupped; don't make a tight fist.
- Hands swing only as far as the center line of the body.

POOR FORM: OVERSTRIDING

Lower Body

- Footstrike is soft and quiet on the midfoot or forefoot (ball of the foot).
- Knee is slightly bent as foot makes contact.
- Foot rolls forward to the front and off of the big toe for power.

POOR POSTURE

- During the recovery phase, the foot lifts to a position that is level with or slightly below the knee.
- Contact time between the foot and the ground is minimal.

The figures shown here illustrate some of the most common mistakes. By focusing on proper posture and developing a more economical stride, you can avoid both of them.

Running Posture

When you are running, you might find that you have a very slight forward lean (3–15 degrees depending on speed and incline). Your ears, shoulders, hips, and foot should be in alignment at midstride. This means that you are maintaining an upright position, similar to when you consciously stand upright with your shoulders back. If you do lean forward slightly, your body is tilting forward from the ankles, not from the waist. I like to think of this as running tall. You are creating space between your hip bones and your ribs. Tuck your buttocks in and tip your pelvis back slightly to avoid leaning back. Your inner abdominals should support your lower back. Running with good posture will enlist your core muscles.

An Efficient Stride

There has been a lot of debate over proper stride, mainly centering on overstriding and heel striking. Overstriding occurs when the foot lands out in front of the knee, and this typically means that the heel is hitting the ground first. Kinesiologists advise against heel striking because it is thought to impede a runner's forward momentum, acting as a brake. If you first make contact with your heel rather than the middle of your foot or your forefoot, you are most likely spending more time on the ground, which typically slows you down. Furthermore, if you are landing heavily on your heel, heel striking can increase your risk of injury. Some people are naturally heel runners (I am one of them). I am convinced that heel striking may not be as bad as the exercise physiologists claim. My advice is to experiment with your stride by making gradual adjustments. Try a shorter stride and see if it makes you faster. Try to run with a turnover of at least 180 to 190 footstrikes per minute. Make it your goal to minimize your time on the ground.

Eliminate any other excessive motion in your stride. Your feet should cut a course directly underneath you, avoiding any side-to-side movement. If objects on the horizon appear to be bouncing as you run, you are directing too much energy vertically, which will negatively impact your forward momentum. To correct this, check the height of your knees as you initiate the stride and the height of your kick as you finish the stride—both errors will prevent smooth forward movement.

Faster running is accomplished by increases in stride frequency coupled with the optimum stride length. Running at an optimum turnover rate and stride length minimizes fast-twitch muscle-fiber recruitment and impact stress, reduces the need for vertical displacement (or bouncing), and provides the greatest energy return for the next stride, all of which means better running economy.

THE QUICK SIX

Here are the "quick six" symptoms of poor running styles:

Error	Effect
1. Feet slapping loudly on the ground	Leg, ankle, and foot stress
2. Shrugged shoulders	Upper-body tension
3. Arms and hands high, clenched fists	Tension, wasted energy
4. Flapping arms and hands	Wasted energy
5. Slouching forward	Excessive impact
6. Bouncing high with each stride	Wasted energy, muscle strain

One of the best ways to check your form is to study your reflection as you pass the glass windows of storefronts, have a friend take a video of you running, or find a large mirror at the gym so you can see yourself running. If you can, get a coach or someone knowledgeable about running to watch you run and give feedback. Your goal is to convert all energy and effort to forward motion.

Changing your running form is like changing your handwriting—it's something you must constantly practice to instill new patterns. Dedicate one day a week to training in your new efficient form, and work on it so hard that it becomes imprinted as your new signature. Just a few subtle

ECONOMY VERSUS EFFICIENCY

Running economy is different from running efficiency. Economy is a measure of the energy cost of each stride that you take, whereas efficiency is mechanical power output for a given level of energy consumption.

In running economy, the energy cost is measured using the gold standard of energy-use measurement in aerobic activity—oxygen consumption. Oxygen consumption is stated in terms of how many milliliters of oxygen you use per kilogram of body weight at each of the different speeds. The faster you run, the more oxygen you need and the higher your oxygen consumption.

The best way to know your running economy is to get a fitness test called a "metabolic cart" that assesses oxygen use and cardiovascular and respiratory responses. The test should cost between $125 and $250. The results will tell you your rate of oxygen consumption per minute (milliliters per kilogram per minute, or ml/kg/min.) or per kilometer (ml/kg/km) at submaximal speed. If you use less oxygen at a given speed, you have better running economy than a runner who uses more oxygen at that speed.

When we measure efficiency, we connect the power produced to the movement intended. Since exercise physiologists and coaches can't measure power output in running like they can in cycling (using a power meter), running efficiency isn't measurable at present. Efficiency is important in cycling and swimming, however, where anatomical structure and biomechanical skills are critical to performance.

changes could give you speed and help you avoid injury. When you have it down, efficient running is like being on cruise control—you can just set the form and the speed and run effortlessly for what seems like forever.

Breathing

To maintain good form you need to keep your upper body relaxed—it's the same with breathing. Breathe deeply and smoothly, not shallowly or through gasps. When you take a breath your abdomen should expand to accommodate it. Concentrate on fully exhaling every breath; this is even more important than breathing in. When training aerobically, you always should be able to pass the "talk test," which means you are able to carry on a conversation while training. If you can't, then you have crossed over the threshold to the high-intensity zones.

WARMING UP

The following three exercises are dynamic warm-ups that will better prepare your body for a run and help to prevent injury. These warm-ups are preferable to stretching, which is now thought to be more effective after a workout.

Grapevine

This drill opens up the hips and the iliotibial band (ITB), which runs from above the hip joint to below the knee on the lateral side. It also promotes agility.

1. *Moving laterally, step to the right with your right foot and cross the left leg in front of your right leg.*
2. *Again step with the lead (right) foot, and following with the left leg, now stepping behind your lead leg.*
3. *Start slow and then pick up speed.*
4. *Twist at the waist, swinging your arms forward and backward to follow the movement of your hips (as your hips move left, your arms will swing right).*

FIGURE 7.1: Grapevine

Monster Walks

This drill opens up the hamstrings.

1. *Lift one leg up and straight out in front of you.*
2. *With the opposite arm, reach forward as if you were going to touch your toes.*
3. *Step forward with the other leg, again reaching forward with the opposite arm.*
4. *Repeat the movement five to ten times with each leg.*

FIGURE 7.2: Monster walk

Leg Swings

This is yet another drill to work the hamstrings.

1. *Stand near a wall or stationary object.*
2. *Use your right arm on the wall for balance and swing your right leg forward and upward.*
3. *Your leg will then swing backward as far as is naturally comfortable, roughly 30 to 45 degrees. Your body should remain upright.*
4. *Repeat 10 to 15 times, then switch sides and do the same number of repetitions with the other leg.*

Another variation on the drill is to swing your leg laterally in front of your body, crossing the centerline of your body. This lateral movement stretches your quadriceps.

FIGURE 7.3: Leg swing

RUNNING DRILLS

These drills are fun to do, but that's not the only reason to do them. By using slightly different muscles, you will be helping to prevent injury, becoming stronger, and developing some of the specific muscles used in running to a greater degree. Do one or two of these as part of your main workout on run training days.

Skipping Drills

Try several variations on skipping—it's the same skipping you did as a kid, but with some new twists, all of which will improve your agility for running.

1. *Skip with low, quick feet.*
2. *Skip with high knees.*
3. *Skip with your knees pointed downward and your feet kicking up toward your butt.*
4. *Skip for height.*

FIGURE 7.4: Skipping drills

Butt Kicks

This exercise works on hamstring firing.

1. *Start out standing with your knees slightly bent and your feet in alignment with your hips.*
2. *Kick back with your right leg and try to touch your buttocks with the heel of your right foot.*
3. *Do five to ten repetitions, then repeat the motion with your left leg.*

Another variation of this drill involves the same movement while running as you kick back with the opposite heel on every footstrike.

FIGURE 7.5: Butt kicks

Strides

This drill will vary your stride cadence. Try each of the variations below while running in place, then while running. Each set should be 15 to 30 seconds. Focus on maintaining good technique and form throughout the drill.

1. *Begin by running in place and using a high cadence.*
2. *Add high knees while running in place.*
3. *Try out different cadences and find one that feels natural.*
4. *Start running while keeping same cadence.*
5. *Gradually pick up the pace to go faster, and then slow down.*

RUN WORKOUTS

For run training, keep the concepts of aerobic and above-threshold training in mind (discussed in Chapter 2). What follows are some descriptions of what the different types of workouts will look like: steady-state, combinations, intervals, and recovery runs.

Steady-State Runs

The steady-state training run lasts 30 to 60 minutes and is usually done at a light intensity level. For example, you might go 5 miles at an easy pace. If you are a slower runner, you would run for a set time, being conscious of your exertion level. These are aerobic workouts to help you build strength and endurance.

You can combine this workout with a steady-state heart rate test. Warm up for 5 to 10 minutes, then run 1 mile at a steady heart rate (the middle of your aerobic zone, or 75 percent of your maximum heart rate). Time yourself. This gives you a baseline speed against which you can test your improvement. After several weeks of training, you should be able to run the same distance at the same heart rate with a faster time.

LONG, SLOW DISTANCE RUNS

When you are building endurance to run farther, your steady-state workout will be run at an easier pace. Long, slow distance runs are submaximal workouts performed at a low intensity over a distance that is significantly farther than your typical training run. This is also known as "overdistance" training. The purpose is to develop long-distance endurance.

Your training heart rate for these runs will be zone 2, or about 60 to 70 percent of your maximum heart rate. Usually, your pace will be slower than your racing speed by at least 1 minute per mile. Try to maintain a steady, easy pace throughout the run. Your goal distance will depend on how far you are currently able to run. Build gradually. From one week to the next your total volume shouldn't increase by more than 5 or 10 percent.

TIME TRIALS

Time trials are runs where you go for a specific distance, at a constant (high) intensity, while being timed. They are used to measure improvement when the same run is repeated and timed after a given number of weeks or months. They are also called "pace training" because they teach you proper pacing, but ultimately they also increase your speed. If you are a beginner, repeat the 1-mile test until you build endurance and fitness.

When you do time trials wear your heart rate monitor and record your highest sustainable heart rate number in your training log. When you repeat the run, see if you can increase this number by a couple of heartbeats per minute. Ultimately, your goal is to become a more efficient runner, but pushing your highest sustainable heart rate will ultimately increase your aerobic capacity.

Interval Runs

As you may recall from Chapter 4, the purpose of interval workouts is to alternate between stress and recovery, hard and easy. Doing this type of workout will increase your running power, which is the product of your stride cadence and the force of your push-off. You are developing your power output in interval runs. With speed and distance data coupled with heart rate data from your monitor, you can track your power gains over time.

ABOVE-THRESHOLD RUNS

Training that involves an intense effort over a relatively short period of time, commonly from 30 seconds to 2 minutes, allows you to stress your anaerobic energy system with a near-maximal output. These above-threshold intervals are done for both strength and speed gains. When you are running, a good distance for an above-threshold interval would be a 400-meter run (one lap around a track). In between the hard intervals, do recovery intervals at an easy pace to rest from the last hard interval and get ready for the next one.

For an above-threshold running workout, run for a total of 1 to 5 miles, and during the main part of the run (after warming up), sprint for up to 2 minutes and then rest for the same amount of time or less. Your heart rate should be in zone 4 for the above-threshold interval. Toward the end of your sets, your heart rate might even reach zone 5 on these efforts. The recovery intervals should allow your heart rate to recover to zone 2. If you are a beginner, you might be walking the recovery intervals to allow your heart rate to adequately recover. A more experienced runner can do jogging recoveries.

THRESHOLD INTERVALS

Long intervals involve work periods of 2 to 15 minutes with intermittent rest periods between the hard efforts. The length of time for the rest period is such that you can maintain each of the repeats at a constant rate throughout the training period—usually 2 to 5 minutes. Do this type of interval work to increase your endurance capacity or your ability to maintain zone 3 for long periods of time.

Here are some more specific instructions:

- Alternate between the bottom of zone 2, 60 percent of your maximum heart rate, and the middle or top of zone 3 for efforts of 4 to 12 minutes, with the timing for the work interval and the number of repeats depending on your fitness level.
- For example, if you are moderately fit, do three repeats of 8 minutes each (3 x 8 min.), starting at the midpoint of zone 2 for 3 minutes and increasing to zone 3 for 5 minutes for the work interval.
- If you are a beginner, stick with three repeats, but change this interval time to 4 minutes in zone 2 and 4 minutes in zone 3.

Doing intervals is a great way to make long runs go by faster. Experiment with different variations to keep things interesting.

TECHNIQUE FOR HILL RUNNING

When you are running uphill, concentrate on your form. Good form can give you momentum to carry you up the hill with less effort:

- Use your arms more; pump them to get momentum.
- Keep the same cadence as on a flat course.
- Concentrate on using your hip flexors to swing your bent leg up the hill.
- When running downhill, try the following techniques for balance and speed:
- Lean forward and let momentum carry you.
- Lower the arms just a bit to keep your balance.
- Keep your footstrike below the knee to avoid "braking" or putting unnecessary pressure on your quad muscles.
- Maintain a quick cadence downhill.

RESISTANCE REPEATS

For another type of interval training, try resistance repeats. These are repetitions using some form of resistance for the increased workload interval, such as running up hills (with the rest period being the downhill) or running in sand (then heading back to the hard sand or the boardwalk for the recovery). These workouts increase your leg strength and allow you to become accustomed to running in various conditions.

ZONE 4 HILL REPEATS

This type of hill-repeat interval training is an advanced workout for the later stages of your training (see below for modification for less advanced runners). It is designed to improve your running economy and strength.

- Select a hill with a moderate grade, preferably not on pavement. Ideally, it will be a hill that takes approximately 3 minutes to climb. If you select a longer hill, find a landmark you can reach in roughly 3 minutes.
- Do three to ten climb repeats at an effort that reaches zone 4, or 80 to 90 percent of your maximum heart rate.
- Time yourself on each run to the top and check your monitor for average heart rate when you reach the top (or your marker). Focus on efficient form and relaxed breathing as you ascend (see sidebar "Technique for Hill Running").
- Jog or walk to the bottom of the hill, recovering to the bottom of zone 2.

If this workout is too strenuous to fit your current fitness level, modify it for your level. For example, only run up the hill for 1 minute, then stop and come back down. Extend the time by 30 seconds each week until 3 minutes of uphill running is attainable.

SPRINT INTERVALS

Sprint intervals are maximal efforts of 10 to 30 seconds, such as a 100-meter run. Try these on a high-school or college track. This activity is great for increasing your speed. You can do these intervals with complete rest or active rest between sets. Begin each workout with 5 to 10 minutes to warm up; include some drills before the interval sets. Beginners should start with a set of five sprinting intervals of 10 to 30 seconds each. Finish with a 5- to 10-minute cooldown in zone 1 or 2.

Over the course of your training, gradually increase the timing of the work interval to 10 to 15 minutes and add more sets. As you gain confidence, sprint for distance instead of time so you can see your progress. These workouts will build strength and speed.

Combination Runs

Any run that combines steady-state and interval running is a combination workout. Fartleks are a great example of this type of workout. You can make them as easy or challenging as you'd like.

FARTLEK RUNNING

Fartlek is a Swedish word that literally means "speed play." It's a method of training in which there are relatively long-duration, high-intensity periods mixed with low-intensity training (which serve as rest periods), but you still do a continuous workout overall. Fartleks are designed to increase your strength and to help you have fun with your running and stay interested in training. Most fartleks are a combination of intervals and steady-state running.

For one fartlek workout, you could go for 3 miles, running for 30 seconds then walking for 60 seconds for the whole distance. You can mix up the amount of time you do for each repeat; it doesn't have to be consistent (that's why it's called "speed play"). If you are on a treadmill and listening to music, you might choose to run quickly to the fast songs and slowly to the slow songs. Your heart rate should go up and down accordingly, reaching into zone 3 (aerobic zone) during the runs and zone 2 (temperate zone) when you're walking. Remember to warm up for at least 5 minutes before you begin the intervals, and give yourself enough time afterward to cool down.

More examples of zone running workouts are available in the monthly newsletter section of my website, www.heartzones.com.

That's it—you now have the information you need to improve your running biomechanics as well as a variety of run workouts to choose from to build skills, speed, strength, and stamina.

~~~~

When I was growing up, most girls simply didn't run; it was a boys' sport. As running started to slowly grow in popularity with the advances in footwear (specifically running flats), and eventually, the development of women's lasts (running shoes), women's participation in running became a reality and slowly grew.

My competitive running career started with a challenge from my college sweetheart. He said he could outrun me in the mile. We raced. I won. That's another story. But that was just a mile, and I thought, "If I can run 1 mile, I can run 6 miles." And I did. With each finish line I wondered if I could run farther than the time before. "If I can run 6 miles, could I run 10 miles?" I could. I ran a half-marathon next. Then it was the Pepsi 20 Miler south of Sacramento, California, my hometown. I finished that one in good time and found myself on the podium! That finish put the marathon (26.2 miles) in sight. It was 1976 and I led for the first 20 miles of the Silver State Marathon (Nevada) right on schedule for a 3-hour and 15-minute finish when the wheels came off for the first time. I hit the wall, hit an injury, hit the walk pace, and finished in 4 hours and 10 minutes with humility and a vow rather than wonderment—a vow to finish faster, not farther.

That vow didn't last long. Jump forward to 1978, when I set the Oklahoma women's marathon record of 3:06 minutes and said, "What would it take to break 3 hours?" I did that, and then the cycle of wonderment began again. If I can run a fast marathon, could I run 50 miles? That same year I finished my first 50-mile race and immediately entered my first 75-mile race, running the circumference of the deep blue waters of Lake Tahoe in northern California. I finished that one in 12 hours—a long 12 hours because of another injury during the race. And when I crossed the finish line I vowed to run 100 miles. Eventually I did that a bunch of times.

It's the process as much as the outcome in running and triathlons that I love so much. I love to run and swim and bike—and I love to just run. When it was announced that women would be allowed to run in the 1984 Olympics in the marathon, and that the top 200 women in the United States would be invited to participate, I vowed to be among them by qualifying. That race, the Women's Olympic Trails, was a race I'll never forget because it proved that women were not the "B" team or the second string or second-class citizens. The Women's 1984 Olympic Trials marked the beginning of the explosion in women's participation in long-distance running events. The race was on national television, and one of the all-time finest and fastest American women, Joan Benoit (later she added the last name Samuelson) won the race and later the gold medal. She demonstrated the joy of taking home the gold by crossing the finish line with the U.S. flag in her hands, a smile, and a big lead.

The moral of this tale is that you can go farther and you can go longer. You can test your endurance and your willpower by running on trails, running in organized races, running farther with each accomplishment. That's because the finish line really isn't a finish line. It's the starting line of your next adventure.

It's now time to start thinking about what to expect on race day.

Other Resources on Running Form

- See the website of Bobby McGee, coach and author of *Magical Running*, at www.bobbymcgee.com, for information on biomechanics and mental skills.

- See www.posetech.com, for information on the POSE running method developed by sports scientist Dr. Nicholas Romanov.

- See www.sportsinjurybulletin.com/archive/pose-running-technique.html for injury-prevention and treatment information.

- See www.walkingconnection.com/Walking_Technique_Form.html for information on fitness walking techniques.

The Art of the Transition

Transitions are unique to triathlons—there is no other sport in which you must make a quick transition from one sport to a completely different one in a matter of seconds or minutes. Throughout the transition time, the race clock is ticking, because there are no time-outs in triathlon. If you choose to hang out with your friends, relax to get a break, or take your time with a snack, you pay the price for it with your final time. The break might make you feel more energized, but the clock won't forgive you—or give you credit for it.

If you are a beginner, and especially if you are entering your first triathlon, don't stress out too much about the transition. Do be organized, and make sure you have everything you need laid out in a logical way. But you need not be worried about shaving seconds off your time. Taking an extra minute or two in the transitions to prepare yourself for the next challenge is fine. However, if you are at a more advanced stage, you are probably interested in learning how to make those transitions as smooth and fast as possible. Either way, this chapter will cover what you need to do to prepare for the transitions: what to pack, how to organize these items in the transition area before the race, and how to move yourself through T1 and T2 once you are there. If getting through the transitions efficiently and effectively is your challenge, this chapter is for you.

THE CHAOS OF THE TRANSITION

First, let me paint a picture of the transition scenario. It's essentially a circus with three rings simultaneously showing different acts. Picture this: swimmers running into the transition area, dodging cyclists in bike cleats who are jogging their bikes out of the area, who in turn are encountering other cyclists running their bikes back into the area to get ready to start the run—and all the while, race volunteers inside the area are trying to help organize traffic flow and maintain safety. Perhaps a bike rack collapses—because there are more bikes racked on it than it was designed to hold—or a triathlete can't find her transition place, or someone is cold or injured and in need of aid. In short, the scene becomes total bedlam—a spectator's delight and a participant's challenge.

That's the nature of the transition area. How do you avoid getting caught up in this situation? You can't. All you can do is be polite, avoid the congestion, laugh at the chaos, and smile inside, because through it all, it's fun. A triathlon is all your favorite activities—swimming, cycling, and running—blended with a little chaos, and much of the chaos is right here, in the transition area.

Nonetheless, you'll want to eliminate as much chaos as you can from your own transition experience. This will require a new set of tools and skills. Think of transitioning as the fourth discipline of triathlon, and realize that although it does not require the intensive training that swimming, cycling, and running demand, it still takes practice and planning. Getting the transitions right matters a lot at the advanced levels: Given two competitors who are about even in the three sports, it's the transitions that can determine the winner. If you have ever been "out-transitioned," it means you fell behind your competition because you were slower getting through the transitions.

To speed up my transitions, I break the concept of transitioning into two parts. There are transition activities—the tasks you perform during the transition, and there is the transition area itself to consider, the place where these activities occur. You can save energy and time both by streamlining your transition activities and by using the transition area to your advantage.

HOW TO GET ORGANIZED FOR TRANSITIONS

Planning your transitions in advance—and practicing your plan—is an essential part of triathlon preparation. During your "transition training," you can even time yourself just as you do in the actual sports, and challenge yourself to think of ways to reduce that time. There are some ways to minimize transition fuss by having the right equipment (covered in Chapter 10). But you don't have to spend a lot of money; just being well organized can do wonders to turn transition chaos into transition calm.

To get organized, first prepare a list of all of the equipment you may need, and save it for future reference (see my checklist later in this chapter for ideas). Keep in mind as you consider "must-haves" that the fewer the items you bring into the transition area, and the fewer pieces of clothing you need to change when you are wet or just starting to tire, the faster and easier your transitions will become. Keep your needs to a bare minimum. Even putting on socks before running shoes or pulling on bike gloves requires 20–45 seconds, and time is precious in triathlon.

> **TIP** For every item that you believe is essential, do a simple test: Practice putting it on or using it under conditions that are similar to those you will experience at a triathlon, and time yourself with it. Now do you think it is truly needed? Was it worth that many seconds, or could you do without it? One thing you can be sure of, veteran triathletes have less stuff in their transition areas than newbies do.

As for the transition area itself, remember that the space allocated for your gear is very small, no larger than 10 to 12 square feet. That's not much room, so don't bring a suitcase and the kitchen sink. Your transition footprint is for the essentials.

Some things can be done ahead of time. Pump up your tires after you remove your bike from your car, not in the transition area, then leave your bike floor pump and maintenance tools in your car. In fact, do anything that must be done with bike maintenance ahead of time—at home or in the hotel room if necessary. This includes putting your race number on your bike and attaching it to your race belt or shirt.

When you are putting your race number on your bike, if it is difficult using the "twisty ties" that are provided, a stapler and tape often work well. Similarly, to avoid waiting to be body marked, you can mark yourself if you know where and how to do it. It takes time when you arrive at the race venue to do all of these tasks, so save the time and the hassle and do them in advance.

Packing for the Race

Before you even begin to pack, get a triathlon backpack. Any gear bag will do, but a triathlon pack makes it easier for you to maneuver as you walk or ride to the transition area, since you can wear it on your back and keep your hands free to hold onto your bike. This is much safer than trying to manage a bike as you carry a gear bag.

Once you have your backpack, it's time for you to figure out what's worth going into it. Here is a checklist of what many triathletes consider to be essential. Copy it and annotate it. Transition gear is unique to every woman, so there are probably a few things you'll want to add (see Chapter 10). Some things are usually provided by the race organizers, such as a swim cap, a timing chip and hospital ankle bracelet, and, of course, the race number. I've broken down the rest of the items into groups to help you organize them for T1 and T2:

GENERAL GEAR

- Personal ID, such as USA Triathlon membership card
- Trisuit or other racing clothes
- Towel
- Sports gels or bars and drinks
- Something to distinguish your spot in the transition area on the bike racks (for example, a balloon or brightly colored towel—more on this later)
- Sunblock
- Ankle bracelet (optional, depending on whether you'd like to wear one that is more comfortable than the one provided by the race officials)
- Personal or motivational item, such as a picture or an inspirational quote (optional)

SWIM GEAR

- Goggles—preferably open-water goggles
- Swim cap (if not provided) or an extra one for additional warmth and comfort
- Wetsuit (optional)
- Flip flops or something similar to run in from the swim finish to T1, if needed
- Swim goggle defogger (optional)
- Earplugs, if you are prone to swimmer's ear

BIKE GEAR

- Bike
- Helmet
- Seat pack with flat repair kit
- Large plastic bag (to protect drive train and saddle if you have to leave your bike racked all night)

- Frame pump or air cartridges and adapter
- Eyewear for safety
- Bike shoes
- Full water bottles or hydration system

- Tool bag with extra inner tube, tire irons, etc.
- Bike computer with heart rate monitor (optional)
- Cycling gloves (optional)
- Socks (optional)

RUN GEAR

- Race belt or safety pins to pin your racing number to your shirt
- Running shoes with lace locks or elastic laces

- Sports gel
- Hat or visor
- Tank or microfiber shirt

EXTRAS

- Change of clothes and a towel for cleaning up after the race
- Camera or camcorder for a family member or friend to use
- Plastic bag for wet clothes
- Extra safety pins

- Sports gels or bars to eat before, during, or after the race
- Lubrication or glide for anywhere you might chafe
- Medication
- Reading glasses

Arriving at the Race

When you arrive at the race venue, give your bike a final inspection while still in the parking lot. Check the tire pressure and brakes, pump your tires, and leave the floor pump in the car. You'll need to head toward the transition area to organize your things as soon as possible, but first, take your bike for a final test ride, putting it into the gear you would like to start the race in.

Spectators are not allowed in the transition area, so say good-bye to your friends or family, then roll your bike into the area and look for your designated bike rack, which should be labeled with your name or number (unless it is an open-rack race). It can be a little overwhelming at first: The space is tight, almost everyone is nervous, and the lines to the portable toilets are ridiculously long. Arrive early enough that you will not feel rushed—when determining how early to arrive, take into account that you will need at least half an hour to organize your transition area. You will need time to wait in line for the bathroom, time to put on your wetsuit if you are using one, time to warm up and stretch, and so on.

HAZARD-FREE TRANSITIONS

Here's a suggestion of what NOT to do: Don't bring a bucket into the transition area. Buckets are used by some triathletes in transition to dip their feet to remove grit and sand that collects after they leave the swim and before they mount their bike. Others turn them upside-down and sit on them in order to comfortably put on their shoes. I caution against using buckets because they create congestion and a hazard.

The transition area is a busy place, with athletes moving quickly and often somewhat recklessly. Rather than bringing a water bucket or pan, I'd recommend an extra water bottle that you can use to wash your feet and an extra towel to rub them dry. It's less gear to bring into the transition area and takes up less room; a bucket just isn't necessary.

Racking Your Bike

There's another reason to arrive early: In the sport of triathlon, the early bird most often gets the prime real estate in the transition area if it's an open-rack triathlon. And the place where you rack your bike is where you will be setting up your transition area. Find out in advance what the racking situation will be.

Some triathlons have you rack your bike on race day; others get this task out of the way on the afternoon before the event, so you need to know what the arrangement is in advance so that you can allocate the time for racking. If you rack the day before, just take your bike at that time and a large plastic bag to cover your saddle and drive train overnight, not all of your gear.

As you've gathered by now, transition areas have two types of setups: open racks and designated racks. You will most likely have to rack your bike in a position determined by your race number, your age, or your wave. In an open-rack race, you can choose wherever you want to rack your bike.

In an open-rack race, keep in mind that where you rack your bike can have substantial time advantages. Take a moment before choosing your spot to notice the location of the two entrances and exits. You may want to rack your bike at the racks that are closest to the entrance you'll be coming in after the swim. Or you might want your bike by the bike start instead. It may be advantageous to be at the end of a rack so that your bike is more visible and you will have a bit more space to move around. Find the spot that you feel the most comfortable with, keeping the time factors in mind.

Once you've found your spot, rack your bike safely:

- Rack your bike by the back of the seat or by the handlebars. Racking it by putting the back of the seat over the bike rack can offer you a quick exit but makes your bike less stable on the rack.
- Situate your bike so that you can easily take it off the rack and run or walk, depending on the transition rules, to the bike exit.
- Racking can be easier said than done if you have a mountain bike or hybrid. Usually you can hang your handlebars over the rack or put your wheels in a ridge, but if you have wide tires, no dropped handlebars, and can't hang it by the seat, you may have to come up with some other solution. You can't lean your bike against a rack because it might knock the whole rack over, ruining it for everyone else.

Finding Your Transition Location

Once your bike is racked, put down your gear and do a location check. Finding your transition spot in a race of several thousand can be difficult, especially upon your return from the bike leg, as you will be entering from a different direction. Note, too, that unless you are among the first in the first wave, many of the bikes will be gone when you come in for your T1, and the transition area will look very different because so many bikes are out on the course. In addition, as you become more fatigued during the race, confusion sets in. Losing the location of your transition spot can cause both frustration and delays.

There are four basic ways to remember where you have racked your bike:

1. *Take note of permanent markers.* These might include trees or poles, for example. Make sure that you are looking at something unique when you memorize your location by this method. It's not very useful to remember that you are next to the big pine tree if there is another one on the opposite side of the transition area!
2. *Create your own visual marker.* Some triathletes use markers such as helium-filled balloons, which they attach to the bike racks. If you choose this method, purchase your balloon the day before the race, and use Mylar, not latex, so it will stay aloft. Find one that others are not likely to have. For example, you could select one depicting a favorite character of a child in your life and give it away afterward. (Some races do not allow balloons, so look into it ahead of time. Also, leave the balloon at home if it's a windy day.)

3. *Use a colorful transition mat or towel.* Place a brightly colored towel over the seat of your bike to serve as a marker when you come out of the swim (this means bringing two towels, as one will be on the ground for you to organize your other things on). Or try one of the nifty new transition mats from Lickety Split to organize your gear on—they are also colorful.

4. *Take note of your position relative to other racks.* I walk to the entrance to T1 and then walk back to where my bike is, counting the number of rows and then the number of racks in my row to determine the exact position of my bike transition spot. This position might be, for example, "5 rows by 3 racks on the left." Next, I go to the finish of the bike leg and follow the same procedure of counting bike racks so that I can find my towel and gear for T2. This second rack counting might be "10 bike rows by 5 bike racks." I memorize the numbers—5 by 3 for T1 and 10 by 5 for T2. Or you could write them on your wrist with permanent marker (not something that would wash off in the swim!).

~~~~

Take a deep breath and walk the route that will take you into the swim area, out of it onto the bike, and off the bike and out on the run—all transition-area navigational tasks that will have to be completed efficiently during the race even though you're fatigued and in a congested situation.

LAYING OUT YOUR TRANSITION GEAR

This section presupposes that you will only have one transition area, but in some cases you will have two—make sure you know which plan your race follows because you may have to set up separate T1 and T2 spots. After racking your bike and taking note of your location, place a small towel under your bike parallel to either your back wheel (if you rack under the handlebar method) or your front wheel (if you rack using the back of the bike seat). Empty your gear bag of its contents and store your bag next to the wheel and out of the way. (You don't have to completely empty the bag, as there is no need to take out post-race items like your snack for after the race or the clothes you will be changing into later.) Race etiquette calls for every participant to be courteous to those around her, so be sure not to take up too much space.

Place all of the items you will need during the transitions on the towel in the sequence in which you will use them. Organize your bike gear first. These items will include your bike shoes or cleats (unless you have them attached to your clipless pedals), with socks inside them (if you use socks); your helmet, open side up, with your sunglasses inside (or you can hang your helmet from your bike frame); and your jersey (if you are planning to wear one), which you can put on top of your helmet. You may want to put a nutrition bar or gel inside a jersey pocket. Now set up the items you will need for the run: your race belt or shirt with your number pinned onto it; running shoes; a visor or hat (optional); and any personal items you will use, such as sunscreen. Keep a water bottle for rinsing your feet next to the shoes.

You're now done, unless the transition areas are in two different locations. In that case, set them up separately with their own towels and gear arrangements. Make one last check to make sure your race number is in the transition area—affixing it to a race belt may save as much as fifteen seconds, as you can grab it and put on your belt as you are on the move. If the race is using "chip timing," affix the computer chip. Make sure your water bottle is full of fluid. Double-check that everything is organized and that you have been thorough in setting up your transition area. Take one last look at your transition area as the announcer calls you to the starting line, and relax: Your transition area is in order.

Next, grab all of your swim gear—goggles, swim cap, and a wetsuit, if you're using one. You may want to put a pair of flip flops or similar shoes by the exit chute of the swim finish, especially if the run from the swim finish to the transition area is a long or rocky one. Now, enjoy a few moments before the start of the race meeting new friends, taking a quiet moment, using the facilities, lubricating and putting on your wetsuit (if you're using one), hydrating, doing some stretching and warm-up activities, reviewing your strategy, and mentally doing whatever you have found to be helpful to focus your energy on the upcoming eight events (see Chapter 9 for a list) that are the pieces of a triathlon. If you race with a heart rate monitor like I do, look at your heart rate as you wait for the start. Anticipation of the start, better known as pre-race jitters, might drive your heart rate higher than normal, but try to breathe deeply and be confident in your preparation.

You have finished preparing for the fourth discipline, the transition. You are ready to begin.

TRANSITION EFFICIENCY

We train and we train—and sometimes, it is the mistakes we make during our transition activities that can botch the race.

The things that can happen in the transition areas can still surprise me. Your goal for T1 and T2 should be to get in and out of them as quickly and efficiently as possible. Because the race time includes your transition times, the faster you can get through them, the faster your overall finish time will be.

Here are my top five pointers for avoiding transition blunders; to drive my points home, I decided to share these anecdotes:

1. Get to the Race Early

When I was inducted into the Triathlon Hall of Fame, an event held in conjunction with one of the sport's national championships, I invited several training buddies to join me for the celebration and challenged them to enter a low-key event called the "Splash and Dash" to be held the day before the induction ceremony. It was for the sole purpose of having fun. They asked when to meet in the transition area, and I said I needed a mere 30 minutes to set up my transition area. Clearly, after more than two hundred triathlon competitions, I still have a few lessons to learn, because it took longer than 30 minutes to get my gear set up.

The swim part of the race was to be in the ocean north of San Diego. The starters announced two important safety conditions, but we were still finding our transition spot and setting up our gear and missed the announcement. The two announcements were that there was a serious rip tide at the finish of the swim, and that the ocean currents were moving swiftly parallel to the shore and pushing swimmers into the pilings of the pier. Sure enough, we experienced the terror of both as we splashed and dashed into them. No one was hurt, but both dangers could have been avoided if we had arrived at the transition area at least an hour in advance.

2. She Who Enjoys the Event Wins

My friend Lynn Cranmer, who now resides at the Sea of Cortez, Mexico, a multitime triathlete finisher from sprints to Ironman, won't leave the transition area without reapplying her lipstick. At first, this nod to beauty seemed whimsical and vain, but for her it is important, and therefore worth the investment of time and energy. She gives the competition an extra few seconds, but it doesn't matter to her. Lynn is not a pro, and she has always raced purely for the joy of being in the event. Hence, looking good is just as important to her as her final finish time.

The same can be true about the outfit you select to wear during the triathlon. Pros swim, bike, and run in the same item of clothing without adding or removing apparel. But if triathlons are more for fun than for bragging rights, then there is no question that looking good reigns supreme over fast transition times. Bring on the fashion groups—it may be more important to look good than to go fast.

3. Pigging Out

I volunteer to finish last as the "sweep athlete" in many triathlons that I compete in today so that no one else has to. I prefer being the last to finish: It's the best place in the race for one reason—the vantage point of being behind thousands of women competing in their first triathlon.

As the last woman out of the water, off the bike, and finishing the run, I get to see things that others can't even imagine. One of those is the "party" that many women have in the transition area. I see leftover cans of pop, pieces of chocolate cake, cookies, ice cream, and more, remnant of everything that has been devoured as many of the gals refuel while they are transitioning. If you want to pig out in the transition areas, and your stomach can tolerate it, go for it. But I'll tell you, those who finish in front refuel during the race; they eat on the bike and on the run, not in the transition area.

4. Stress Makes Us Stupid

Dozens of times I have watched women leave the transition area on the run wearing their bike helmets, forgetting their race numbers, or leaving their hats or sunglasses behind. That is because when we enter the stress zones, it is nearly impossible to think clearly.

Stress is our perception of emotional strain. Because of the pressure to transition fast, because of the effects of physical fatigue and our high heart rates going into and out of transition areas, our brains get foggy. If this is a problem for you, learn to calm the mind and cool the heart. When you are in the transition area, breathe deeply, relax, take a drink of water, and stay focused on the activities required there—apparel and equipment changes. Taking a few extra seconds in transition areas to remain coolheaded is worth it if it saves you minutes during the next leg.

My friend, training partner, and business partner Kathy Kent is proud of her lightning-fast transitions. She likes to chew gum on the run because she believes it keeps her mouth wet. She takes the time during her transition setup to put the gum out so that during her T2 she can quickly grab a piece. She is sure that it helps her run faster. The moral is: If it works for you, then do it.

5. And the Winner Is . . . Whoever Makes the Fewest Mistakes

A few years ago, in Austin, Texas, I was serving as a sweep triathlete, riding with a water-logged gal who was in an early swim wave but whose swimming skills needed major improvement. We had been biking for about 30 minutes at 10 miles per hour, her fastest speed, when a motorcycle cop rode up beside me to say there was a triathlete behind us.

Astonished, I did a careful U-turn on the course (closed to traffic) to discover a frustrated woman indeed riding behind us. As we rode along, I asked how she had gotten herself in the situation of being probably twenty minutes behind the second-to-last triathlete. She described her experience of exhaustion and panic: She had lost her helmet in T1 and had to run back to her car to get a spare, which cost her about 40 minutes. Ironically, she was an Air Force officer responsible for logistics. I wondered how this specialist in organization and execution could now be dead last in the triathlon, especially with her background in logistics.

Her experience serves as a paramount example of how planning and logistics are at the heart of triathlon events. Be organized. Follow the Girl Scout motto, "Be prepared," and you won't be swimming, biking, or running with me in the Trek Women Triathlon Series as the final finisher.

TRANSITION DRILLS

Many experienced triathletes still practice transition training, because doing so can make a big difference in their performance. You should train the same way. Training for transition requires that you practice organizing your gear and using it in a way that simulates the race experience during some of your training sessions. Time yourself in practice and see if there's a way to expedite this fourth leg. Can you replace a piece of equipment with something that works better? Is it better to sit down or stand up as you put on your bike or running shoes? Time it different ways until you feel confident that you have both transition routines as streamlined as possible.

Transition training sessions can be fun and rewarding. You'll learn a great deal from them. For instance, most first-timers learn the wet-feet-and-dry-sock lesson. It may surprise you to find out how long it takes to put on a pair of socks in T1 when your feet are damp! After practicing that particular transition, you'll either get faster at putting on socks or eliminate them altogether. Pay attention to how your gear performs. Again, the rule for triathlon transition gear is: Less is more. The less clothing you can wear, and the less gear you need, the faster, and usually—but not always—the better you perform.

To smoothly transition, you must be well rehearsed. Make a transition spot for this exercise, such as in your driveway or backyard:

- Go through your transition the first time slowly; practice "thinking through" the transition. In subsequent rounds, time yourself.
- Place your bike, your water bottle (if you choose to wash off your feet), and all of your other gear on a towel just as you will have them on race day. Practice different configurations if you like. See if you're faster doing everything standing up or sitting down.
- If you will be using a wetsuit on race day, go ahead and put it on for your transition drill, and get it wet. On race day, you will be taking off a wet wetsuit, not a dry one!
- Get your feet wet under your outdoor spigot, put on your flip flops if you'll be using them, then run to the transition spot and practice your T1 transition. Do everything you will have to do at the actual event, including riding off on your bike.
- Then pretend you have finished biking and practice your transition to running. Bike into your practice T2, transition, and then run away from your transition spot.
- Your goal should be to change from one sport to the next in less than 2 minutes! And if you really practice, you can get it in under 60 seconds.
- Practice transitioning five times and write each completion time down in your log.
- Repeat this exercise each week until the race. You'll be amazed at how fast you can become at transitioning from one sport to another.

You get the added benefit of keeping your neighbors guessing what you're up to as you time yourself changing clothes, gear, and sports in your driveway!

EIGHT MORE WAYS TO GET FASTER IN TRANSITIONS

There are a few secrets about transitions that I haven't mentioned yet. If you're a first-timer, ignore them, because they are advanced techniques. If you are a veteran triathlete, give them a try if they sound like good ideas to you:

1. **Do it on the bike. Do it on the run.** If there's anything you can do on the bike or the run rather than in the transition area, save it for that time. Sometimes, it's faster to grab and go than to hang out in the transition area changing or fixing something. For example, don't drink if you can do that on the bike or the run.

2. **Get the fast gear.** Trade in your slow gear for fast gear. For example, use speed laces or elastic laces for your running shoes and Velcro closures for your bike cleats. Use a race belt instead of pinning on your race numbers.

3. **Get slippery.** Do whatever works for you to make your apparel slide on rather than having to tug at it. Use baby powder to make slipping on your shoes easier after the swim, for example, by putting the powder inside your shoes in advance. Use lubricant on your body before the swim to help you slip off a wetsuit faster. Tugging off gear takes a lot more time than slipping it off.

4. **Do it like a pro.** Go to a race that you are not competing in and watch to see how the pros transition. Although as someone who is not signed up for that race you will most likely not be allowed into the transition area, you can probably position yourself someplace close by where you can observe the transition. You can even time the racers in the transition so you can compare their transition time to yours. Video some of them transitioning if you can, because if they can transition in 10 seconds and you transition in 120, there's something you can learn by studying them carefully. That's the difference in some races of twenty-five finishing places.

5. **Don't add and don't subtract.** Unless vanity calls, wear one outfit throughout the race. The less you have to change clothes, the better. That's why I prefer to go without socks, though many people prefer them for comfort and blister protection. The bottom line is this: No matter what you change, changing takes valuable time.

6. **Put it on the bike, not on you.** Attach your extra gear to the bike and not in your clothes. It eats up time to put small items into your pockets. One

way to do this is with a bike top-tube bag. It sits right in front of you and can keep all of your extra gear, such as sports gels, in a place where you can access it easily and safely while on the bike.

7. **Mount and dismount like a cyclocrosser.** Watch a cyclocross race, or a video of one on the web, to learn how to get onto your bike like a cyclocross bike rider. It's a running start with a leap that ends with a gentle landing on the bike seat, almost like mounting a moving horse. Learn how to dismount like a cyclocross rider, too—they never come to a stop but rather slow and dismount while moving.

8. **Learn how to push your bike.** You can walk your bike out of the transition area or you can save time by safely pushing it. This is a learned skill, especially with bike cleats on, so try it in a parking lot as one of your transition skills. Observe a more advanced triathlete doing this before trying it.

The trick is to push the bike with one hand while you swing the other arm back and forth in running form. If you have to make a turn in the transition area, you will have to know how to do so with one hand, leaning the bike in the direction of the turn. Don't drop the bike! Practice turns until you feel confident that you can do this without losing control of the bike.

If transitions are like a three-ring circus, as I suggested at the beginning of this chapter, then you'll be prepared for its acrobatics if you follow these instructions for transition training and organization. In fact, if you practice your transitions and organize them as I've suggested, I'm sure you can learn how to breeze through them with the greatest of ease, no matter how much chaos surrounds you.

Racing:
You Go, Girlfriend!

Participating in a triathlon can be as large or as small a step as you make it. You can aim toward competing in an Ironman (as an Ironwoman), or simply sign up for your next local "Tri for Fun"—a low-key, fun triathlon without a lot of competitive energy. In any case, be reasonable with yourself. Success at racing—just doing a triathlon—always involves honestly evaluating your strengths and weaknesses as well as setting realistic goals.

Race preparation has many mental components. Take some time to figure out how to frame this challenge to suit your own temperament. If the idea of "racing" puts you off, think of it as an "event." If you don't like the idea of competing against others, choose to think about the race as a personal quest to do something new or better than you have before: Challenge yourself to simply finish, if this is your first race; if you have done other triathlons, set a goal of doing better than you did in your last race. Both of these goals are just as respectable as beating the competition, and just as rewarding. Then again, if the idea of competition is what motivates you, go ahead and enjoy your competitive spirit.

THE EIGHT STAGES OF A TRIATHLON

Most people think of a triathlon as a combination of three events. It is that—but it's also more. A triathlon begins when your swim wave starts, continues with your bike segment, and ends when you cross under the finish banner at the end of the run. These are the eight parts of a triathlon, and each has its own set of skills for you to master:

1. Start of the swim
2. Finish of the swim
3. Transition 1 (T1)
4. Start of the bike
5. Finish of the bike
6. Transition 2 (T2)
7. Start of the run
8. Finish of the triathlon

Training—mentally and physically—for each of these eight segments is what this book is about, and this outline can help you see the big picture: Many of the participants will be thinking of the race as just a swim-bike-run event, but this concept of the eight legs of a triathlon will give you a different vantage point. Think of each event as having individual start and finish lines (they do). Then, link three great races together with two fast and efficient transitions, which you learned about in Chapter 8.

PREPARING TO RACE

Here's what to do in a nutshell: Be meticulous with your equipment, hydrate, and eat and sleep well. Be sure to get a good night's sleep two nights before the race, since you may be too nervous or excited the night before the race to sleep well.

The day before the race, there is often an expo and pre-race registration. Use this time to review the course. Go to every informational session you can, especially if there is a "First-Timers Talk" and this is your first race. Often there will be a course review, speakers on special topics, and a chance to soak up the energy of the pre-race activities. There is no such thing as too much information about the course or about race-day conditions. If body marking is being done at the expo, get it out of the way, as it means one less thing to do on race morning.

The night before the race, set out all your gear and make sure you have everything you need for the race (see Chapter 8 for more details on setting up your transition area and a full gear checklist). Check that you have the essentials, the tri-suit or shorts and top, the swim cap, and your goggles. Make sure your bike helmet, cycling gloves (if you plan to wear them), sunglasses or other eye protection, and bike shoes are in your race bag.

Don't forget your race number and running shoes. Put the bike number on the bike, and clip your number onto your race belt or pin it to the shirt you'll wear for the run. Put your full water bottles in the bag or on the bike, have an energy bar or other quick food in your bag in case you need it, and bring along some clothes to wear after the race. Pump your tires. Mentally walk yourself through the entire race, and see if you've forgotten anything. Then you'll be ready to go in the morning without having to worry about your equipment.

RACE-DAY PREPARATION

Race-day preparation can seem a little overwhelming at first. But if you break it down into various steps, it becomes less daunting. So let's do just that: Examine the various pieces of the puzzle so you can put it all together, from the time you wake up in the morning until you reach the finish line.

First Things First: Early Preparations

Get up and have the breakfast you have worked out beforehand as being best for you on race day (see Chapter 11 for some healthy and satisfying suggestions). Finish eating 2 hours before the race begins. Don't try any new foods on this morning. Hydrate in advance of the race, especially if the race is longer than an hour, and nibble on something if you are in one of the last wave starts—which, in a big race, may be as long as 2 hours after the first wave hits the water.

RACE-DAY HAIR

If you have short hair, this is not going to be an issue for you, but if your hair is long, there are a few things you should consider before the race. In putting your hair up in a ponytail or headband for racing make sure that you use a hair accessory that grips your hair effectively (e.g., the Goody StayPut hair bands). If you notice in training that your hair comes out of the ponytail and bothers you by getting in your face, you can use the pockets in your tri-suit for bobby pins to quickly pin your hair out of your face while on the move (try this out in training first). If you wear your hair in a ponytail, experiment with different bike helmets and with putting your ponytail low at the nape of your neck for comfort. The last thing you need is for your race to be hindered by your hair getting in the way or feeling uncomfortable.

Arriving at the Race

Plan to arrive early to the transition area to choose your position and get your personal items organized. Once you've completed that very important task (which we examined in detail in Chapter 8), you just have a few final preparations to take care of before getting ready to take the plunge.

Next, you will go to be body marked (a number will be written on your arms and legs with felt pens); if you brought your own marker and you know how to do this, you can mark yourself that morning or the night before. Then, go stand in line for the bathroom—it may be a good idea to bring tissue to the portable toilet since often there are none.

Now make your preparations for the swim. Put on your wetsuit, first putting wetsuit lubricant on your neck and other body areas where abrasions might occur (nonstick cooking spray will also do the trick). Don't be too heavy-handed with it. Be sure not to touch your goggles when you have the lubricant on your hands.

Finally, put your swim cap on. The race organizers will provide you with a latex cap, but some people find that putting a stretchy Lycra cap on under the latex one makes it easier to grab the cap and take it off after the swim. To put the cap on, place both hands together inside of it and pull your hands apart to stretch it open.

Once you're ready for the swim, your physical preparations are done and it is time to mentally prepare.

Mental Preparation

Acknowledge that there will be pain. Exhaustion and discomfort are part of the entry fee you pay to reach the finish line, so be prepared to pay the price, but only up to a point. If the pain is verging on bodily overextension or breakdown, be prepared to back off. It's better to finish upright than to practice the "triathloid crawl."

Tap into and refine the source of your energy—the mind/body union. Listen intently to both the sounds of your mind's chatter and the feelings of your heart and lung exertion. Fine-tune both to maximize your efficiency, and relax into the experience as best as you can. Now is the time to reflect on your expectations of the race ahead. Warm up your mind before the race as well as your body. Think through the whole race day so thoroughly that you know the race as well as if you had already completed it. This will help you to eliminate the pre-race jitters and get you into a performance mind-set.

Last, remember to live it up. Doing a triathlon is like a big party—you've done all the hard work to get here, so you deserve to enjoy it. And while the actual event may be the main attraction, the sideshow is almost as much fun. Meet new people, share stories, and let your spirits soar. Although you will be careful about what you're eating and drinking, you can still be merry—so be the merriest of them all. Head to the starting line with the knowledge that the woman who starts the race is not the same as the woman who will finish it.

Gathering for the Swim

As you walk over to the start of the swim, don't forget to select markers, such as buildings or trees, that you can use as sighting points during the swim, because it's almost impossible to swim in a straight line without them. In most triathlons, you will begin the race in "waves." Waves are groups of individuals in the same age division who start separately, with delays of 2–5 minutes between each wave. Stand with the individuals who are marked with the same age division number as you; usually everyone in the age group is wearing the same color cap. The announcer will call your group to the starting line when it's time for your wave to start. Don't go in the wrong wave or you will have the wrong time.

Keep in mind how strong a swimmer you are and let that decide where you position yourself in the wave as the race begins. It depends on your talent, your confidence level, and your preferences. If this is your first race, place yourself near the back so that you don't have to worry as much about kicking someone or being kicked. If you feel more confident that you can handle a more crowded start, seed yourself closer to the front. Many triathletes benefit from getting in the water before the triathlon begins to get used to the water, but don't do this so early that you start to get cold while waiting for your group to launch—getting wet first is more useful if you are in an early wave.

THE SWIM LEG

You have already been practicing swimming in open water, but, if you are a beginner, today you will experience a new dimension of open-water swimming: swimming with dozens of other people. It is difficult to be at the start of a swim wave when many, many people are starting at the same time. You may get kicked or hit in the water, which may be choppier than you are used to because of all the swimming bodies around you. You may even want to wait a few seconds after your wave starts until you feel comfortable swimming.

If you are new at triathlon, enter the water with measured caution when the starting signal sounds for your wave. After a few strokes, stop and take a few extra breaths. Sight on a buoy or other landmark, and then start again. Have a backup stroke, such as the breaststroke, to do in case you have any trouble. Get into a rhythm, and sight the buoy every fourth or fifth stroke, using the technique for sighting that you learned in Chapter 5.

In a race situation, even the water can be different from what you expected. It may be, for example, that you have done your open-water swimming in fresh water and have not experienced salt water, which can make your mouth taste salty no matter how firmly you shut it and can make some people feel nauseated. If the water is choppy, you might feel disoriented by the waves. If you've been training in a relatively clear body of water, cloudy water with vegetation may be disconcerting, or if you've been swimming in a lake, swimming in a river may be harder than you were expecting because of the current. Take the time to get your bearings. Breaststroke for a few yards if you need to, and remember to follow the most important rule of swimming: Keep breathing.

> **TIP** You're midswim, nature calls, and maybe your bladder isn't what it used to be after a baby or two. Save a few minutes and urinate in your wetsuit or tri suit! If you're well-hydrated, it's clear anyway; it's sterile, it will all get washed away, and you're not the only one out there doing it.

As you may know, drafting on the bike is not legal for most triathlons, but drafting in the swim is, and it can make you faster while saving you effort. A 2008 study showed that you can experience up to 44 percent less drag than a lead swimmer if you are approximately 2 feet behind her and 16 percent less drag if you are 20 feet behind. To draft, stay within 2 feet of the swimmer—but try to feel for her bubbles rather than looking up. It is also possible to draft by staying to the side of a swimmer. Be warned, drafting is not always the best race strategy. You may be following someone who is off course, or you may be going slower than you might have gone without drafting. Do an occasional reality check to make sure you are actually benefiting from drafting. In addition, be courteous to the person you are drafting and don't hit her feet.

About 100 yards from the finish of the swim, you reach a turning point: You go from step 1 of the triathlon (start of the swim) to step 2 (finish of the swim), because it's then that you'll begin to visualize the swim finish line. Always visualize what is going to happen next, because your calculated thoughts become your immediate actions.

As the water becomes too shallow for swimming and you put your feet down, you might feel dizzy—most of us do. Your equilibrium may be thrown off as you come

> **TIP** Walking through water expends much more energy than swimming. So save yourself a little bit of energy and swim until your hands are touching bottom. You can even pull yourself along the sandy bottom with your hands until that becomes impossible as well.

from a prone to an upright position, but you'll regain it quickly. Once you do, run through the water with high knees. There may be volunteers in the water to help you; listen to their instructions. Take off your goggles and swim cap, then, after you leave the water, the top portion of your wetsuit (if you are wearing one) as you move toward transition. In a controlled

STRIPPING OFF THE WETSUIT

The first time I met a "stripper" was at Ironman Canada, where volunteers were assigned the task of pulling off our wetsuits after the 2.4-mile swim. It probably gained me only 5 to 10 seconds in the 11-hour race, but it was helpful and I appreciated the consideration. It also was worth it because my hands were too cold to strip off my suit with any grace.

In most races, though, removing a wetsuit is your responsibility. It sometimes helps to coat your calves and ankles lightly with something slippery and non-petroleum-based that doesn't degrade the neoprene in the suit (Suit Juice wetsuit lubricant will work). The benefits of wearing a wetsuit far outweigh not using one because it keeps you warm and buoyant during the swim leg. If your wetsuit fits well, you can shave minutes off your swim time. Using a wetsuit changes your body position in the water. You swim faster because your body position is higher, and that means less drag. I once came across a triathlete who was struggling with her wetsuit during the swim. I discovered she was wearing it backward! This will definitely slow you down (*note:* almost all wetsuits zip in the back).

fashion, walk or run through the flagged area that has been constructed for a finishing chute. Don't forget your flip flops if you left them at the end of the chute. And remember, the clock is running, so each added item (like flip flops) may take more time than it saves.

T1: SWIM-TO-BIKE TRANSITION

Your gear will be waiting for you in the transition area (because you organized it there before the race; see Chapter 8). Don't sacrifice comfort for speed in your transition. You will want your feet to be as dry as possible before putting on your socks and shoes for the bike segment. Nevertheless, speed in the transition areas can make a big difference in your race time, so streamline your transition routine well before race day through practice.

Some athletes decide to change their clothes for each of the three events. I don't recommend it. To avoid the time-consuming process of clothes changing, I recommend a tri-suit. You can wear a singlet or shirt for the run as well, but don't wear it on the bike unless it's cold, because the shirt will create greater wind resistance.

If you took the time to get your T1 things properly organized before the race, this should be a breeze. Slip on your bike shoes or cleats, put on your shirt and shorts if you prefer them to a tri-suit, then add your sunglasses and your helmet (it must be buckled). If you've practiced it in advance, you can save time by clipping your bike shoes onto the pedals ahead of time and putting on your shoes while you ride.

Finally, walk with your bike out of the transition area (or run if you can do it safely). As you get on your bike, enjoy that fresh and high-energy feeling of "Oh, girl—it's the bike leg and I love to ride my bike."

THE BIKE LEG

I love the start of the bicycle leg. I am fresh, happy, and excited. I've learned from experience that what I need to do at that point is to relax and ride according to my pre-race strategy—first, at a set speed, not at the pace that my heart is going, then at a set heart rate or power output from my power meter, not pace. That said, the bike part of the triathlon is the most dangerous; whatever your race strategy is, it is important for you to focus on keeping yourself safe.

Be wary of the sometimes questionable riding skills of other riders. Give yourself the benefit of the doubt—you may be a better rider than many of the other participants. As you start, remind yourself not to draft,

TAKING IT SLOW

When I'm involved in a triathlon as a volunteer, I always want to make sure the final finishers are doing okay. So it was that at one triathlon, I watched a woman walk up the entrance chute to the bike transition area after the swim, the last person to finish out of 2,000-plus women in the race. I don't know her name—she was one of thousands of women immersed in their first triathlon on that day. She met two of her supporters there who had managed to get into the transition area to help her (against the rules), and she said to them, "I can't believe I did it." It was clear that this was one of the happiest moments of her life. She hadn't known if she could swim that far, in open water, in a strange lake, with thousands of other women, but she did it.

"I have never been so scared in my whole life," she confided. Now that the swim leg was completed, she wasn't worried about the 20 km bike leg or the 5 km run. There was no urgency in her voice, no hurried actions. She sat down and ate a sandwich, chatted with her friends about the joy and thrill of her accomplishments, and finally left the swim-to-bike transition area about 10 minutes later.

Compare that to an Olympic women's triathlon competition, where transitions are generally between 10 and 30 seconds long. It's easy to get caught up in the chaos—that's the nature of transition for most triathletes. However, that doesn't mean everyone has to approach the race in the same competitive way. Every racer needs to decide what her objectives are beforehand and approach the race accordingly.

which is officially cycling within three bicycle lengths of another bike (see illustration on page 109). Most triathlons don't allow it, and you can be disqualified if you do draft.

Always pass to the left, but don't ever cross the centerline of the road. Shout out to other riders before you pass them. As you approach the rider in front of you, call out loudly to say, "Passing on your left." Giving other riders advance notice that you are near them will keep them from crashing into you as you pass, and it will let them have a safe race as well.

Being safe also means starting to drink water almost immediately. If the bike portion of the race is more than 25 miles, you may need to eat during the ride as well. Don't depend on the race organizers to provide water bottles or food along the bike course. Bring water bottles with plain water or your favorite sports drink (diluted if you prefer it that way), and be sure that you have tested this hydration choice in training so that you know it will work well for you. As for snacks, bring items that you have tested while training (for suggestions to try, see Chapter 11).

If you notice that your legs are tighter than usual, stand up on the pedals and stretch, or backspin on the downhills, to allow for some recovery. As you near the second transition, remember to go slowly through the chicane (the traffic cones that are set up to slow you down as you ride into or out of a transition area). Get off and walk your bike in the transition area, because runners will be exiting down the corridors between the bike racks. Find your bike rack location and prepare to "rack your bike." The second leg is over.

T2: BIKE-TO-RUN TRANSITION

Like the first transition, the second transition starts before the finish of the segment. This time, however, it's when you start to prepare mentally for the run. Drink as much fluid as you possibly can at this point so that you are fully hydrated as you set off on your run. Visualize yourself slipping off your cleats, sliding on your running shoes, grabbing your visor, and leaving the transition area.

That said, stay focused on safety as long as you are still on the bike. Don't unbuckle your helmet until you've gotten completely off the bike— that's a rule in nearly every triathlon. Once you're in the transition area, find the spot that is assigned for your bike and rack it. Slip off your bike shoes, unless they were clipped to your pedals and you took them off as you got off your bike (something you can practice before the race). Slide on your running shoes, put on a visor, add a shirt if you want one, put on your race number, and take off.

Many racers hang out in the transition area, eating, drinking, and resting. You can do so, too, but remember that you will be using up time that you will value later. The transition area is a checkpoint; if you need help with equipment, motivation, food, or drinks, now is the time to seek it. It's better to get help now than to wish you had it later.

THE RUN LEG

You are finished with six of the eight parts of the triathlon that I identified earlier in the chapter. The run has its own challenges, but if you are prepared for them, you will soon be celebrating your finish.

Check your watch or heart rate monitor as you exit the transition area, and try to set an even pace. This may be difficult at first, because as you take those first few running steps away from your bike, you may feel what triathletes call the "bike-to-run grip." The changeover from using cycling muscles (those in the front of the thigh—the quadriceps) to using running muscles (those located in the back of the thigh—the hamstrings) results in an incredible tightening. Your quadriceps feel as though they have rigor mortis; they can be so tight that it's hard to take a normal stride length.

The feeling is normal and happens to everyone. You will notice that you can't extend your legs as far as you would like and that your stride frequency (turnover rate) is impaired. It usually takes several hundred yards or even a couple of miles before your legs recover from the triathlon grip, but eventually you'll settle into your chosen pace. You will probably have to run or run/walk for a mile before you feel truly comfortable at your chosen speed; the musculature needs some time to adapt to the transition. Brick-training can help to alleviate the challenge of the grip. If you do experience it, reach down inside yourself for strength and perseverance.

Another issue is this: To drink or not to drink? You will find that at every half-mile to a mile there will be opportunities to drink, whether it is some sort of sports drink or water. During training, you should be practicing the skill of drinking on the run so that you know what your stomach can tolerate. You may find it is sometimes better to pour a cup of water over your head to cool yourself down, or to sip small amounts rather than chugging a whole cup.

Other runners will pass you, just as other swimmers and cyclists have passed you during those portions of the race. You will pass other runners as well. Jockeying for position among those with the same single-sport specialty makes triathlon fun. Those with a strong cycling background pass the swimmers and the runners in the bike leg of the race, while those with a strong running background sail past the strong swimmers and bikers in the run segment. Those with strong backgrounds in all three are rarely passed. That's why the "secret" to coming in at the top of your age group in this sport is really no secret at all—you simply have to be the best you can be in all three of the sports.

THE FINISH LINE

Finally, you'll see the finish line—very likely a sight you will never forget if it's your first triathlon. Even if it's your fiftieth triathlon, it will be a welcome sight. It's what you've worked so hard for over a period of months, so let the moment soak in as you cross under the banner.

While you're starting to celebrate, there are a couple of things to remember. As you approach the final finish line, look up—there will be a finish clock with the time. It's guaranteed to display the wrong time, because it will be measuring the time from the first wave, and you are probably in one of the later ones. Remember the time that it is displaying, though, so that you can subtract your wave handicap when you are thinking more clearly. Better still, look at your wristwatch or heart rate monitor and rely on your own timing. Okay, now that you've noted the timing, throw your shoulders back, hold your head high, and run across the finish line with a huge smile spreading across your face—you are now officially a triathlete.

Some of the most vivid highlights of my athletic career have occurred at the finish lines of races. Running toward that finish banner, with the spectators applauding and the announcer saying my name over the loudspeaker, and looking up at a finish clock that reads the numbers that match my goal, is pure exhilaration. I have one overriding thought that always hits me at that moment. I think that if I had just known how good the finish-line experience would be, I would have trained more.

THE RACE YOU DIDN'T EXPECT

Grow from the triathlon experience. If you have a disaster—a broken bike, a slow swim, or a person who looks less fit who passes you—use those experiences for what they were meant to be: lessons. Link the lessons together, and you will watch your performance grow.

If you end up with a triathlon disaster story, you're in good company. Take Estelle Gray, for example. Estelle is one of my training partners. She is also a world record holder in ultramarathon cycling and an elementary school special ed teacher. One time, when she was racing at a new venue, although she had followed her pre-race ritual of counting bike racks and memorizing the numbers and landmarks, after the swim she couldn't find her bike. At the last minute, race management had changed the location of the entrance to the transition area, and with 2,500 bikes and about three acres of transition area, she was lost. It was a serendipitous time for me, though: After finding her bike, Estelle decided that continuing her race was pointless because of the lost time and instead joined me as the sweep cyclist.

As we rode up next to the last rider on the bike course after the first mile, Estelle casually said to her, "How would you like to make your bike go faster?" The woman grinned in agreement. Estelle, the bike aficionado that she is, said, "Shift gears," and with the ease of lower gears and higher pedal cadence, the two left me behind in a heartbeat.

She showed me that a "disaster" is whatever you make of it: That day, Estelle made a friend. After you finish your race, even if you've experienced a disaster, watch others finish, share in their joy, and commiserate with their difficulties. Don't worry about the race you didn't have—just enjoy the race that you did have. And if you can stay to celebrate the final finisher, and if I am in the race, I'll be there to give you a high five.

Tools of the Triathlon Game

Triathlons synthesize three sports, and if you want to maximize performance and minimize risk of injury, choosing the right equipment for each event is almost as important as training. The things you will need for all three events can add up to a formidable list, not only in quantity but in cost as well. As in other sports, triathlon has its extremists on both ends: On one side, the fanatics who will swim only in a certain brand of suit, pedal only with a specific bike fork, or run only in a shoe made for pronators; at the other, those who ignore the value of the right equipment, confident that fitness is everything and that brand names and the latest technology are of little importance.

The truth lies somewhere in the middle. Think of the equipment, clothing, and other items you use in triathlon as the tools of your game. Just as a pianist needs a piano that is in tune, or a homebuilder needs a drill and a nailgun, you need a good bicycle, comfortable and functional clothing, the right shoes, and so on. If you are a beginner or intermediate triathlete, you might simply consider what is needed to participate safely and successfully. The farther you go in the sport, the more important it becomes to seek out the latest technology or spend top dollar for something that could shave seconds off your race. But even as a beginner, you should purchase the best equipment you can afford. Why disadvantage yourself right from the start with outdated equipment?

Triathlon equipment has come a long way since the inception of the sport. Back in 1979 when I was preparing for my first race, there were fewer than ten races in the whole country; today there are thousands. At that time, I knew very little about the tools of the trade. In this race the run came first, then the bike leg, and finally the swim. I strode off on the run, my specialty, in high-fashion racing gear. Winning the foot leg, I hopped helmetless onto my ten-speed clunker and began pedaling furiously, taking myself to what I would now call heart zone 5 (red-lining) in a matter of moments. I soon heard that sound. It hits you right over the left shoulder, the whoosh as a hot cyclist on a fine racing machine passes you, moving with such smooth quickness that the air flow is barely audible.

At the lake I dismounted from my bike and its painful saddle and stripped to my swimsuit, which hadn't seen service since my college days fifteen years earlier. Gingerly entering the frigid water, I immediately started to chill. No goggles, no swim cap, no wetsuit, no experience—it sapped my heat. After one lap of a double-loop course, I edged my bone-chilled frame to the side of the lake and spent an hour shivering. All the while, I was vowing, "As soon as I get warm, I'll swim that last lap." I never kept that vow. The cold drained my will. I had a DNF (did not finish) in my first triathlon. I still fell in love with the sport, but you can bet that I also figured out how to become better equipped for the next time.

We are fortunate today to have so many options in triathlon equipment. But deciding which items to purchase can also be difficult *because* there are so many choices. Along with the many manufacturers come controversies about what is most suitable. There is a wide range of costs, there are constant changes in design, and your own needs will change over time. In the end, you just have to analyze each sport to determine what is needed, make a grocery list of gear, decide on your budget and your true needs, and slowly accumulate the tools of your triathlon game. In this chapter, I've done part of the analysis for you. But you are the only one who can make those final decisions, depending on your individual circumstances and experiences with triathlon. First we'll look at some things you'll need for all three sports, then we'll examine each of the sports individually. You can easily research equipment using online triathlon retailers or a friendly staff person at your local tri shop, but I've included photos of some of the specialty gear to give you a better idea of what you'll be looking for when you start shopping.

BASIC NECESSITIES
HEART RATE MONITOR

Heart rate monitors (see Figure 10.1) have become more than just an accurate way to measure your heart rate. Some can even store times and training zones for each segment of your workout ("splits"). With many models, you can time your repeats and, at the end of the set, download and replay your exact splits. But it's not just the increase in the data that I'm talking about. What I find most fascinating is that, when used to its fullest, a heart rate monitor is a personal training tool. With a heart rate monitor you can experience a new way to train that can change the way you work out.

FIGURE 10.1:
Heart rate monitor

You can spend as little as $50 and up to $500 for a heart rate monitor, depending on the features you want. Choosing a heart rate monitor is a lot like the process you'd go through when buying any other electronic device, such as a computer, a PDA, or a mobile phone. Once you begin the shopping quest and find out what's available, you need to decide on which features you'll need (or can't resist), and which ones you can afford. If your budget allows, try to take into account how you might make better use of your heart rate monitor as you become a more capable triathlete. However, if you are not a gadget girl, and it's highly unlikely that you will ever read the user's manual to discover and download all that your monitor has to offer (for example, recovery heart rate, time in zones, heart zones points, and heart rate lap data), keep it simple and spend your money on something else.

Today, there are nearly two hundred different models and more than twenty manufacturers of heart rate monitors. Each monitor has a different set of functions and features (see Table 10.1), and each requires unique programming. As you add more functions and features to the monitor, you generally add both cost and complexity to the tool.

There are two different kinds of downloadable monitors: manual and device-based. Device-based downloading of workout data is growing quickly with the inclusion of mobile phones, GPS devices, and various

TABLE 10.1 Heart Rate Monitor Functions and Features	
HEART RATE FUNCTIONS	**Current heart rate**
	Average heart rate
	Percentage maximum heart rate
	Percentage threshold heart rate
	Zone alarm: audible or visual
	Peak heart rate
	Personal heart rate zone settings
	Sum of training load (Heart Zones Training Points)
	Switch function mode to transmitter by touch
OTHER RECORDED DATA	**Total exercise time**
	Time in zone(s) memory
	Stopwatch function
	Lap timing with heart rate (including best lap and current average and peak heart rate)
	Dynamic memory stores and displays of recent workouts
	Calories burned
	Fat burning
	Oxygen consumption
	Altitude and weather (setting)
ADDITIONAL FEATURES	**Water resistant or waterproof**
	Wireless transmission
	Common interval settings (5, 30, 60 seconds)
	Custom interval settings
	Speed and distance
	Display workout results graphically
	Fitness tests
	Multiple user profiles

Note: I've highlighted in bold the functions I consider to be mandatory for beginners.

types of sport watches where the data can be captured and analyzed or transmitted to a web-based application. The heart rate output data is invaluable in measuring fitness improvement and permanently recording your workout sessions. It allows you to save the stored data for post-exercise time interpretation and evaluation and provides validation, quantification, summary data of time in zones, and zone training points, a measurement of training load. Manual downloading requires that you enter the data manually into your log or a computer spreadsheet.

There are also two types of heart rate monitor transmission—digital and analog. The analog monitors use radio-like transmissions, and frequently you will experience cross-talk or interference from another transmission that makes your numbers go crazy. Digital transmission is pure with no interference because it uses digital packets.

SUNSCREEN

It is extremely important that you protect yourself from the sun's damaging rays because of the skin cancer risk. This becomes even more important when you train for hours outdoors in the sun and compete in triathlons. Each of the sports requires prolonged exposure to sunlight, and in swimming the risk increases even more because of the reflection of sunlight off the water.

> **TIP** No product should be called "sunblock," "waterproof," or "all-day," for the simple reason that no sunscreen can live up to these claims. You will need to reapply sunscreen during any triathlon longer than a sprint in order to protect your skin because the sunscreen you use will be compromised by the effect of water and time.

Be sure to select a broad-spectrum sunscreen with an SPF of at least 40. Broad-spectrum products provide protection against both UVA and UVB radiation. Remember to try your sunscreen well in advance of race day to make sure your skin does not have an adverse reaction to the perfumes or dyes. Your sunscreen should be "water resistant"—no sunscreen is "waterproof" because they will all wash off. Liberally apply it—use at least one ounce (the size of a shot glass)—to exposed body parts, and don't forget to get just under the edges of your clothing as well. (Bring extra for friends who are training with you.) Apply the sunscreen a full 30 minutes before sun exposure, then reapply it every 2 hours. It's worth the extra time in transition to protect yourself from skin cancer. Use sunscreen even on cloudy days—you never know if the weather will change, and it is possible to get a sunburn through cloud cover. Pay attention to expiration dates: Sunscreen should last for up to three years—but you need to make sure you are using enough of it if it is not new.

IDENTIFICATION

While you are training it is a good idea to have identification with you. You could carry identification in your saddlebag, but if you are knocked unconscious or separated from your bike your rescuers may not think of looking there. For that reason you might want to try the Road I.D. (see www.roadID.com).

SWIMMING

All you really need for swimming is someplace to swim, a swimsuit, and goggles. There are some other things that are nice to have, too. But if you want to get started quickly, just get those three figured out and you are ready to dive in.

Ideally, you should have access to both a pool (especially for interval sessions) and a good place for open-water swimming, such as a lake or the ocean. You don't need to move to the beach or dig a hole in your backyard, though; swimming space is available at low cost. As mentioned earlier (Chapter 5), there may be several pools to choose from in your city or town. Once you make a choice, you've decided on the biggest piece of "equipment" for swimming. Now you can proceed to the personal items.

CHOOSING A POOL

Visit the public swimming pools in your community and ask questions about fees, hours of operation, and the like before deciding. Don't forget to check out university pools as well as community centers such as the YMCA and the JCC. Here's a list of variables to consider when deciding on a swimming pool:

- Cost of membership or admittance fees
- Hours of operation and lap swimming
- Times reserved for masters swim groups
- Prominent pace clock to time your repeats and determine your departure times
- Width of the lap lanes
- Use of lane dividers
- Proximity to home or work
- Size and shape of the pool (avoid the kidney-shaped ones)
- Indoor or outdoor facilities
- Cleanliness
- Traffic
- Frills: weight room, whirlpool, sauna, and so on

Swimming Equipment

GOGGLES AND DEFOGGING SOLUTIONS

If you're a beginner and you're not used to wearing goggles, you may find them a bit uncomfortable at first; once you get used to them, you'll probably wonder how you ever did without them. In any case, they're essential for triathlon. Goggles will protect your eyes from chlorine and help you see better while your face is under water. All goggles fit differently, and some are better for certain sizes and shapes of faces than others. Be sure to try several different models. Place the eyepieces up to your eyes and press gently, without using the elastic band, to test for the correct fit. If they stay on for a second or two (from their own suction), then they should work for you. If they fall right off, try another brand. Try women-specific goggles first, because they'll most likely fit your face better.

One of the easiest ways to boost your swim performance is to wear open-water swim goggles, called a "swim mask," instead of pool goggles (see Figure 10.2). These will improve your peripheral vision and enable you to see the turn buoys more clearly.

When you shop for goggles, one of the first things you'll notice is that some are clear and some are tinted. Clear goggles are much better for open water, especially in murky conditions, but tinted ones can be better if you're swimming in bright sunlight. So if you'll be swimming in murky water on a sunny day, it's a toss-up! You're the only one who can make that choice: If your eyes are very sensitive to sunlight, you might want to go with the tinted ones. If so, choose the shade of the tint according

FIGURE 10.2: Swim mask and hand paddles

to your own preferences, just as you would with sunglasses. If you're not sure, you can always buy two types and experiment with them in different conditions. It's a good idea to have two pairs of goggles anyway, in case one pair breaks on race day.

If you are nearsighted, you now can purchase prescription swim goggles. Some manufacturers offer goggles with replaceable lenses; you can pop out each lens separately and replace them as your eyes change.

Swim goggles fog easily, but this can be prevented in a number of ways. You can either put a commercial defogging solution or saliva on the inside of your goggles, or you can buy antifogging goggles.

SWIM CAP

Often triathlon organizers supply swim caps that are color coded to aid in organizing everyone for different start times. But you'll need your own swim cap for training—especially for open-water swims. Choose a brightly colored swim cap to be more visible to boaters and to your swim buddies.

A swim cap also keeps your hair out of your face and goggles as you swim, and a waterproof cap made of a material such as silicone or latex protects your hair as well. To further reduce chlorine damage, you can pre-wet your hair or put chlorine-resistant conditioner on first for pool swims (if hair is wet already, it will not absorb as much of the chlorinated water). A Lycra cap will not protect your hair from water but is easily taken on and off, and for that reason it can be useful to put one on underneath the swim cap given to you at a race.

PULL BUOYS AND KICKBOARDS

Usually cylindrical pieces of Styrofoam, pull buoys (Figure 10.3) allow you to rest your legs by floating them in a natural position, isolating your upper body during area-specific workouts. Pulling drills can also be conducted by using small black inner tubes, called "pulling tubes," around your ankles. They provide greater resistance in training than do pull buoys, since they aren't buoyant and therefore don't hold your legs up.

Kickboards, held with your hands and arms to allow them to rest as you isolate

FIGURE 10.3: Pull buoy

leg movement, are also usually made of Styrofoam. Kickboard exercises are great for conditioning your legs and improving the biomechanics of your kick.

SWIM FINS

Used as a training aid, swim fins (Figure 10.4) can increase the flexibility of your ankles, build the strength of your quadriceps (thigh muscles), and provide a tougher workout by increasing your cardiovascular load. They also allow you to swim longer, since you are using your legs more and thus sparing your arms and back. This can help you get up to the yardage or time you need in the pool to prepare for a triathlon. Fins are not allowed during the race, however.

HAND PADDLES OR GLOVES

These are either flat pieces of thin plastic you secure to your hands or webbed Neoprene gloves. Used as training devices, they improve your arm stroke by forcing your hands and arms into the correct stroking pattern. Paddles also increase stroke force, but some research has shown that with overuse they may cause shoulder tendinitis. (Figure 10.2 shows hand paddles in use.)

EARPLUGS

If you are prone to swimmer's ear, in which excess moisture in the ear introduces a bacterial infection, or you frequently get water in your ears, you might want to try waterproof earplugs.

FIGURE 10.4: Swim fins

Swimming Apparel
SWIMSUIT

When buying a suit, don't just try it on and look in the mirror. The ladies in the dressing room might think you're a little strange, but practice a dry-land version of the freestyle with a few kicking motions and arm circles to see if it fits comfortably on contracting muscles. It should not slip or rub. The shoulder straps shouldn't fall down or feel too loose, and they should allow for about a 2-inch stretch when pulled toward the ears.

Lycra suits are standard racing apparel for competitive triathletes. The Lycra stretch fabric adheres tightly to the skin, preventing drag as well as providing some breast and stomach support. There are different cuts and styles—some suits are triathlon specific and even have slightly padded crotches, which are useful on the bike and run stages of a triathlon. The suits dry quickly and should last one or two years without stretching out and losing their shape. Chlorine-resistant suits can be useful for frequent training.

TRIATHLON WETSUITS AND SKINSUITS

Wetsuits come in a variety of styles and are made from different thicknesses of Neoprene. The quality can vary greatly. Skinsuits are thin bodysuits (usually just 0.5 to 1.0 millimeters in thickness) and are used primarily for warmth when training in colder conditions. The use of a wetsuit or skinsuit is usually optional in triathlons, and there may be restrictions on their use. In USA Triathlon–sanctioned races, they can be used only if the water temperature is up to and including 78 degrees Fahrenheit if you are racing for prizes and awards.

Wetsuits (see Figure 10.5) are useful in that they improve buoyancy and body position, and you swim faster as a result. If you decide to purchase a wetsuit or skinsuit, be sure to choose one specially designed for triathlons rather than for surfing or water skiing. Try on

FIGURE 10.5: Wetsuit

many different models to make sure you're getting a good fit. They are not unisex, so make sure you are not talked into purchasing a men's suit.

CYCLING

To the cycling aficionado, buying bike gear is simple: Get the finest wheels attached to an ultralight frame, make sure the name Shimano or Campagnolo is stamped on all the other components, drop on a pair of aerobars, get a power meter that is also a heart rate monitor and bike computer, and then set up the bike aerodynamically. All this technical babble can be intimidating to people accustomed to less complicated sports such as running. Not only must you buy an expensive thoroughbred machine, but you must also custom design it, fit it, adjust it, understand it, conform to it, power it, and babysit it.

This is only partly true. Figuring out the best bike for your needs will take a little time, but it's a fun process. You get to visit bike shops, talk to lots of knowledgeable folks about the pros and cons of different models, and test-ride bikes. In the meantime, you'll be meeting cycling enthusiasts—you might even find some training buddies.

Cycling Equipment
THE BIKE

This is a gotta have—a good bike. Not just a good bike, a really good bike. And not just a really good bike, but a really good bike that fits you perfectly.

Why? Because if you settle for anything less, you will be plagued by sore shoulders, wrists, knees, and ankles, not to mention posteriors. You can spend a lot of money and buy the best possible bike, with a great paint job and the finest components, but if it doesn't fit you, you are likely to be miserable. No, it's more than likely—you will be miserable. So for step one, get a bike-fit analysis (see sidebar "How to Measure Up").

Obviously, anatomical differences affect how bikes fit the human frame. If bike fit depended on height alone, there would be no need for different frame sizes. But there are two different measurements—torso length and leg length—that matter the most in bike fit. Women and men, on average, are very different from each other in these two measurements, and these differences necessitate modifications in bike design. The bottom line is to find a bike that you will be comfortable riding. To determine your comfort level with different types of bikes, once the bike-fit analysis is complete have the salesperson put the ones that should be most compatible with your body type on a trainer so that you have adequate time to try them out.

BOOKS ON CYCLING

I suggest that one of your first biking purchases be a good bicycling book. There are plenty available today that are written especially for women cyclists. Here are some of my favorites:

- *A Woman's Guide to Cycling*, Susan Weaver
- *Every Woman's Guide to Cycling*, Selene Yeager
- *Bicycling for Women*, Gale Bernhardt

These books include detailed information on everything from selecting a bike with the right gears to training methodologies to bike fitting. Arm yourself with information to be a savvy buyer. I've just touched on the basics of equipment in this chapter, so if you are planning to invest in a really good bike you'll want to do more research on how different frames and components will affect your ride.

Your reach to the handlebars is one of the most critical parts of your bike fit. Some women are comfortable stretching out and leaning down and others are not. Once a bike is on the trainer and you hop on, start your evaluation with the bars and seat level. Sit up straight (hands off the bars) with your shoulders back, chest out, and head held high. Rotate your feet so that the cranks are parallel to the ground. Now bend or hinge from your hips, without moving your neck or bending your back. Reach down to the handlebars, just until your hands are slightly above the brakes but not touching. Now gently rest your hands on the brakes (or bars if it has upright bars), putting very little pressure on them. You are looking for the position where you have some bend in your elbows, no pressure on the front of your saddle, and just a little on your hands. If you can move the bars up or down to achieve this position, then you're all set. If not, you will want to purchase a new stem that will position you in this manner. You want to be able to sit there comfortably for half an hour or so before you have to change your position. Of course, you probably won't sit on the bike for that long in the shop. But if you try several bikes, you should start to get a feel for the ones that seem best.

In short, it doesn't matter what you look like on the bike; what matters is how you feel. If you need to sit up because of a back or neck injury, do it. If you're comfortable on your bike, you'll feel good when you get off it. If your back is sore whenever you dismount, you'll suffer in the running segment in any triathlon you enter.

HOW TO MEASURE UP

Most people just go to a bike shop and let the salesclerk take a guess at what size bike to buy. I can assure you, that won't work. All you know about that salesperson sizing you up is that he or she gets paid to do it. He or she may not have any expertise; what you need is an expert in bike fitting.

Bicycle frames used to be measured by sizes, usually in inches such as 17, 19, 21, 23, 25, and so forth, or in the metric equivalents thereof. This represented the distance between the top of the seat tube and the middle of the bottom bracket. Today, frame geometry is more important than frame size. Do you want a triangle frame or a dropped top tube or a beam bike? To determine the type of geometry and frame size best for a particular cyclist is an art; the old methodology just isn't adequate today. Take this advice instead—go to a specialty bike shop and get measured. To figure out the best bike shops, find some serious cyclists in your area and ask them for recommendations.

About once a year the major cycling magazines publish articles on sizing and bike fit, which are also often available at their websites. Commercial sizing systems such as the Fit Kit, BioRacer, and Serotta's Size-Cycle can be very helpful. One of these bike-fit systems is available in most quality bike and triathlon stores. A store might even apply the cost of the bike fit against the purchase price of a bike if you ask in advance.

The bike-fit analysis takes about 30 minutes to complete, and you will be given a written set of measurements when you are finished. These measurements will tell you what will fit your individual anatomy: saddle height, frame size, crank length, handlebar stem length, and much more. If you go into a shop to get a bike fit and the salesperson asks you to straddle the bike so he or she can measure your clearance, you know you're being fitted "the old way." Don't accept this. Bike-fitting may be an art, but it also requires precision right from the start, or the fit is compromised.

Once you've been measured, test-ride several different bikes that are the right frame size and geometry. Don't make a snap decision, though, because there are other elements of the bike to consider.

CONSIDER THE SHIFTER

Besides bike fit, frame geometry, and a comfortable seat, consider the humble shifter. Shifter configuration may not be at the top of the list for most bike shoppers, but smooth gear shifting sure makes a big difference when you're on your bike.

The type of shifters you like could determine the kind of bike (road, mountain, hybrid, or tri) you ultimately end up with. Some systems are grip shifters, on the ends of the handlebars, and these require using your wrist. Others are finger shifters. Campagnolo shifters involve a push with the fingers and thumbs. Shimano requires a larger-than-average-sized hand, because you have to push the brake lever. Take a look at different types, and don't rule out trying shifters made for children if you have smaller hands. They are of equal quality but might make the reach to the brake lever easier for you.

While you're trying out bikes, be sure to try some women-specific designs. Although most bikes are still designed for men's anatomies, not for the size and shape of women's bodies, today you can find more bikes designed for women than in the past. You'll want to try some of these before making a final decision. Many larger bike companies, such as Trek and Specialized, are making them. Rather than being scaled-down versions of men's bikes, they are specifically designed to fit a woman's body. They may have shorter top tubes, narrower handlebars, smaller reach levers, smaller diameter grips, steeper seat tubes, or a women-specific saddle (wider at the back to accommodate a woman's wider sit bones). The shorter top tube more evenly redistributes weight between hips and hands to eliminate lower back pain and reduce neck and shoulder stress. If the tubing is the same on a women-specific bike as on men's bikes, the bike may be heavier than it needs to be. Figure 10.6 shows some different types of bike frames in women-specific designs.

Consider a custom bike if you can afford one. These are one step better than women-specific bikes because they take your unique size and riding style into consideration. After riding most bikes on the market and struggling with the fit, I ordered a custom bike, and it has made a huge difference for my riding and my comfort. No longer am I stretched out over a top tube with brake levers that are too long and far apart for me to use effectively. Even though I'm a standard-size woman—at 5 foot 6 and 135

HYBRID/COMMUTER BIKE

ROAD BIKE

TRIATHLON BIKE

FIGURE 10.6: Women-specific bikes from Trek

pounds—stock bikes don't fit me well. I recommend at least investigating this possibility before deciding on a stock bike.

If you are a beginner and funds are tight, another option is to buy a used bike. As with any used item, you must be cautious when purchasing a bike from a stranger. Find out everything you can about a used bike before you purchase it—how old it is, how much use it has seen, what kind of use, how well it has been maintained—the same things you would find out when buying a used car. It's also important to know if the bike has been in an accident, as stress fractures on the frame usually are not obvious to the naked eye.

Roadies are always looking to trade up, just as sports-car nuts are. You can get a good used bike for 50 to 75 percent of what a new one would cost. But unless you know bikes really well, find somebody you can trust who is knowledgeable enough to help you make your selection. Don't purchase one that isn't a perfect fit just because it's a "good deal." It's not a good deal if you end up with back pain from using it.

Beyond size and comfort, another important element is the material used for the frame. Standard stock bikes, from 10-speeds to 18-speeds, are constructed of either some sort of metal (steel, aluminum, titanium) or a carbon-fiber composite. Aluminum, titanium, and carbon-fiber bikes have the advantage of being lightweight, which typically makes them more expensive. You should decide what's in your budget and test-ride some different frames. But don't assume that the most expensive bike is the most desirable bike. You might find the steel frame to be more comfortable and easier to handle.

Whether you are purchasing a stock bike, a custom bike, or a used bike, and whether it is made of a traditional material or carbon fiber, take the time to select one that is right for you, and spend as much as you can reasonably afford to spend. The bicycle, after all, is a machine that has been designed around you, the human engine. If the bicycle is compatibly matched to you, the energy expended in pedaling is efficiently converted into power and forward motion—the direction to the finish line—and it is a joy to ride.

HELMET

A helmet is the single most important item you will purchase for cycling. In fact, one saved my life a few years ago. After my bike accident (and after I awoke from the concussion), I looked at the two cracks and the skid marks that cut deeply into the side of my helmet, and I was unbelievably thankful because the helmet cracked open and not my cranium.

Helmets must meet the safety requirements set by the Consumer Product Safety Commission (CPSC) or one or more of the voluntary bicycle helmet certification organizations, such as the American Society of Testing Materials (ASTM) or Snell. If the helmet meets their rigorous testing, a sticker is attached as a seal of approval. There are three other requirements to take into consideration: fit/comfort, ventilation, and weight. My unbreakable rule is that I won't ride with anyone who doesn't wear a helmet—either my cycling partners wear a helmet, or we don't ride together. It's a good rule.

Some people have a good helmet, but they never wear it correctly or even make the minor adjustments needed to customize the fit (see Figure 10.7). Once you find a helmet that fits you, take the following steps to make sure it will protect your head as much as possible:

TOO HIGH

TOO LOW

JUST RIGHT

FIGURE 10.7:
Proper helmet wearing

- Put the helmet on so it sits evenly between the ears and rests low on your forehead—it should only be one or two finger widths above your eyebrows.
- Put foam pads inside the helmet so it feels comfortable but snug. Usually, the helmet includes more than one size of foam pads that can be attached inside with Velcro for a better fit.
- Tighten the left front strap so that the buckle is under the center of your chin and the straps make a "V" beneath your ears with the buckle under the earlobe.
- Adjust the left back strap, pulling any slack away from the front of the helmet.
- Adjust the right back strap, continuing to pull the slack in the strap so that it lies flat against the head.
- Adjust the right front strap so that you have a "V" under this ear with the buckle under the ear lobe.

• Adjust the chin strap so that it is snug and holds the helmet level. You should be able to put one or two fingers between the strap and the chin and be able to yawn, chew, and talk with the helmet staying secure.

After you've adjusted your straps, double-check the fit by doing the following:

With one hand, gently lift the front of the helmet up and push back. If the helmet moves back to uncover the forehead, tighten (shorten) the front straps to junction under the ears while leaving the back straps in the same position. Retighten the chin strap as needed. Also, adjust the padding thickness and position, especially in the back (and/or front). If this doesn't work, the helmet may be too big.

With one hand, gently lift the back of the helmet up and push forward. If the helmet moves forward to cover the eyes, tighten (shorten) the back straps. Make sure the chin strap is snug. Also adjust padding thickness and position, especially in the front (and/or back as needed). If this doesn't work, the helmet may be too big.

Put a hand on each side of the helmet and rock it from side to side. Shake your head "no" as hard as possible. If the helmet slips from side to side, check the padding on the sides and add thicker pads. Make sure the straps are snug and evenly adjusted.

Open your mouth (lower jaw) as wide as possible, without moving your head. The top of the helmet should pull snugly against the top of your head. If

HELMET BASICS

• When you're not on your bike, hang your helmet on the handlebars by the main buckle and not by the straps that you have fitted to go under your ears.

• Helmets are good for one crash and one crash only.

• Helmets need to be replaced after three years even if they haven't been in a crash. Check the "birthday" inside your helmet to make sure you don't continue to wear it after it has "expired."

• Cut the straps off before throwing a helmet away. If it is not safe for you, it is not safe for anyone else to wear.

• Write your name and contact information inside your helmet with a permanent marker.

it does not pull down when you open your mouth, tighten the chin strap. Make sure the front and back strap junctions rest under the earlobes.

GEARING

A certain elitism is built into the high-tech sport of triathlon, a snobbery that usually pertains to lightweight bikes with only a double chainring for the front chain wheel. (The front chainring is what your chain travels around on the front; the rear chainring, or rear cog, is the set of gears on the back that the chain rotates around.) I strongly recommend a triple chain wheel in the front—it's worth the weight to have enough gears to climb steep terrain easily for long periods of time.

Examine the different gearing setups for road bikes and touring bikes. Typical racing time-trial bikes have front chain wheels with 53 teeth on the large one and 42 teeth on the small one. Touring bikes have front chain wheels of 52 teeth and 36 teeth, respectively, with the 14 to 34 teeth on the rear cogs. In both, the high gear combinations are necessary for good speeds on level roads or downhills. The touring bikes and cross bikes have more gears for pulling grades with heavier loads.

TIRES

If you use a mountain bike or a hybrid in a triathlon with a course mainly of asphalt, change the tires to a tread that maximizes your effort, such as slicks. Although I have seen the behinds of many faster bikers on road bikes, I have rarely been passed by anyone riding a mountain bike in a triathlon, and certainly never by anyone on a mountain bike with knobbies (tires with mountain bike treads).

SADDLE

The main thing to remember when purchasing a saddle is to find one that fits your rear end rather than forcing your rear end to fit the saddle.

Once you find a good saddle, you'll need to get it positioned properly on the bike. There are basically three saddle-adjustment settings: angle, height, and forward/backward position. Individual preference plays a big role here. Some women prefer the nose of the saddle slightly tipped upward, some (like me) prefer it tipped downward, and still others like their saddle positioned parallel to the ground. You'll need to experiment with this.

Saddle height is the next adjustment. There are many different ways to align the saddle over the crank, and making even slight changes can lead to differences in comfort and performance. To make adjustments, place your bike in a stable position with your heels on the pedals, barefoot. Choose a saddle height that you think is too low and pedal backward. Raise your seat height a quarter inch until your hips slide up and down as you complete a revolution of the crank. Once this sliding occurs, lower the seat position about half an inch. Again, you'll need to experiment. If you experience any numbness, your seat may be too high or too low.

HANDLEBARS

The type of handlebars you should have and the way they're set up on the bike will depend on your riding style and your anatomy. For conventional drop bars, select the width that best corresponds to your shoulder width. Position them so that from a side view, the tops of the bars are parallel to the top tube.

Drop handlebars work fine for triathlons. If you can upgrade, add a pair of aerodynamic bars with elbow pads. These are especially useful in long-distance triathlons, such as international-distance events. Aerobars are aerodynamic, but they also sacrifice bike-handling ability because they place your upper-body weight on your forearms.

PEDALS AND SHOES

For every 2,000 miles you ride, you will rotate your pedals about a million times. That means your knees will be rotating a million times, too, so never underestimate the importance of pedal selection and adjustment.

As for adjustment, the ball of your foot should be directly over the pedal axle. There's no question that clipless pedals are the safest and lightest option, but they are usually an upgrade to a standard bike. Your bike will probably come with toe clips, or cages. For pedals that come with a cage, you need the right size cage. They come in small, medium, and large; have the salesperson help you with sizing and fit.

As soon as you can, upgrade to clipless pedals. In these pedal systems, such as those offered by Look, Crank Brothers, Speedplay, and SPD, the pedals themselves hook into a pair of bike shoes. Clipless pedals will increase your speed and power because you can pull the pedal through the full rotation of the pedal stroke. You will find that you can pedal much more efficiently this way. (See Chapter 6 for tips on how to get used to this type of pedal for the first time.)

TWO PUMPS

When you purchase your bike, get a frame pump to go with it, installed on the bike. This is a must because it's inevitable that you will have a flat. (See Appendix B for instruction on bike maintenance, including how to fix a flat.) But you can pump a bike tire to only about 60–80 psi (pounds per square inch) with a frame pump. Frame pumps are designed to get you home so you can use the second pump. Your second pump should be a high-pressure floor pump with a pressure gauge. You will use the floor pump to pump the tire to the recommended psi number that appears on the tire sidewall.

You might also consider carrying a CO_2 canister with an adaptor, a quick alternative to hand pumping your tires when you get a flat on the road. There are also dual inflators with a Co_2 canister on one side and a hand pump on the other. These are especially useful when racing.

TIRE REPAIR ACCESSORIES

Buy a bike accessory bag that will fit under your saddle, and put these items into it, at minimum: cell phone, speed lever, new tube (for the first flat), a patch kit (in case of a second flat), and your personal identification information, including an emergency phone number and medical insurance information.

CAGE AND WATER BOTTLES

If your bike doesn't come with a water-bottle cage, buy either a light-weight alloy type or a tough plastic one. There are also cages that attach behind your saddle or on your handlebars for ease and aerodynamics. I recommend carrying two water bottles for those hot days when you will really need them. For longer rides you might like to bring along a hydration system such as a Camelbak.

REFLECTIVES

Any gear that provides reflective properties is a plus—and if you ever end up riding at night, these items are a must. Reflective clothing, equipment, patches, vests, reflectors attached to pedals, and tape for your helmet all light you up in a world where, as a cyclist, you are difficult to see. Attach a rechargeable, nickel-cadmium, battery-powered lamp with halogen bulbs to your frame if you are going to ride at night. The beams are bright enough that you can see the road well. You should also have a taillight if you will be riding at night.

BIKE COMPUTERS (CYCLOMETERS)

These small computers that attach to your handlebars are a delight because they give you useful feedback as you ride. There are two types of transmission: hard-wired or wireless. They both use a magnetic impulse that is transmitted to a computer chip from a pick-up device mounted on the wheel. Bike computers measure pedal cadence, speed in miles per hour (or kilometers per hour), average speed, distance traveled (trip distance), total distance traveled to date, time of day, and elapsed time, or the duration of the ride. Some cyclometers can display several of these data functions simultaneously.

> **TIP** Stock bikes are frequently equipped with unnecessary accessories. For example, kickstands are heavy and serve no useful purpose for a cyclist. Reflectors on your wheels slow you down; if you're going to ride at night, you will wear reflective gear and use a front and rear light. Nor do you need valve stem caps, those little black plastic caps that screw onto the tire's valve stem. They slow you down when you want to fix a flat and serve no useful function.

POWER METERS

Power meters measure your wattage, which is the product of how fast you are pedaling (rpm) and how hard you are pedaling (the amount of force you exert on the pedal). To generate more power, you pedal at the highest gear that you can push (force) at the highest possible cadence. More power means faster speed on the bike. Power meters are the preferred training tool of competitive cyclists because they measure exactly what these cyclists need to know—the force, or work, exerted on the pedals over time. Power data can be difficult to interpret and apply to your training. If you are an experienced cyclist and you want to know more about training with power, read *Training and Racing with a Power Meter* by Hunter Allen and Andy Coggan.

Cycling Apparel

It's as important to dress in performance wear as it is to invest in performance components and equipment. Researchers have used wind-tunnel tests to measure performance differences among cyclists wearing different types of apparel and have demonstrated that wearing tight-fitting cycle wear can save the rider 10 percent or more in energy costs and time.

JERSEYS

Cycling shirts are snug and often wick moisture away from your body. The term "bike jersey" comes from those olden days when the shirts were made from black wool jersey material to match the color of bike grease, with pockets sewn onto the back. Today, like cycling shorts, cycling jerseys are constructed from performance fabrics and cut in fashionable styles. Some women prefer a Lycra bra-top with an overshirt that can be removed once they are warmed up. However, if you crash and your shoulders aren't covered, you risk serious abrasions.

In colder weather, multiple layers of apparel are recommended: A durable wind-jacket (preferably water resistant) over a long-sleeved performance-fabric turtleneck, over a short-sleeved shirt, over a performance-fabric tank, will give you four layers, and that should be enough to keep you warm in most conditions. If you want more, add arm and leg warmers to your ensemble.

As for those pockets sewn on the back of bike jerseys, most triathletes prefer to carry their extra stuff—food, sunscreen, tubes—in fanny packs or under-the-seat accessory packs. It's easier to carry your gear in a fanny pack that can be taken off than to wear everything stuffed into pockets worn on your back.

SHORTS

The two concerns for all cycling apparel are warmth and moisture control. Back in the day, riders wore black wool shorts with a chamois patch sewn into the crotch. A good design change is that chamois-lined pads have been replaced with softer and more hygienic polyester pads. Today, there are new fabrics and methods of construction that have brought about even more advances. In cold-weather riding, the new high-tech fabric blends are warmer and wick sweat better than wools. In hot weather, Lycra stretch blends contour to the body more comfortably, reflect the heat, allow perspiration to evaporate, and dry quickly. You can also train comfortably without pads in Lycra fitness or cross-training shorts.

Cycling shorts are designed to be worn without underwear, which is generally uncomfortable and annoying while bicycling. Therefore, because of the heat and sweat, cycling shorts must be washed after each ride. If you have problems with yeast infections, try different types of fabric blends in the inner lining. You will probably need several pairs of shorts if you ride frequently.

GLOVES

Cycling gloves are cut off at the knuckles for gripping power. They are designed to protect you from the road shock that is transferred to your hands through the handlebars as well as to protect your hands if you crash. However, I've always preferred to pad my handlebars, not my hands, with handlebar material like foam rubber—and to avoid crashing. This means that I don't wear cycling gloves for rides under 20 miles unless I need them for warmth. It's your choice.

SOCKS, HATS, AND EYEWEAR

If it's hot, I wear neither a hat under my helmet nor socks. If the weather turns cool, all of that changes. I hate to be cold, so I adopt the attitude that there's no cold weather, only warm clothing.

Investing in quality protective clothing is the key to never being cold. Wearing polypropylene socks (with plastic baggies over them if it helps) and bike booties over your shoes is usually enough to keep your feet warm. Placing a hat under your helmet may cause a problem with a good fit, but it does keep your head warm. Plastic-framed glasses or sunglasses will protect your eyes from both bugs and the elements, and ski masks or balaclava can further cover and warm your face.

Some people prefer to wear socks for comfort even when it is warm out. If you are one of them, be sure to use socks made of a breathable fabric that wicks moisture away from your skin.

Dress for the occasion: the temperature, the sun exposure, the rain (hopefully not snow), the fog, the wind speed, and the strenuousness of your ride. Dress for success, and be prepared to strip it off or pile it on as needed.

RUNNING

I love the sport of running because of its simplicity. All you really need is a pair of top-of-the-line running shoes and you can be on your way. You should also have a heart rate monitor, however. In addition, wear reflective tape or a vest that makes you more visible at night, and carry identification with you at all times, such as the Road I.D. mentioned at the beginning of the chapter.

Running Equipment

SHOES

If you have never run in a pair of real running shoes, go immediately to a specialty sports shop, try some on, and run up and down the aisles in the store. They are so incredible, compared with cross-trainers, walking shoes, or tennis shoes, that you won't leave the shop without them.

Don't rush your choice, though. Spend time getting a professional fit, and invest about 30 minutes to try on at least six different models. Trust your feet, not the salespitch—they know best. That said, it's a good idea to cultivate a relationship with the people at your local running store, because they are often knowledgeable and can help you find the proper shoe for your feet and running style. If they do not know running and running shoes, go elsewhere—in most medium-sized and large cities you can find an athletic shoe store with well-trained salespeople who are runners themselves.

Manufacturers of running shoes have specialized to such a degree that you should be able to find a shoe designed for your specific biomechanics. If you're heavy, have narrow or wide feet or ankles, are hard on shoes, want lots of rear foot support, are a pronator, or need more cushioning, don't despair. There's a running shoe out there for you.

With new styles being released every six months and old styles being discontinued just as quickly, it is impossible to describe training shoes based on model or style. In the past, runners would find a style they liked and then keep buying the same kind year after year. This is no longer the case. Nowadays, new models come and go so quickly that your favorite style will probably be discontinued before you can wear out your first

BEYOND "SHRINK IT AND PINK IT"

When I first started selling athletic shoes in the retail chain I cofounded in 1976, Fleet Feet Sports, I ran into two problems: First, there were few styles specifically designed for women's feet, and second, the ones that were sold for women were simply smaller versions of the shoes made for men, with the word "lady" added before the name, such as the Nike "Lady Cortez." Today the situation has changed. Manufacturers now recognize female athletes as "women" instead of "ladies," and shoe companies have taken to building women's shoes around the shape of a woman's foot instead of just producing scaled-down versions of the men's shoes.

pair. To find the right pair of shoes for you, look for good shock absorption, stability, adequate flexibility, a last that matches your foot's shape, pronation support (for the way the foot rolls inward after contact with the ground), and motion control. The biomechanics of your foot should match perfectly with the structural performance of your running shoe. Only a specialist who knows the current technology in performance footwear can help you with this.

Your basic choice is between racing flats (which weigh about 5 ounces) and running shoes (about 10–14 ounces) (see Figure 10.8). For now, select the heavier but more stable running shoes. Later, if you are so inclined, buy a pair of the racers—they are heavenly and make you feel almost barefooted when you run. If you have a wide foot, you might want to experiment with men's models, so keep in mind that an equivalently sized men's shoe will be 1½ sizes less than a women's shoe (for example, a women's 8 equals a men's 6½). Your new shoes don't generally require a break-in period; just lace them up, put on a pair of lace locks (plastic devices that prevent your laces from coming untied), and take off for an enjoyable few miles.

FIGURE 10.8: Racing flat

When you reach the half-life of your running shoes (at roughly 300 miles or 6 months, whichever comes first), purchase another pair, but of an entirely different technology and style. Then alternate wearing the old pair with the new ones. A primary cause of running injuries is wearing the same shoes for every run. If you have a biomechanical weakness and you wear the same pair for every workout, you could fall prey to a cumulative injury effect.

Don't use your running shoes for other sports; these are sport-specific footwear, not cross-training shoes. Save an old pair for the gym. Occasionally check the wear points on your soles, and if the treads look worn out, especially in one place, either buy some patching goo from the running/ triathlon store or get a new pair. The midsoles are probably shot anyway, although the outsole should last for a thousand miles unless you are a foot dragger.

Another word of advice from an old shoe dog: Buy the best pair you can afford. Choose value over price, because running shoes are an investment. It's cheaper to buy top-of-the-line running shoes than it is to pay for a visit to the doctor's office for a foot injury.

SUNGLASSES

Sunglasses reduce glare and help keep the face muscles relaxed, and they protect the eyes from the sun's harmful rays as well as from particles in the air. For running, look for a rubber nosepiece that will keep the sunglasses from sliding as you sweat, lightweight frames, and adjustable nosepiece and temple arms.

SKIN PRODUCTS

Don't bother with cosmetics before your run—you'll look worse afterward if you do. Skin-care products, though, are an exception. Body Glide or Vaseline can protect your hands and feet from chafing and blistering, though Vaseline can stain. Sunscreen, again, is a must—apply it to all exposed areas. Take care of your skin; it is with you for a lifetime.

Running Apparel

SPORTS BRAS

When I first started running, there were no sports bras. Women either wore a Lycra swimsuit (interestingly, we still do today as triathletes) or a support bra. Now many companies make sports bras, and no longer are bras uniformly white—they are designed with wild patterns and prints and can even be worn as outerwear.

Bras that are designed for athletics, rather than aesthetics, serve two primary purposes. First, a good sports bra can prevent a variety of possible injuries to breast tissue: contusions, soreness or abrasions such as jogger's nipple (raw and/or bleeding nipples due to prolonged rubbing against a bra or shirt), or hematomas. Second, sports bras provide support to breast tissues from excessive movement. Large-breasted women in particular need to make sure their sports bras give them enough support, and may need to wear two bras together. If you fit into this category, use one that is tighter and smaller first and layer a slightly looser and larger one over it for better support. Finally, a sports bra distributes the weight of the breasts evenly over the ribcage and the back rather than the shoulders.

Proper bra fit is the key to preventing breast movement and bouncing during vigorous activity. In addition, look for the following features:

- Wide straps that are nonelastic and designed not to slip off the shoulders, such as the Y-back design
- Covered fasteners that will not cause abrasions
- A nonmetal underwire, such as a wide cloth band, that prevents the bra from riding up over the breasts
- Construction from absorptive, nonallergenic, and nonabrasive materials with little elasticity, such as the CoolMax fabrics
- Good upward support

Try on several different bra styles and test them in the dressing room by jumping up and down and swinging your arms, both over your head and in running style. Also take a few deep breaths, as a bra should not interfere with breathing; a sports bra should be firm but not too tight or restrictive to body motion.

TOPS AND BOTTOMS

As in cycling, performance apparel can make a big difference in running. Apparel that fits and is of the right fabric can prevent chafing, wick perspiration away from your body, maintain warmth, and lower wind resistance. For any one of those features alone, it's worth it to be choosy. Cotton is not recommended for training apparel, since it retains water and thus keeps the moisture next to your skin, which can cause chafing and chills when it's cold.

A technical-fabric shirt wicks moisture away from your body, which helps to keep you cool. Cotton t-shirts absorb your sweat and end up getting drenched. The layered approach in running apparel works both for its insulating properties and for its convenience. In cold weather, layering starts with a sports bra (always, for me, and I highly recommend you wear one), then continues with a performance-fabric short-sleeved top, a long-sleeved shirt, and a jacket or vest. All that remains is to add a few turtlenecks made of fabrics such as Dry Zone or polypropylene to your wardrobe, and you'll have your top half covered.

As for your bottom half, you have a lot of choices. First, fitness shorts, sometimes called "compression shorts," are made of stretch fabrics and cut slightly longer than normal shorts, usually extending to just above the knee (to prevent thigh chafing). Running tights are full length, sometimes with stirrups or zippers at the bottom so you can pull them on over shoes, and are great for cold weather. Tricot nylon shorts, with liners cut to a woman's body shape, are lightweight (so light you may feel you have nothing on) and durable. They also often have a key pocket. Briefs, or "butt huggers," might work for elite runners, but they leave nothing to the imagination and don't work for me.

OUTERWEAR

Overheating presents a more immediate danger than cold-weather exposure. When it's hot, expose as much of your body as you can and wear light, loose-fitting tops. Don't tuck in your shirt, and do wear a visor or cap to shade your face. Also take care to drink lots of fluids during your workout, and run through sprinklers, if possible.

> **TIP** Remember the 20-degree rule—add 20 degrees (Fahrenheit) to the ambient temperature, and that's how hot it will feel during your run. Dress with this in mind.

Cold-weather running is easier because you can add layers that trap heat. A stocking cap and gloves are standard fare. Wear polypro-type blended fabrics for warmth; they have wicking properties that allow moisture to escape and warmth to stay in. To combat wet weather, wear waterproof fabrics such as Gore-Tex (which is also breathable). A run in the cold or rain can be as enjoyable as any other if you dress appropriately.

HEADWEAR: HATS AND VISORS

A cap will help to keep the sun out of your eyes and prevent sunburn (although you should still wear sunscreen if you wear a cap). Hats made specifically for running (as opposed to a cotton/twill baseball cap) are made of mesh technical fabric that is breathable and moisture-wicking. They'll feature a sweatband around the inside, and some have a black underside on the bill to prevent reflection of glare from the street.

SOCKS

Whether to wear socks when running is a matter of personal preference. Some of my training partners never wear socks, and others wear blister-free socks that are double-layered on the bottom. Most runners wear socks for hygiene reasons, since it's easier to wash socks than shoes. Some people may get blisters without socks, some do with them, and some get them either way. It's up to you to experiment to see what makes you most comfortable. Socks that wick away moisture help prevent blisters. Cotton "tube socks" absorb a *lot* of sweat and moisture, which can lead to chafing and blisters. Check different styles of running socks—you can find thin and cushioned styles, and there are many fun designs!

RACE DAY

If clothes don't really "make the woman," they may well make the race. There are a wide variety of triathlon clothes that will make you more comfortable during your race. They will also improve your performance because you will not have to change clothes in transition.

Tri-shorts look like cycling shorts, but the padding is usually a light fleece and is quick to dry. A tri-top is a tight-fitting Lycra top that goes down to the waist. The fabric dries quickly, so you can swim, bike, and run in it. It provides more coverage than a sports bra, usually has a front zipper, and sometimes has pockets in the back. It may be advisable to wear a Lycra/nylon sports bra underneath the top.

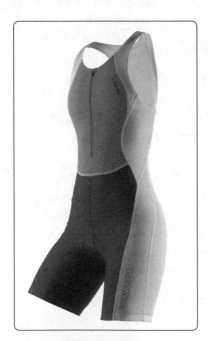

FIGURE 10.9: Tri suit

The tri-suit (see Figure 10.9) is a one-piece Lycra suit that is like a tri-top attached to tri-shorts. There is usually a zipper in the front and light padding in the seat. The downside to a tri-suit is that it is more difficult to take the tri-suit off for quick calls to nature.

A swimsuit and nothing else may also be worn in a triathlon. It can be a one-piece or a two-piece suit.

Other possibilities for race day include wearing a swimsuit for the swim, then adding running shorts and a running singlet in T1. Do not try to put on cycling shorts after the swim. It's too hard to get them on over wet skin, and the shorts themselves can become waterlogged. You could also wear a sports bra and tri-shorts (look for Lycra/nylon blends for the sports bra, not cotton blends).

SHOP AROUND

Shop for your triathletic gear in specialty sports shops, especially your local tri-shop or Web retailer. Salespeople in discount, department, or hardware stores are not trained for the triathlete's specific needs. Members of the sales staff at specialty stores are trained to sell bike, swim, and footwear gear and often very knowledgeable about their products. They will help you select the right equipment to meet your needs, your body size and shape, and your budget. The running-shoe shop should have a wide selection of top-quality brands, and bike shops can set your bike up properly, measure you for it, and provide repairs. Ask around to find out which businesses are best known for their service and expertise. In a good specialty store, you will find friendly people who understand athletes, because they are frequently athletes themselves.

Thankfully, we have crossed into the twenty-first century with sportswear and equipment. Taking advantage of today's innovative products and specialty technologies will make a big difference in your training and racing. Gone are the old days of heavy everything, from bikes to warm weather clothing. Gone are the ancient days of training by perceived exertion without personal training tools like heart rate monitors, power meters, and smart fabrics. Gone are the archaic days when women couldn't be seen in public wearing a sports bra or tight, compression fabrics.

Welcome to an era of constant innovation in products, training systems, and science-based coaching. They will enhance your comfort, your speed, and your enjoyment of multisport. Watch for even more innovation as manufacturers create new solutions to our training needs. Who can say what the next generation of triathlon products will bring?

11

Eating for Training and Racing

For most people interested in health and fitness, the million-dollar question is this: "What is the best diet for me?" In other words, what combination of fuels will best clean out your pipes, rev up your engines, and fire the motor that takes you through the rigorous physical and mental demands of a typical day, or a hard training day?

Nutritional experts, health faddists, and successful, experienced athletes expound at length on the subject of nutrition and diet, bombarding us with a mass of conflicting theories and recommendations. It's no wonder we're confused. And yet, research on diet and nutrition has come a long way in recent years, and it has confirmed some nutritional principles again and again so that we can recommend them with some degree of certainty. In this chapter and the next, I will summarize how these nutritional principles apply to you as a triathlete.

This chapter is about eating an optimum diet that fuels you with energy to live a healthy lifestyle as a triathlete. We are interested in top performance, but the same principles are involved in basic wellness. In Chapter 12, we'll explore the concept of weight loss and how it may affect you as a triathlete. Weight loss has physical, emotional, and metabolic components, and I'll explain how to manage your weight by taking all three into consideration and eating in the "low food zones."

An optimum diet can be defined as that particular combination of foods that stimulates the body to perform with maximum comfort and efficiency in a predictable variety of situations. A well-balanced diet is necessary for everyone, but it is particularly important for individu-

als in highly stressful situations—such as the female triathlete. How can we gauge the relative values of different food types in this search to find the best fuels? We do know that it makes a difference whether they are high or low in nutrients, and how they rate in other measures of quality. People who make fitness a priority know to choose whole grains over processed flours, to keep their intake of fruits and veggies up, to stay away from trans fats, and to seek out high-quality proteins. Those who are especially savvy may be aware of how a food rates on the glycemic index scale, or take the time to balance their caloric needs with their athletic activities.

There is one basic formula for overall good health that all experts can agree on:

Balanced nutrition + physical activity + quality sleep + fresh air + good genes + moderate exposure to sunlight + low stress + staying mentally active = Your best chance for good health

All of us, and especially triathletes, should closely evaluate our eating habits, monitoring the amount, type, and nutritional value of the foods we ingest. Probably the most optimum diet for a triathlete is one that will both tune up the engine and turn on the high performance. After almost 40 years of training and racing, I have found some simple criteria that help me unravel the confusion caused by obsolete nutritional theories, commercial interests in the advertising that surrounds us, and the fad diets that sometimes take the country by storm. Before I eat any food, I ask myself, "What will it give me, and what will it cost me?"

Food gives the body a source of fuel that it can burn for energy and provides certain nutritional benefits (for example, protein to repair muscle tissue). However, food can also cost the body. It may provide empty (non-nutritious) calories, or it may be difficult to digest. To use an economic metaphor, there is a cost-benefit ratio that applies to the act of eating. It makes sense, therefore, that the food we put into our incredible machines must pay some dividends—it must give us more than it costs us.

TRIATHLETES AND ENERGY NEEDS

As a triathlete with a rigorous training program, you will be burning more total calories in your day than the average person. As a result, you will need more calories—but not just empty calories. You also need these calories to be rich in nutrients in order to support all the increased demands you are placing on your body. This is probably the biggest difference between you and the average American when it comes to nutrition.

Your energy requirements depend primarily on your training load, or the duration, intensity, and frequency of your workouts. A rough estimate of caloric costs and therefore energy requirements in training is that you

What will it cost me?

will expend approximately 500–700 calories per hour if you are training at a moderate intensity, or at 60–80 percent of your maximum heart rate (zones 2 and 3). (To find out how to measure this, see the sidebar "Metabolic Fitness Testing").

But there are other factors in your total daily caloric cost, or daily energy expenditure (EE). It is actually the sum of these three things:

Basal metabolism (resting metabolic rate)
+ physical activity + digestion =
Daily energy expenditure (total calories burned per day)

The basal metabolic rate is where energy expenditure begins—these are the calories you burn just to keep your heart beating, your lungs breathing, and your other organs doing all the other things organs do. Muscles burn more calories than fat even when you're just sitting around, so to increase your metabolic rate, also known as your *burn rate*, you must change your body composition, the ratio of fat weight to fat-free weight. Triathlon training increases your muscle mass and therefore increases your burn rate at rest. In other words, triathlon training increases your caloric output because you are exercising more, but it also increases your caloric output when you are just sitting around, because your basal metabolic rate is higher than that of the average person. The final part of the equation is the caloric cost of digestion, which is based on the types of foods you eat. Each food has a caloric cost for digestion that can be measured.

With all this focus on energy expenditure and caloric cost, you might assume that I would recommend counting calories. However, in all my years of manipulating this calories-out side of the energy-balancing equation, I have never found that counting calories works well for most triathletes. It's not that counting calories is cumbersome—it isn't, because there are personal calorie-counting tools to simplify this—but that it simply doesn't work. There are a lot of reasons why, and one of those is how smart your body is at making changes to adjust for energy in and energy out.

However, I do believe that it can be helpful to familiarize yourself with the caloric estimates—and these are very rough estimates—of the expenditure of calories based on data and training levels. Table 11.1 will help you understand how many calories per day you may metabolize based on your physical activity level. Also, notice how increasing the physical activity part of the formula makes enormous differences in your daily burn rate.

TABLE 11.1 Daily Calorie Allowance to Maintain Current Weight

WEIGHT (lbs.)	COMPETITIVE TRIATHLETE	HIGHLY ACTIVE	ACTIVE	MODERATELY ACTIVE	NOT VERY ACTIVE	COMPLETELY SEDENTARY
80	1,600	1,440	1,280	1,120	960	800
90	1,800	1,620	1,440	1,260	1,080	900
100	1,900	1,800	1,600	1,400	1,200	1,000
110	2,000	1,980	1,760	1,540	1,320	1,100
120	2,200	2,160	1,920	1,680	1,440	1,200
130	2,400	2,340	2,080	1,820	1,560	1,300
140	2,600	2,520	2,240	1,960	1,680	1,400
150	2,800	2,700	2,400	2,100	1,800	1,500
160	3,000	2,880	2,560	2,240	1,920	1,600
170	3,200	3,060	2,720	2,380	2,040	1,700
180	3,400	3,240	2,880	2,520	2,160	1,800
190	3,600	3,420	3,200	2,660	2,280	1,900
200	3,800	3,600	3,360	2,800	2,400	2,000
210	4,000	3,780	3,520	2,940	2,520	2,100
220	4,200	3,960	3,680	3,080	2,640	2,200
230	4,400	4,140	3,840	3,220	2,760	2,300
240	4,600	4,320	4,000	3,360	2,880	2,400
250	4,800	4,500	4,160	3,500	3,000	2,500

METABOLIC FITNESS TESTING

I recommend that you take a metabolic exercise test to measure your caloric expenditure at both rest and during exercise. This lab-quality test can be taken at most health clubs, chiropractor or physical therapist offices, or college exercise labs.

There are two different tests: the resting test, which measures basal metabolic rate, and the exercise fitness test. Your basal metabolic rate is the number of calories you would burn each day if you were sedentary. This is the caloric cost of all the functions your organs carry out, that is, the sum of the energy spent for your heart to contract, your brain to work, your lungs to pump air, your endocrine system to balance hormones, and so forth. This test takes about 20 minutes, and all you have to do is rest comfortably, remaining motionless, and breathe while an analyzer measures your oxygen consumption and the amount of carbon dioxide that you expire. Actually, it's useful data to have because it tells you how many calories you would expend each day if you didn't move. It you have a low resting metabolic rate, then you don't have to burn very many calories to stay alive and awake. That can be a problem if it means you don't have much muscle tissue (muscles burn more calories than fat when you are just sitting around). The remedy is to stoke up your metabolism, build up your muscles, and increase the burn rate.

Exercise fitness testing, also known as a VO_2 max test, uses the same equipment, a respiratory gas analyzer, but this time you do a graded exercise test that slowly ramps up the speed on a treadmill or the power output on a bike to measure the amount of oxygen you can process (called the volume of oxygen, or VO_2). I love this test because it gives me the seven big numbers that reveal rich physiological data on my metabolic response to exercise:

1. Total calories spent in each of the five training or heart zones.
2. Fat and carbohydrates used in each of the five zones (so I know at what intensity I am burning the most calories and what the ratio of those calories is in terms of fat and carbs).
3. My threshold heart rate number (the crossover point between aerobic and anaerobic exercise).
4. An estimate of my maximum heart rate number (so that I can set training zones more accurately).

CONTINUED →

← METABOLIC FITNESS TESTING, CONTINUED

5. Recommendations on how I can improve my fitness and caloric expenditure.

6. A ranking of my fitness compared to other women in my age group (whether I'm in the top 25 percent or somewhere below that level, and as a competitive athlete, this is the number I really want to see).

7. The maximum volume of oxygen that I use, my VO_2 (which provides me with information on the caliber or ranking of my athletic talent—am I average or world class?).

Each test takes about 20 minutes. Each session for each test takes about an hour because a metabolic specialist will explain what the numbers mean (but not what to do to improve your metabolism). To improve your metabolic response—to get fitter—you need to hire a certified metabolic specialist (CMS). My company, Heart Zones USA, offers these tests and has trained people on staff to interpret the results for you. The cost of the tests varies, typically ranging from $75 to $125 for the resting metabolic fitness test and from $150 to $200 for the exercise fitness test.

If you get these tests done, I recommend that you commit to a retest 8 to 24 weeks later to see how much you have improved. If the change is not as great as you had hoped, you may be able to get better results by ramping up your training and making further improvements in your nutritional program.

The bottom line is that we get done what we measure and monitor. Measuring and monitoring your metabolism is one of the most important things you can do for your health and your performance.

EATING FOR ENERGY: CARBOHYDRATES

As you learn to fine-tune your diet, your body begins to regard food as fuel, the fuel that makes your muscles operate efficiently. Muscle burns primarily glucose and glycogen. Researchers have shown that the muscle tissues can consume 90 percent of all calories burned in a day's activities in an active individual. It would seem reasonable, then, to feed our muscles those fuels they can make the best use of—complex carbohydrates, the primary source of muscle sugars.

When I eat, I do so to meet my metabolic needs for supplying my fat-free mass, my muscles and essential tissues. Everyone's nutritional needs are different. I know from experience that my muscles prefer carbohydrates because I work out a couple of hours a day. So I feed them just that. I don't eat to feed my body fat; my body already stores sufficient amounts of fat without my encouraging it to store more. Protein, needed to rebuild or resynthesize tissues, is required only in small quantities. For me, the breakdown among these three principal food sources for percentage of daily caloric intake (plus or minus 5 percentage points) comes down to a basic formula. Although it works for me, that doesn't mean it will work for everyone. I use it as a guide, not as a stringent rule:

- Complex carbohydrates: 60—65 percent of total daily calories
- Protein: 10—15 percent of total daily calories
- Dietary fat: 20—25 percent of total daily calories

By maintaining a diet that is balanced and full of nutrients and that consists of a healthy ratio of fats, proteins, and complex carbohydrates, I am feeding my engine a blend that results in a high-octane fuel—energy for my triple-fitness body.

In this day and age there are many mixed messages about the amount of carbohydrates you should incorporate into your diet. Some weight-loss fads have promoted a low-carbohydrate, high-protein diet. However, pick up any sports magazine and you'll see all kinds of advertisements touting carbohydrate drinks, bars, and gels, all for the purpose of better sport performance. For an athlete who wants to manage her weight and perform well in sports, it can be very difficult to know how much carbohydrate, fat, and protein to include in one's diet.

Since I love carbohydrates, let's take a long look at them. Carbohydrates, a.k.a. carbos or carbs, are basically sugars and starches. Your body breaks them down into glycogen, the primary source of fuel for your muscles and your brain. How hard you are training determines the ratio of fat to carbs used. When you exercise at a low intensity, such as when you are walking, you are using fat as the main energy source (in technical jargon, fat is the substrate). As your exercise intensity increases to moderate level, you are using both fat and carbohydrates as your energy source in about a 50—50 ratio. At harder intensities, glycogen from carbs becomes your primary fuel source.

Carbohydrates are stored as glycogen in your liver, muscles, and blood. When your muscles are glycogen depleted, they are no longer able to function at a high performance level. You may have experienced this as muscle fatigue, "bonking," or "crashing." As you train for an event, you train not

THE COMMONSENSE DIET

Your diet does not have to be complicated. Usually eating well simply means putting commonsense rules into practice until they become habits. Here are the sensible nutritional guidelines that I follow:

- **Eat whole foods.** This means foods that are complete, unfragmented, unrefined, and neither fortified nor enriched. Fill your grocery cart with nuts, spinach, tofu, fresh fruit, beans, tomatoes, rice, barley, and so on. Avoid engineered and genetically modified foods.

- **Eat complex carbohydrates.** These foods form the gasoline that fires up my motor—grains, breads, and potatoes. They digest more slowly than simple sugars such as cookies, ice cream, and cake, and do not produce a rapid rise and fall in blood-sugar levels—that is, they have a low glycemic load.

- **Eat modest amounts of protein.** The old-time nutritionist said, "Eat what you are made of." The modern-day nutritionist says, "Eat what gives you energy—complex carbohydrates."

- **Eat living foods.** Such foods as apples, bananas, carrots, sunflower seeds, and sprouts are examples of living foods because they are usually in their original state when you eat them.

- **Eat unprocessed foods.** These are foods with no chemicals, preservatives, artificial sweeteners, flavor enhancers, stabilizers, food dyes, and the like added, or those that have not been chemically altered.

- **Eat unpackaged foods as much as possible.** Packaged ones are much more likely to contain unnecessary additives. Choose the same foods in their natural state, preferably from a local farmer (although, if you do use packaged foods for the sake of convenience, try to purchase brands that use all natural, organic ingredients.)

- **Eat foods in combination.** To assimilate and digest foods optimally, present them to your stomach in balanced combination.

- **Eat to feed your muscles, not your fat.** Eat only as much as you need, not as much as you might want. Fat is nonworking tissue, so there is little need to feed it.

- **Eat for physical energy, not for emotional comfort.** I know, it's hard, because in our culture we are constantly bombarded with messages telling us to eat, drink, and be merry rather than to stay fueled, hydrated, and happy.

- **Chew your food well, and take your time.** The saliva in your mouth begins the chemical breakdown of the food; this is the start of the digestive process.
- **Breathe while you chew.** Breathing will enhance the flavor and contribute to overall satisfaction and satiation.
- **Eat in a relaxed, pleasant environment.** Don't combine eating with loud, disruptive activities, such as animated conversation, noisy music, or watching television. Concentrate on the process of eating and enjoy it.
- **Be aware that food nutrients are easily lost.** Eat fresh foods and cook them lightly, if at all.
- **Eat when you're hungry, not just because it's the conventional time for a meal.** Let real hunger be a guide to when you eat, how much you eat, and how often you eat. Eating small amounts more frequently may be a better eating pattern for you than having three large meals a day.
- **Eat at home rather than when you're out and about.** If you eat home-cooked meals you can control portion sizes better and concentrate on eating slowly. When you grab food on the run, it's more likely to be unhealthy, and you're more likely to gulp it down quickly.
- **When you eat at a restaurant, share the meal with another person and order an extra salad.** This saves you money and keeps you from overeating.
- **You don't have to eat everything on your plate.** Try to be in tune with feelings of hunger. When you are full, stop eating. Try this as an exercise to develop a conscious connection to the satiety center in your brain, and you can learn to have more control and power over your eating patterns.

only your muscle strength and cardiovascular fitness but also your body's ability to store glycogen and then assimilate it into blood glucose used by the muscles. A well-trained athlete can store two to three times the amount of glycogen in his or her muscles as an untrained person. You want to train your body to be a good fuel burner, and one way to do this is to teach it to store fuels, especially glycogen. If you can store carbs as glycogen, you will be able to tap into this abundant fuel source on race day.

Carbohydrates are categorized by how quickly they release glucose into the bloodstream. High-glycemic-index carbohydrates release glucose quickly into the bloodstream. These are the carbohydrates you'll want to consume during exercise, to give you quick energy, and after exercise, to help with muscle recovery. Low- to moderate-glycemic-index carbohydrates release glucose slowly into the bloodstream. These are the carbohydrates you'll want to consume before exercising to provide a sustained energy level for your workout or race.

Keep in mind that along with a food's rating on the glycemic index, it makes a big difference how much of the food you eat. Glycemic loading refers to eating a large amount of high-glycemic-index foods. Though these foods raise your blood sugar levels for quick access to high-energy carbs, the amount that you eat—the load—is just as important.

Table 11.2 shows the glycemic index for some common foods.

FOOD SUPPLEMENTS

An area of heated debate with regard to diet today is the use of food supplements. Some people feel that if you eat multiple balanced meals a day, you will receive all of the MDR (minimum daily requirements) of the vitamins, minerals, and other nutrients your body needs. On the other hand, the supplement industry lobbies fiercely to raise those MDR levels, and advertises extensively to get you to feel that you must swallow several vitamins every day.

What's an endurance athlete to do? Here is my thinking on the subject. As an athlete, I frequently stress my incredible energy machine to its fullest capacity. Then I demand that my immune system resist breakdown and rebuild my body to higher levels of work capacity. This stress-and-rebuild regimen requires more from my system than a sedentary lifestyle would. Many women add to the stress-recovery cycle other substances that truly damage their bodies: toxins such as cigarette smoke, overindulgence in alcohol, and processed or fast foods. Complicating this is the fact that many sedentary women lack natural and daily stress reducers such as hobbies, exercise, healthy relationships, and joyful pastimes. Still others struggle with too much "screen time": overexposure to computers, electronic games, and television.

It thus seems logical that a triathlete would have different minimum daily nutritional requirements than the average person. When it comes to supplements, I therefore ask myself the same question I ask about other nutritional matters: "What will it give me, and what will it cost me?" If the intake of food supplements above the MDR passes this test, then a well-

TABLE 11.2 Glycemic Index of Common Foods

LOW GI <55	MODERATE GI 55–70	HIGH GI >70
Apple	Apricots	Baked potato
Grapefruit	Banana	Bread, white
Green beans	Boiled potato	Cereal
Green peas	Bran cereal or muffin	Crackers
Lentils	Bread, wheat/whole grain	Sports drinks
Milk	Corn	Sports gels
Oatmeal	Fruit juice	Watermelon
Yogurt	Honey	
	Muesli	
	Oranges	
	Power Bar	
	Rice, white/brown	
	Split peas	

Note: Look for more detailed food listings online. Remember that it's your total glycemic load that matters more than the index of a particular food.

thought-out vitamin and mineral supplement program may be reasonable for some. If your goal is to strengthen your immune system, for example, then consider adding a blend of vitamins and minerals that might help you do just that.

I supplement my diet with antioxidants. It works for me. I remember the ingredients of my antioxidant cocktail by their acronym, ACE, which represents vitamins A, C, and E. Most multivitamins have all three ingredients, but if you are hoping to get your antioxidants in a multivitamin, check for the amount of vitamin C and vitamin E. I have found that the amount of these usually included in a multivitamin is too low for me. As for the amounts of each that you need, check with your doctor about your specific situation. Be careful not to get too much of the fat-soluble vitamins A, D, E, and K. And even the water-soluble vitamins can cause problems if the dosage is too high.

You should also ask your physician about supplementing with calcium and iron in amounts beyond the usual multivitamin and mineral dose. There are many factors, especially age, that would affect whether or not extra amounts of these minerals are advisable for you. Omega-3 and omega-6 fatty acids, often called "good fats," are thought to prevent heart disease and strokes, so ask your doctor about supplementing with these substances as well (although you can get these in food sources such as flaxseeds and flaxseed oil as well as certain fish and fish oils, olive oil, and nuts).

Listen to the nutritional needs of your body by paying attention to its signals. I like to keep a nutritional performance journal to analyze those messages. If a food or vitamin improves my performance, I use it; if not, I don't. After all, eating is one of the few variables you can control. Eating well is certainly worth the expenditure in time that it takes to achieve. It's a sobering thought that by eating with intelligence, we can maximize the benefits of the foods we consume. And when you're a triathlete, it's a factor in athletic performance that you can use to improve in the sport.

EATING FOR RACE DAY ENERGY

You've trained diligently; you've practiced drills and techniques, gained speed and strength, and prepared yourself emotionally for a race. You've even broken the budget for top equipment. But what if you've neglected to find out the best way to eat before and during a race? Can it affect performance? You bet. Read on to learn some basic concepts in eating for race day.

Pre-Race Meals

The night before a race, or during the race itself, many endurance athletes will "carbo-load," or eat complex carbohydrates, in order to build glycogen stores to keep them going throughout the event without "hitting the wall." This procedure often involves consuming a plate of pasta the night before the event, or it could be a carbohydrate drink during the event. This practice may well not be needed for a shorter race, like a sprint, because you have enough glycogen on board, stored in your muscles, liver, and brain, to get you through the race easily. Carbo-loading for sprint triathlons by eating too much volume of food can also cause problems the next day. For an Olympic-distance race and higher, however, moderate carbo-loading can be useful.

On race day, the pre-race meal should be composed of foods that will keep moving through your GI (gastrointestinal tract) during the swim. If you are like some people, food in the stomach during exercise may cause nausea, probably because of the "nervous-stomach syndrome." Nervous or irritable stomach is caused by the release of hydrochloric acid into the stomach, combined with the fact that during competition blood normally sent to the stomach is shunted to the working muscles to provide them with oxygen and nutrients. The result of an upset stomach during the race is impaired breathing, flatulence, and diarrhea, which can lead to performance losses.

It is advisable to consume 300–500 calories 1 or 2 hours before a training session or race to keep your blood sugar (plasma glucose) levels high. It is important to consume familiar foods and to focus mostly on carbohydrates, since it takes them a shorter time to digest than it takes for fats and proteins. A little bit of protein will give you some slow-burning energy to help sustain your efforts. Fat and fiber take longer to digest; thus they will stay in your system longer. If you eat them before training, you may feel a heavy, full sensation when you begin to work out. If solid foods simply do not agree with your system pre-exercise, try a liquid meal or sports drink.

Experiment to find out which foods sit best in your stomach. Generally, 2 hours before my wave starts, I eat a light, complex-carbohydrate meal of about 400 calories. My pre-race meal might include a muffin or bagel, a banana or energy bar, whole-grain toast, or pancakes, but no juice. For me, juice is so high in sugar that it triggers a glycemic response that leads to an acidic stomach. Foods high in protein are generally a bad choice for the morning of the race, since they remain in your stomach a long time. I avoid dairy products for 48 hours before a big race; for me, they tend to result in loose bowels, unpleasant at best.

Your pre-race meal should be substantial enough to eliminate both physical weakness and hunger. Eating 1 to 2 hours before the race ensures that your stomach and upper bowels are relatively empty during the race and that your bloodstream has carbohydrates to deliver to the working muscles. Here's a tip: I'm a coffee drinker and I enjoy a cup of coffee during this meal, as that also seems to help my bowels to eliminate everything before the race begins.

GOOD FOODS FOR A PRE-RACE MEAL

Try the following before training sessions before using them as pre-race foods. The meal should be eaten at least 1 or 2 hours before your wave starts, but again, experiment with the timing in training. Limit this meal to 300–500 calories.

- Banana
- Oatmeal
- Bagel with peanut butter
- Muffin
- Whole-grain toast
- Whole-grain pancakes or waffles
- Carbohydrate-based smoothie

Eating During the Race

If you know you will finish a triathlon or a training workout in less than 2 hours, you don't need to read this section. For most people, eating during a short race or training session provides little energy benefit. For triathlons that last longer than 2 or 3 hours, eating during the race is as important as eating beforehand.

During exercise, it is important to maintain blood glucose levels by ingesting about 200–300 calories per hour. Since the amount of carbohydrates our bodies can store is limited, it is important to replenish them during a long event. Energy gels or sports drinks—and for me, oddly enough, Coke—are very easy for the body to digest during exercise. (Soft foods such as ripe bananas are also easy for most people to digest.)

During your training you should try different gels, bars, sports beans or gelatin blocks, sports drinks, and soft foods to see which combinations will give you the best workout. It's always good to have a race food plan firmly established before race day. *Never try new foods on race day!*

I know that what I eat during the race can contribute substantially to my performance. Another way of saying this is that I know that when I eat properly during the race I will enjoy my performance and finish faster. Therefore, I want to begin a fat-metabolism cycle as early as possible. Carbohydrate sparing means training the metabolic system to prefer fats as the source of fuel above carbs. This is the goal.

I don't start eating during the race until I'm out of the water and onto my bike. For long races, I stash foods in my top tube box to eat during

SALLY'S TEST FOR RACE DAY NUTRITION

Again, each of us is different in our training and nutritional needs. I've had my fair share of involuntary stomach emptying while racing and have developed the following criteria for acceptable food to eat during a race:

- Food that is in season, low in fat, and free of dairy products
- Food that is easy to chew
- Food that tastes good
- Food that is not monotonous but has variety
- Food that does not result in dehydration
- Food that can be assimilated rapidly, so that the muscles can make use of the energy
- Food that is in liquid form

the bike leg; I organize the foods there earlier when arranging my T1 area, so they are ready to go when I grab my bike. Some that work best for me are pulped fruits (bananas, apples, or strawberries). They can be easily packaged and easily eaten on the bike, and they meet all of my criteria—variety, flavor, chewability, complex carbohydrates—and they are easy on the stomach (though a little difficult some-

> **TIP** Ask race management in advance if there will be food at the aid stations, and, if so, what kind and where, so that you can plan your nutritional needs.

times on the bowels). Though not as enjoyable, liquid meals have been an excellent energy source for me during my Ironman-distance races. During extremely hot-weather races, I like watermelon diced into small pieces with a little salt on top. Ah, what a joy to find an aid station with salted watermelon and potato chips.

After experimentation, I've found that it is easier on the GI tract to eat small amounts frequently than to eat large amounts infrequently. Rather than eating an entire energy bar at once, I spread it out in small bites. When I race I also like hard rock candy that dissolves slowly in my mouth (seven minutes for a small piece—I timed it!). This gradual intake of simple carb calories helps to minimize the massive changes in blood-sugar levels that occur with high-intensity exercise, and it reduces the pancreas's response of dumping insulin into the body in massive amounts after you've eaten the high concentrations of complex sugars found in energy bars and gels.

Some triathletes perform well eating special liquid meals, the kind originally developed for hospital patients unable to eat solid foods. Liquid meals are high in calories, provide for hydration, and are easily ingested. Do not confuse them with instant powdered meals or meal supplements, as these are generally mixed with milk and are high in fat and protein. Liquid meals are convenient, easily digested, soothing to a nervous stomach, high in carbs, and low in fats. Some brand names to look for include Ensure (Ross Products), Sustacal and Sustagen (Mead Johnson), Power Dream (Imagine Foods), and Nutriment. Or you can make your own concoction and not have to worry about the additives in these packaged, engineered foods.

I advised you earlier in the chapter to eat when you're hungry; that rule doesn't hold during a race. Heat and exhaustion extinguish the feeling of hunger, so eat by the clock.

HYDRATION

Your need for fluids during a training session or a race is totally individual. Your body depends on proper hydration for normal metabolic function. A typical 150-pound woman carries approximately 90 pounds of water on board, and half of that is stored in the muscle tissue. Your body is a water reservoir; you need to keep it full.

During the race and hard training, fluid intake is crucial. The quantities you drink depend on how much you sweat, which depends on individual conditions:

- Temperature
- Humidity
- Your current training state
- Intensity of your exertion
- Your individual sweat propensities

If you sweat a great deal, you must drink more fluids. As the relative humidity increases, your ability to be cooled by sweating decreases. If you begin to feel thirsty, you are already dehydrated. Water poured over the body during the race will help cool you as well. If the racecourse lacks shade and the sun is blazing, your need to drink increases. Wear a hat with a bill that will help cool you, especially if you keep it wet. Wearing white or light-colored clothing will help, too. Drinking chilled fluids will also lower your core body temperature—but use caution, because cold liquids can give some people severe abdominal cramps or headaches.

How much water loss you experience through sweat, and how well you replace it, is critical to your continued performance. For every 1 percent of body weight lost in water, your blood volume drops by 2.4 percent. With a water loss of 4 percent, your performance is reduced considerably, and there is a marked reduction in strength and endurance. A 6 percent water loss results in exhaustion, but it should never come to this because you know better, and you will be constantly topping up your water reservoir.

Hyperhydration, or loading on fluids in advance of a race, is a practice I follow when the event is staged in hot climates. If you are hyperhydrated, you should weigh more on the morning of a race because you are carrying more stored liquids on board your system.

You need to stay hydrated during your training and racing because water loss reduces your ability to perform. When you become dehydrated, your blood thickens because there is less water in the bloodstream. This limits the bloodstream's ability to transport nutrients and oxygen. And as you sweat, mineral loss occurs. Therefore, it is important to replace both the water and the minerals by drinking an electrolyte-replacement drink if you are training or racing in hot climates.

Before the advent of electrolyte-replacement drinks, those of us who raced in the 1970s made our own concoctions adding table salt, bee's honey, and other ingredients to water—keeping the details of our own recipes a secret. These are less expensive, but you might prefer the commercial products to your own recipe if they work for you. There are dozens of commercial drinks available today that are a combination of fluids and minerals, such as Gatorade, Ultima, Accelerade (PacificHealth Laboratories), and Revenge (Champion Nutrition). I don't endorse or recommend any of them in particular but I do recommend using something.

It is best to drink water on a timed schedule rather than wait until you feel thirsty. The body's hydrostat, its hydration detector system, does not always tell you how much fluid you need. As with food, fluid is better taken more frequently in smaller amounts than less frequently in larger amounts. How much and how often you drink depends entirely on your needs, your ability to utilize fluids, your body size, and the ambient temperature and humidity. When I train in the heat, I carry a handheld 8-ounce water bottle or wear a portable hydration fanny pack or backpack, depending on the length of time that I am working out for that session. During the race, I take water at every aid station, consuming 4 to 6 fluid ounces, and hope that the stations are spaced about 20 minutes apart if it's hot. To cool my "radiator," I pour water over my head (though I try not to get water in my running shoes because wet shoes invariably give me blisters).

At the end of a race, the body needs fluids and rest. It is good to get some carbs and protein within the first 30 minutes following exercise. This is the time to focus on eating foods that have a high glycemic index, meaning they are more quickly absorbed into the bloodstream. Sports drinks are great for this also, since it is sometimes hard to eat solid foods after exercise. Fruits are also a great choice and also supply much-needed fluid. Try to ingest some carbohydrates and protein (in about a 4:1 ratio in grams), and get an adequate amount of fluids. This will ensure a faster recovery, which will allow you to exercise sooner after your event.

Water is absorbed faster than any other fluid (it takes about 20 minutes to absorb juice). If the weather is particularly hot and dry, you will need to drink two to three glasses of water almost immediately after crossing the finish line. Then slowly drink some fruit juice or commercial electrolyte-replacement solution. The water will replace the lost fluids and increase your blood volume; the juice will replace lost electrolytes (sodium, potassium, and magnesium). Next, do some heavy-duty resting. Massage will help, as will hot and cold whirlpools.

ERGOGENIC AIDS

By definition, an ergogenic aid is anything introduced into the body that provides performance enhancement. Among the substances and nutrients that can influence performance capacity are electrolyte or sports drinks, vitamins, caffeine, aspirin, creatine, amino acids, L-carnitine, substances with an immune-modulating effect (medicine or drugs), and energy bars and gels.

Most triathletes who use ergogenic aids do so to help improve their ability to train harder (load tolerance) and to aid in regeneration (recovery between training sessions). Consumption of some substances can be advantageous in these situations. However, all active substances or drugs having a clear performance-enhancing or -influencing effect that give an athlete an advantage are banned and placed on a doping list, which is determined by international sports governing federations. Consumption of these aids is a doping activity that not only presents a health risk but also is unethical. Items on the doping list include stimulants, narcotics, anabolic substances, diuretics, growth hormones, banned methods (such as blood doping), alcohol, and other substance groups. To see a list of such substances banned in triathlon, refer to www.usantidoping.org.

GOOD NUTRITION AS A LIFESTYLE

Proper nutrition is essential for health maintenance and fitness. This is of even greater significance if you are training for triathlons, because you are exposing your body to positive physical strain that results in fitness improvement. To perform well, recover from training sessions and races, and perform well again, you have to eat well—not just sometimes, but as a healthy and enjoyable habit day in and day out.

Many star triathletes feed their fires with junk food and still win races. They believe that the body is a garbage disposal—that when foods are broken down, the body will take what it needs and eliminate the rest. Some do succeed with this philosophy for a time. These athletes conclude that speed, strength, and stamina—not carrots—make champions.

This philosophy is badly flawed, however. We owe it to ourselves to live life in the best way that we can. If we are not willing to settle for junk living, we certainly should not settle for junk food. So take a hard look at your eating habits, find out what works for you as an individual, and adapt that into your individualized nutritional program. Sadly, the ones who win races even though they are eating junk will one day find out that it has caught up with them. And if they think they are succeeding on junk, think of what they could have achieved on good, healthy fuels. When you eat right, you not only ensure optimum performance, but a life of optimum health.

For me, health is more than merely the absence of disease. It is a positive state of being that pervades our minds and bodies, enabling us to live long, productive, active, and energetic lives. The food we eat should make a positive contribution to that state of being. Eating, like everything else, should be an integral part of life. That is what this book is about—making sports and nutrition second nature, our lifestyle, not just an afterthought in our lives.

Finally, take a moment to consider your physical and emotional performance. If you are a performance-motivated female triathlete, you want to extend your athletic career, your performance life span. My goal is to continue racing until I'm 100 years old—and to do that I know I need to pace myself. Otherwise, the competitive years may be relatively few. If you are in the midst of those few peak racing years and you want to PR, set personal records, you owe it to yourself to act on the best nutritional and diet information available. This chapter is a starting point for learning more about fueling your fires. Clearly, this information recommends that you should put the best possible fuel into your incredible energy machine. Socrates said that others lived to eat, while he ate to live. For the performance triathlete, perhaps you should improve on his maxim by saying, "Other women eat to live, while I eat to perform."

12

Weight Loss for Triathletes

Many women are lured to crosstraining by the promise of losing weight. So, what is the first thing that pops into your head as you reach for your wallet: Buy a best-selling weight-loss book, love yourself more, quit now because it is useless—or work out more? Or maybe you could go to a triathlon camp.

If you want to resolve the complex and confusing matter of losing weight, this chapter is for you. But I should warn you that I'm going to ask you to go beyond the bathroom scale to become healthy and fit.

You may be surprised: It's not all about turning your life into one big boot camp. There are many factors that play into your health. So in reading this chapter, you will likely get a new perspective on how metabolism, emotions, and triathlon training all work together to produce your fitness level—and perhaps a new perspective as well on how to view your current weight.

TIME FOR MYTH-BUSTING

There may be some old belief systems about weight loss that are hard to let go of because they are just that—what you believe in. You have heard it—from U.S. government publications, popular magazines, and weight-loss experts—so it's natural to assume it must be true. I invite you to approach these myths in the spirit of the arcade redemption game called "Whack-a-Mole," where you win a prize by whacking ground moles with a mallet when they pop out of their holes. Knock out old and invalid beliefs to improve your score—ultimately, achieving a weight that's healthy for you.

Maybe you still hold on to a couple of these Whack-a-Mole statements. I recommend that you decide to beat these old beliefs because they simply aren't accurate. They do not represent how the body really works, and science has invalidated them because of lack of evidence.

- Weight loss can be easy, quick, and require little commitment.
- You have to be thin to be healthy and attractive.
- Do whatever the celebrity TV, sports, or movie star says.
- The right fad diet (e.g., high-fat, high-carbs, or high-protein) will guarantee body weight loss.
- If you eat less and exercise more, you will lose weight.
- If you are fat, you are unhealthy and destined to die young.

And so on. Fight the moles with scientific facts, not fads and hype. Neither exercise nor diet alone is sufficient for most people to achieve weight loss. Rather, with a combination of the two, and with emotional health and other support mechanisms, women can successfully lose weight and have more energy. And, a big part of achieving your weight loss goals is to live a healthy active lifestyle by swimming, cycling, and running and by eating nutrient-dense foods.

THE HONEST TRUTH

The first step in getting on track with weight loss is to replace old, invalid beliefs with accurate information based on scientific research and common sense. We always assume we have to be thin, for example, to be healthy. But is this statement true? Should losing weight be your priority? Let's take a closer look at some of these beliefs that we have absorbed from our thin-obsessed culture.

You Don't Have to Be Thin . . .

The truth is that you don't have to be thin to be healthy. You don't have to be thin to be fit. You don't have to be thin, period. If your genetic heritage, body type, and metabolism make you susceptible to gaining weight very easily, you don't have to feel bad about that. You could be one of evolution's triumphs—a success of natural selection.

Why? In prehistoric days, the people who fared the best through times of sporadic food supply were the ones whose bodies made the most efficient use of energy and stored away as much as possible for tough times. Scientists now know we evolved to succeed at a time when food supplies were unreliable and the physical activity demands of life were high.

Imagine yourself in prehistoric times, pitted for survival against that skinny fashion model with no apparent body fat. Who would live longer? To take liberties with Darwin, it all comes down to "survival of the fattest, and yes, the fittest." But, you might be saying "I don't want to be the fattest gal in the cave. I need to go on a diet and get some of the excess weight off. Don't I need to be fit to survive a stroll through the jungle?" That's where you are wrong—dead wrong. Fitness and thinness are not the same thing. They are not connected. Sure, you probably know a lot of fat and unfit people. They got fat in large part because they are unfit, because of their emotional disconnections, and because of their energy level. But it is possible for a person to be fit *and* fat *and* perfectly healthy, emotionally and physically. Fitness correlates to how well your engine is running, not to streamlined fenders or narrow tires.

You Need to Be Healthy

I'm committed to a healthy, active lifestyle. (If you come to one of my events, you might hear me refer to this as "HAL.") This commitment helps me to keep my priorities straight. I designed a program based on healthy, active living for my company Heart Zones Training. Here are the foundational principles:

- It's not about being fat; it's all about being fit.
- It's not about being thin; it's all about being healthy.
- It's not about weighing less; it's all about having more energy.

This program's very foundation is to focus on fitness, health, and energy. The weight will take care of itself as you get fitter and healthier—and you will have more energy to boot. The majority of weight-loss programs focus on food intake, food composition, food types, and various oddball ideas. Rather than focusing all that time on food, you should just focus on putting together all three components of wellness—physical, metabolic, and emotional—for a healthy, active lifestyle.

Fat Is Not the Problem . . .

Fat is a symptom of being overweight, not the cause. It's like looking at a case of measles and calling it "skin lesions," when we really know it's an infection caused by the measles virus. The spots are just a symptom.

Defining fat as the problem ignores what really goes on inside the body. In truth, obesity is the condition by which the complex mechanisms of appetite and satiety (that is, metabolism), have, quite simply, become messed up. In obesity, the body's weight-regulatory system has gone haywire, resulting in physical, metabolic, and emotional abuse of the body.

Fat is a symptom of being overweight, not the cause.

. . . Abuse of the Body Is the Problem

We commit a form of physical abuse when we don't perform the basic physical activity we need to stay healthy. Amazingly, we readily accept that the Labrador retriever needs exercise to stay trim and healthy, but we don't recognize the same for ourselves.

An all-too-common example of metabolic abuse is serial dieting, sometimes called "weight cycling." The body fights against this periodic starvation by making key metabolic changes that facilitate your return to homeostasis, which means you gain the weight back and then some when you go back to eating a normal, healthy diet. Your metabolism can become so dysfunctional that the body can function only by grabbing and storing all the energy that comes its way—and it stores it very efficiently.

Finally, and this one has long been overlooked by weight-loss experts, we subject ourselves to emotional overload, such as stress, anxiety, anger, and depression. All of these, and their pharmaceutical remedies, can throw the body out of synch and disrupt its weight-regulating system. That system is centrally located in the brain, so it is only logical that it is influenced by other things occurring in the brain. Emotional overload results in changes to the brain structure that result in neurotransmitter insensitivity—and hence changes in the release of hormones.

GREYHOUNDS AND ST. BERNARDS

If you have always been a little fat, yet you've cared for the three basic aspects of your health—physical, metabolic, and emotional/mental—then consider your specific biological makeup, your inherited genetics, and your individual physiology. Your genetic heritage extends not only to whether you are gifted as a natural athlete or got your mother's nose but also to the nature of your metabolism and how your body responds to physical fitness training. Your individual biological makeup involves internal biochemical processes that influence your weight, including everything from your adrenaline production to your digestive processes, your personal chemistry of fat metabolism, your insulin regulation, and fluctuations of your sex hormones.

Once you understand your inherited bio makeup, you can stop fretting over the fact that you didn't inherit the physique of a teenage fashion model. Perhaps you should stop trying to be something you can't be—and learn to accept who you are. After all, you'd never buy a St. Bernard dog and think, "Ah, well, if I starve Bernie enough, maybe I can make him look like a greyhound. Greyhounds are so fashionable this year, and I want a fashionable dog." No, you treasure all your big, lovable St. Bernard qualities. As you become more fit, your unique physique will become a reflection of your hard work and you can be confident that you look great.

. . . Unhealthy Expectations Are the Problem

Sometimes, especially as women, we talk ourselves into a corner, saying, "Even though I was born with this body type, it can't be natural for me to be like this, because this is an unhealthy state. How can it be okay that I was born unhealthy?" Such thinking reflects one of the problems the fat-free movement has created for us: We have forgotten why we have fat and what it does for us. We've forgotten that it is natural for some of us to be fatter than others, even if it places us outside of the recommended weight for our height. Fat is a natural thing, an essential ingredient in a healthy woman's body. Most fat works for us in life-sustaining ways, protecting our vital organs, insulating us, and storing energy so we can function without constant eating—and providing us with a figure. Some special types of fat cells perform absolutely crucial tasks, such as dealing with toxins in the body and maintaining a healthy hormonal balance. We need fat, and we need to store some fat.

It's also natural for us to gain more fat as we age. It's natural for some of us to carry more fat than others. But it's *not* natural for us to be unfit. Our bodies require physical activity as much as they require air, water, and fuel. Without it, we die. And this brings us to the crux of the matter: We have become stuck in the mind-set that says fat makes us sick or unhealthy, when, in truth, being unfit makes us sick or unhealthy. When we grasp that fact, we begin to realize that fat loss as a solution to health problems is just a big fat lie.

THE TRUTH ABOUT FITNESS

Let's explore what we mean by fitness and fatness. Fitness measures how healthy you are, how functionally able you are to carry out your daily life and other activities. Fatness measures the amount of padding you carry and how big your fenders are, not the strength of the inner engine that gives you the power to do things.

Fitness may mean one thing to an age-group competitive or professional triathlete and another to a young woman with a family and career, but basically it all boils down to being healthy and in good condition, with the energy and optimism to tackle your dreams and goals. When you attain fitness you are thriving in all three wellness categories (see Figure 12.1).

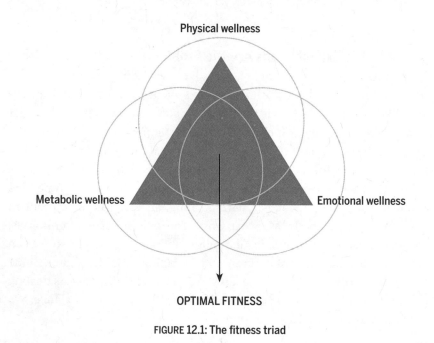

FIGURE 12.1: The fitness triad

- Physical fitness: your cardiovascular fitness (heart and circulatory system), muscular strength, and flexibility.
- Metabolic fitness: your blood pressure, glucose sensitivity, and blood chemistry.
- Emotional fitness: your ability to manage your feelings and your mental capacity.

With this list in mind, consider these questions:

1. Can you possess a strong, healthy heart and be physically strong and flexible even if you are fat?
2. Can you display healthy blood chemistry and a healthy metabolism even if you are fat?
3. Can you maintain emotional balance even if you are fat?

The answer to all three questions is a resounding yes. It's that simple. Fatness does not prevent fitness. The amount of fat you carry around represents but one aspect of your health and fitness, and not necessarily a terribly relevant one at that. In contrast, physical, metabolic, and emotional wellness will result in fitness—the key to a healthy and long life. Being thin will never guarantee you a long life.

Our obsession with weight and weight loss has misled us to blame fat and fatness as the root of all illness. In fact, according to Steven Blair, a professor of Physical Education at the University of South Carolina (see sidebar), nothing can improve your health and reduce your health risks more than fitness.

"USA SCIENTIST: FAT CAN BE HEALTHY"

This was the headline on the CNN News service on July 18, 2001. American researcher Steven Blair had sparked controversy at a meeting of the Association for the Study of Obesity in London by saying that body fat can be healthy. Results from the studies at Blair's institute, the Cooper Aerobic Institute, on obesity and risk of death showed that previous research had missed the crucial link between fitness and health. "The focus is all wrong," claimed Blair. "It is fitness that is the key." In fact, he even went on to report quite simply that "fat people who exercise are at no greater risk from disease than their thinner, lazier counterparts."

Not surprisingly, Blair's claims continue to ignite criticism. In October 2003, the head of the Centers for Disease Control, Dr. Julie Gerberding, told a meeting of the National Health Council that Americans are now much more likely to die from cancer, heart disease, and diabetes caused by smoking, eating too much, and exercising too little than in the past. She claimed that obesity is the number one health threat in the United States.

In recent years, however, the evidence supporting Blair's claim that fitness confers a lower risk of disease and mortality, independent of fatness, has been pouring in:

- A study published in the October 1999 issue of the *Journal of the American Medical Association* found that overweight men who *exercised* had death rates, by any cause, only slightly higher than fit men of normal weight, and twice as low as men of normal weight who were unfit.
- An observational study carried out by three researchers, Chong Do Lee, Steven Blair, and Andrew Jackson at the Cooper Institute for Aerobics Research in Dallas, Texas, demonstrated that it's fitness, not fatness, that really counts when it comes to longevity. In their observational study of 22,000 men, they found that death rates doubled for unfit men. Interestingly, obese men had no greater risk of dying than unfit men, as long as they were fit. The researchers concluded that being fit reduces the health risk of being obese.
- A study of 17,000 men in the Harvard Alumni Health Study found that mortality was lower for each of three degrees of fatness when the men were fit.
- Researchers Steven Blair and Suzanne Brodney at the Cooper Institute, Dallas, conducted a review of all studies that had been done up to 1999, examining more than 700 scientific articles. They concluded that regular physical activity clearly mitigates many of the health risks associated with being overweight or obese, and that fat people who are fit have lower death rates than individuals of normal weight who are not fit.

The American College of Sports Medicine (ACSM) and the U.S. National Institutes of Health National Heart, Lung, and Blood Institute commissioned reviews of all this new evidence, hoping they could prepare consensus statements concerning the benefits of physical activity for overweight people. The review concluded that the recent scientific research had shown the following:

- Overweight and obese individuals who are active and fit have lower rates of disease and death than overweight and obese individuals who are inactive and unfit.
- Overweight and obese individuals who are active and fit are less likely to develop obesity-related chronic diseases and suffer early death than people of normal weight who lead sedentary lives.
- Inactivity and low cardiorespiratory fitness are as important as being overweight or obese as predictors of mortality, at least in men.

Not only does fitness help free you from disease, it can extend your life expectancy, too. But don't just take my word for it.

A new study published in the *New England Journal of Medicine* provides new evidence regarding the relationship between fitness and survival. In it researchers examined more than 6,000 male patients referred to a clinical exercise-testing laboratory and then followed the group for 6 years. They found that the peak exercise capacity (a measure of fitness) achieved by a person during the exercise test was the best predictor of the risk of death, whether the individual suffered with cardiovascular disease or not. For both groups, the fittest, regardless of their fatness, had four times less risk of dying compared to the unfit groups. As with earlier studies, fatness, when accompanied by fitness, did not figure significantly in risk of death. Fitness extends life.

So, there we have it. Don't expect great health benefits from fat loss and dieting. Yes, you may have a problem losing weight, but the problem is not your fatness. Fatness is merely a symptom, not a cause. And fat loss cures nothing and can actually do some harm. The question is not whether you are fit or fat, because you can be both. The most important question is whether you are fit. When you get fit you stake your claim on your health and longevity.

THE FIT AND FAT MATRIX

Now, armed with what you've learned so far, where would you place yourself in "The Fit and Fat Matrix"?

This matrix includes four different quadrants (see Figure 12.2). All of us fall into one of four categories (1) fit and fat; (2) fit and not fat; (3) not fit and fat; or (4) not fit and not fat.

This diagram can help you figure out where you are today and where you might want to ultimately end up. We know from all we have learned so far that the quadrants with the least risk of death, the lowest disease rates, and the best quality of life are the two above the fitness threshold (fit and fat or fit and not fat). If you want to enjoy a long and healthy life, you need to live above the line: You need to be fit.

Now what surprises most people is that the two top quadrants provide the *same* benefits in terms of health and longevity. It doesn't matter for your health or your longevity whether you place in the "fit and fat" quadrant (top left) or the "fit and not fat" quadrant (top right). If at the moment you reside below the threshold, you obviously want to make a change. How do you do that? Well, there's only one escape route: You need to get fit, and that means physical, metabolic, and emotional fitness. Becoming less fat will only allow you to move sideways on the matrix to an equally unhealthy quadrant, not to a higher level of health and well-being.

FIGURE 12.2: Fit and fat matrix

Who Wants to Be Fat and Fit?

It is understandable if many women need some time to digest this information about fitness versus fatness, and even more time to adopt such a dramatically new perspective, even if it's based on science. After all, most of us want to be thin. We've been led into thinking that thinness will win us both fashionable good looks and a good life. However, the scientific evidence says long life comes from health and fitness, not being thin. And health comes from fitness, not lack of fatness. I honestly believe that most of us need to place a long, healthy life first and foremost, and compared to that, put fashion way down the list. That's why getting fit should be your number one priority. Once you gain the health benefits of fitness, natural weight loss becomes considerably easier. When it comes to losing weight, living "above the fitness threshold" gives you a huge advantage.

If you still need convincing, consider this one last reason why you should focus on getting yourself fit, even if you are fat. If you've tried to get thin, you've undoubtedly waged a long, hard battle. In truth, only 5 to 10 percent of people who successfully lose weight by dieting keep it off for the first year, not a very encouraging statistic. If you focus on long-term fitness, your health will improve. It's all a matter of basic human physiology, the way the body works, and how your bio makeup responds. I promise you that if you live a healthy active lifestyle, you will get the health benefits you seek. No matter what your current body weight, you'll enjoy a better self-image, improved self-confidence, *and* will get to swim, bike, and run for health.

You can be fit *and* fat. You can be fit *and* not fat. People who are fit—better yet, triple-fit—even if they are fat, can expect to live longer than similarly fat people who are not fit, and even longer than lean people who are not fit. And you can much more easily achieve fitness than leanness.

YOUR NEW FITNESS PROGRAM

No fitness program should focus on the goal of losing body weight and body fat. Rather, you should concentrate on the goal of gaining physical, metabolic, and emotional fitness (refer to Figure 12.1). Being inactive, eating poorly, and dealing with stress place a tremendous burden on your body. I guarantee that if you lighten these loads, your quality of life will improve. You will be able to do more, increase your energy, and feel happier. It's not a game of counting calories, starving yourself, and feeling guilty, but an empowering way to learn how to give your body what it needs in terms of physical activity, energy, and care. You may not lose all of the fat that you dream about losing, at least not in the short run. But a long-term commitment to living a healthy, active lifestyle will create positive changes that will allow you to ease off plenty of pounds. If you shift your focus from fatness to fitness, it will enable you to reach optimum health and energy.

Physical Fitness

Physical fitness is not a static point, or an on-off switch. It is a continuum that goes all the way from zero-level fitness to your personal, individual, best-ever level of fitness. Think of it, then, as a sort of sliding scale from zero to ten. Your ten will differ from mine. And it is sport specific. You can be fitter in cycling than in running or swimming, for example.

Don't compare yourself to me or to anyone else. Your own fitness is unique to you and your specific biological makeup. Fitness is also activity-specific. Venus Williams is perfectly fit for tennis, but she would not fare well if asked to race against the world's fittest triathletes, like Karen Smyers, or Beijing Olympic gold medalist Emma Snowsill. I doubt whether Venus could finish any one of the three Ironman distances with her tennis fitness, although it would be fun to watch her try. Physical fitness is also affected by how your body uses fuel. Your body might be efficient at metabolizing carbohydrates but not at oxidizing fats, or you might find yourself limited by your body's inability to resynthesize lactate quickly. Finally, fitness is function-specific. You can be fit at lifting heavy weights when you're doing bench presses at your health club, but still struggle to lift a piece of furniture.

Are you fit? You might answer, "Sort of" or "It depends." It depends on where you are on your own fitness continuum, plus where you are with respect to specific activities, fuels, and functions. As you work out and participate more in physical activities that you love, you move toward a ten on the fitness continuum, while if you slack off and do less, you fall back toward zero. Or your goal changes, and so do the demands on your fitness. You may feel fit for a 5 km run, but when you decide to tackle a marathon, you may have a long way to go.

Burn More Fat

As you work to improve physical fitness, your body burns more fat. It's important that you know that you can burn fat in every heart rate zone. The percentage and total amount of fat burned does change in every zone, however. The amount of fat you are burning as you work out depends primarily on these three factors:

- How fit you are
- How hard you exercise
- What you eat (carbohydrates, fat, protein)

Figure 12.3 recaps much of what we learned about zones in Chapters 3 and 4. Figure 12.4 builds on this to show how higher workout intensities (higher zones) result in more calories burned. And in the higher zones, namely zones 3 and 4, more fat is metabolized. For example, 30 minutes in zone 3 is worth about 10 calories per minute, or a total of 300 calories. And about 50 percent of the calories metabolized in that zone are from carbohydrates, while the other 50 percent are from fat. That's about 5 calories of fat and 5 calories of carbohydrates per minute.

Of the many myths in the world of weight loss, one of the worst is the existence of the fat-burning zone. There is no fat-burning zone. The concept was invented to try to simplify a complex subject, but it is invalid. It has led to a great deal of confusion about how fat is utilized in exercise training. What does exist is the "fat-burning range," a dynamic range of exercise intensity where you burn the most fat.

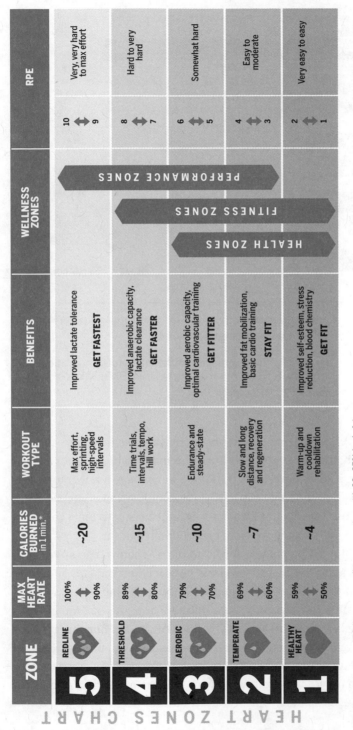

HEART ZONES CHART

ZONE		MAX HEART RATE	CALORIES BURNED in 1 min.*	WORKOUT TYPE	BENEFITS	WELLNESS ZONES		RPE
5	REDLINE	100% ↕ 90%	~20	Max effort, sprinting, high-speed intervals	Improved lactate tolerance **GET FASTEST**			10 ↕ 9	Very, very hard to max effort
4	THRESHOLD	89% ↕ 80%	~15	Time trials, intervals, tempo, hill work	Improved anaerobic capacity, lactate clearance **GET FASTER**	PERFORMANCE ZONES		8 ↕ 7	Hard to very hard
3	AEROBIC	79% ↕ 70%	~10	Endurance and steady-state	Improved aerobic capacity, optimal cardiovascular training **GET FITTER**	FITNESS ZONES		6 ↕ 5	Somewhat hard
2	TEMPERATE	69% ↕ 60%	~7	Slow and long distance, recovery and regeneration	Improved fat mobilization, basic cardio training **STAY FIT**	HEALTH ZONES		4 ↕ 3	Easy to moderate
1	HEALTHY HEART	59% ↕ 50%	~4	Warm-up and cooldown rehabilitation	Improved self-esteem, stress reduction, blood chemistry **GET FIT**			2 ↕ 1	Very easy to easy

*Estimated testing a 150-lb. person walking or running, with 20–25% body fat.

FIGURE 12.3: Five fitness zones

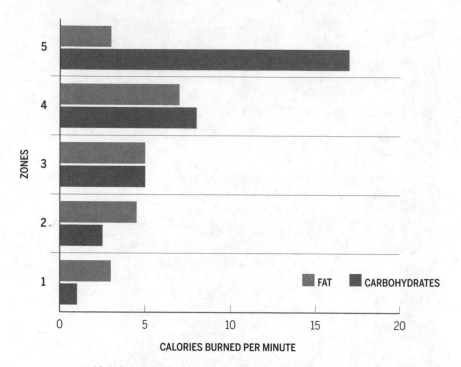

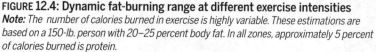

FIGURE 12.4: Dynamic fat-burning range at different exercise intensities
Note: The number of calories burned in exercise is highly variable. These estimations are based on a 150-lb. person with 20–25 percent body fat. In all zones, approximately 5 percent of calories burned is protein.

By definition, the fat-burning range is the exercise intensity and duration at which, metabolically, you burn the most total fat. Your fitness level, diet, nutritional state, level of fatigue during a given workout session, stress level, genetic makeup, and body composition all impact your fat-burning. Still, what is important for weight loss is to burn the most total calories, whether they are from carbohydrates or fat.

Since oxygen must be present for fat to burn, when you go above your threshold intensity, the crossover point between aerobic and anaerobic exercise effort, there is no additional fat burned. To burn the most fat, try to keep your effort aerobic. The ceiling, or top, of your fat-burning range is marked by this threshold. The floor of the fat-burning range is the point where aerobic benefits are first measured, at about 55 percent of your maximum heart rate, or the midpoint of zone 1. As you get fitter, your threshold moves upward toward your maximum heart rate and your fat-burning range expands.

METABOLIC FITNESS

Forget the numbers on your bathroom scale and pay attention instead to the numbers that mean something: your cholesterol, your blood pressure, and your insulin sensitivity. Those numbers reflect metabolic fitness.

Metabolism includes all of your body's energy activities, the chemical reactions and processes that occur every second of your life to provide energy for vital processes and movement. According to Professor Glenn A. Gaesser, Ph.D., at Arizona State University, author of *Big Fat Lies*, "Being metabolically fit means having a metabolism that maximizes vitality and minimizes the risk of disease—particularly those diseases that are influenced by lifestyle, such as heart disease, type 2 diabetes, and cancer." Recent studies indicate that even Alzheimer's could be added to that list. Measures of metabolic fitness reveal how well or efficiently your metabolism works. Metabolic fitness is a relatively new part of the fitness puzzle, one you can measure in a lot of ways, including having your doctor assess your insulin resistance and sensitivity (blood sugar levels), having a specialist determine your resting and exercise metabolic rates, and having your blood pressure and cholesterol levels regularly checked. You can improve your metabolic fitness with a better diet.

The Five Food Zones

There is a vast landscape of choices when it comes to food. The number of new food products grows daily. Every day, you must make decisions about quantity, quality, packaging, preparation, and so forth. One of the most common questions raised at my speaking engagements is this one: "Sally, what should I eat?" The answer is complex on one level, but I have designed a diet plan that should simplify it for you. The Sally Edwards' Food Zones Chart (see Figure 12.5 for an adaptation of this chart or visit my website for an even more colorful version

Eat below the threshold line.

of it) classifies foods based on their inherent metabolic load. That is, the weight of that food on your physiology, your vital processes. The metabolically "light" foods, the low-zone foods, are the healthiest for your metabolism, and you want to select foods from this zone and eat them often.

There are five different food zones in this system. Each zone is numbered, with low numbers (1–3) being low-metabolic-load foods. The

FOOD ZONES CHART

ZONES		FAT	CARBOHYDRATE	PROTEIN	BEVERAGES	CHOCOLATE	FIBER (grams per day)	GLYCEMIC INDEX	QUALITY
5C	TOXIC	Trans fats, nondairy creamer, stick margarine, hydrogenated oil	Table sugar	Fatty meats	Alcohol	<20% cocoa	0	>80	AVOID
5B	UNHEALTHY	Chemically modified fats, saturated fat, beef, whole milk, bacon fat	Fructose	Canned meat, bacon	Espresso, soda	10–20% cocoa, white chocolate	1	75–79	VERY POOR
5A	LESS HEALTHY	Fatty cheese	Cookies, chips, white bread, white rice	Lunch meat with nitrates	Fruit juice drinks	20–30% cocoa, milk chocolate	1	70–74	POOR
THE THRESHOLD LINE									
4	HEALTHY	Monounsaturated fat: olives, olive oil, peanuts, peanut butter, almonds, cashews (salted/roasted), avocados	Processed grains, cereals	Extra-lean chicken/beef	Beer, wine, 100% fruit juice	30–40% cocoa, dark chocolate	1–2	65–69	GOOD
3	MORE HEALTHY	Polyunsaturated fats: safflower oil, sesame seeds, walnuts, salmon, flaxseeds (salted/roasted)	Whole grains	Lean cuts of meat	Decaf coffee, soy milk	40–50% cocoa, sweet dark chocolate	2–4	56–64	VERY GOOD
2	HEALTHIER	Monounsaturated & polyunsaturated fats (unsalted/roasted)	Beans, seeds	Eggs, beans, seeds	Low-fat milk, herbal tea	50–60% cocoa, semisweet chocolate	4–5	50–55	EXCELLENT
1	HEALTHIEST	Monounsaturated & polyunsaturated fats (raw)	Fresh fruit and vegetables	Wild fish	Water	60–85% cocoa, bittersweet chocolate	>5	<50	SUPERB

FIGURE 12.5: Sally's five emotional and food zones

high-metabolic-load zones are above the threshold. You want to eat from the lower zones because foods from these zones will optimize your energy and health. The food zones threshold, like the other thresholds we've discussed in this book, marks a crossover point in your diet spectrum. The less healthy zones are above this threshold. These are the foods to be enjoyed with caution. Below, you'll find the healthier foods. I know that it isn't easy to eat well all the time, for more reasons than I want to discuss. Still, make every attempt to eat foods in the lower zones.

FOOD ZONE GUIDELINES

Here is some of the advice I give to people when they are just getting started with the food zones. I hope it helps you find your way to a more healthy, active lifestyle.

- **Avoid counting calories.** The energy-balancing equation (calories in should equal calories out) is not valid.
- **This is a lifestyle, not a diet.** Think of low zone eating as the way you eat, not as a diet you will endure for a period of time.
- **Eat quality foods.** It is better to eat more quality and less quantity; eat only the amount needed for the next 3–4 hours of activity.
- **Eat in or make food to go.** To better control portion sizes, nutrient density, and less processed food, eating in or packing a meal-to-go is your best choice.
- **Get support.** Surround yourself with other people who use the Food Zones or eat healthy.
- **Eat high-energy foods.** Fruit, vegetables, low-fat dairy products, whole grains, fish, and lean meats are all great options.
- **Allow yourself some emotional foods.** Comfort foods and food cravings are normal. Try to respond by choosing foods from zones 1–4.
- **Find what works best for you.** There is no one-diet-fits-all plan, so tailor one to your needs.
- **Eat diverse and new foods.** Add a variety of foods including new foods to your daily food selection. Each meal should contain the three food groups: carbohydrates, protein, and fat.
- **Be flexible.** Avoid crossing the threshold line, but it's okay to make exceptions. We are all human.

What Does It Take to Keep the Weight Off?

Every year, millions of new diet books are sold in America. There are apparently a lot of ways to take off the pounds. But how have those women and men who have themselves taken weight off *maintained* the weight loss? These are the true experts, because they have successfully discovered what works for their individual physiologies, genetics, and emotional temperaments and applied it consistently over time. They are the applied weight-loss experts; they've done their own personal research and have found weight-management solutions that work.

> **TIP** In discussions around our household, we talk about what zone we've been eating in over the course of a day or a week. For example, "It's a zone 4 day for me but I had a blue zone breakfast." Do the same with your family and friends to improve accountability and support for healthy eating.

One of the worst parts of failing to maintain weight loss is that weight cycling (the process of losing and gaining body weight in a repeated cycle) can result in the redistribution of body fat to what is known as the "upper compartments," your abdomen. This abdominal or "visceral" fat resides in and around your organs, and it has been strongly associated with chronic high-risk diseases. If that weren't bad enough, weight cycling also leads to a reduction in metabolic rates. This process is known in research circles as adaptive thermogenesis. Basically, the more often your weight cycles, the lower your resting metabolic rate—your base caloric burn rate—becomes.

Where's the hope in all this bad news? Well, that's where those weight-loss experts come in—the people who have taken weight off and kept it off. The National Weight Control Registry (http://www.nwcr.ws) is a nonprofit organization that tracks people who have kept more than 30 pounds of weight off for more than one year. The registry has kept noteworthy statistics on more than 5,000 Americans representing a wide range of ages and number of pounds lost. There are both men and women on the registry, and they have kept off the pounds for an average of 5.5 years. The registry participants reported three key factors in their weight loss and maintenance of the loss: (1) low caloric consumption, (2) low fat in their diets, and (3) a high level of daily physical activity. Here are some interesting stats from the registry that should reaffirm your commitment to attaining physical, metabolic, and emotional fitness:

- 98 percent of registry participants report that they modified their food intake in some way to lose weight.
- 94 percent increased their level of physical activity, with the most frequently reported form of activity being walking (and 90 percent exercise, on average, for about 1 hour each day).
- 78 percent reported eating breakfast every day.
- 75 percent weigh themselves at least once a week.
- 62 percent watch less than 10 hours of TV per week.

So while each of us must find what works for our individual metabolism and our genetic makeup, we can thank these strong women and men for discovering the common denominators in losing weight and keeping it off. And we can follow their lead, even if each of us must still take ultimate responsibility on our own.

EMOTIONAL FITNESS

Most women are fairly aware of the spectrum of emotions that they can experience within any given month, week, or even a day. I'm going to invite you to become even more aware of your emotions. Emotions in and of themselves are not bad. It's what we do with them that can be harmful to ourselves and others. Earlier in this chapter I explained that emotional fitness is found through good management of your emotions and an increased mental capacity. After all, all of us will have bad days. The trick is knowing how to make some adjustments that will help us escape those days with our health and happiness intact.

Five Emotional Zones

Figure 12.6 details the five emotional zones. The Red Zone and the Distress Zone (zones 4 and 5) are the zones you should try to avoid. The Performance Zone, the Industrious Zone, and the Safe Zone all fall below the threshold and mark great opportunities for accomplishing your goals. You should regularly gauge your emotional zones and make adjustments when you are above the threshold. Your energy levels and your physical performance will inevitably be negatively affected when you cross the threshold.

On the days when I find myself above my emotional threshold, I often adjust my workout to allow for more recovery and relaxation. You might find these are good days to allow yourself to indulge in some comfort food or a coffee with a friend. All too often I see women try to ignore the warning signs that pop up in zones 4 and 5. This only perpetuates the

EMOTIONAL ZONES

5	RED ZONE	Toxic, harms the health and safety of self and others, body becomes maladapted to the stress response, unhealthy weight gain or weight loss, susceptible to mental disorders and addictions
	OUT OF CONTROL, FRANTIC, TOTAL PANIC, DISCONNECTED, EMERGENCY	
4	DISTRESS ZONE	Elevated blood pressure, high cholesterol, and increased risk of heart disease; increased risk of infections, certain cancers, allergies, and autoimmune diseases; poor concentration, increased muscular stress, hormonal changes that result in weight gain; increased risk of degenerative disease; premature aging
	WORRIED, ANXIOUS, ANGRY, SCATTERED, FEARFUL, REACTIVE	
3	PERFORMANCE ZONE	Heightened awareness and creativity, heightened physical endurance and performance, improved mental performance, faster reaction time, less potential for accidents, able to inspire and energize others
	FOCUSED, COMFORTABLE, POSITIVE STRESS	
2	INDUSTRIOUS ZONE	Improved capacity of undertaking tasks involving mental or physical dexterity, improved learning ability, infectious energy
	HIGH CONCENTRATION, EFFECTIVE, PROLIFIC	
1	SAFE ZONE	Increased patience, compassion, and capacity for love; lowered risk of hypertension, type 2 diabetes, immune disorders, and mental disorders; increased capacity for dealing with pain; decreased risk of stress-related disorders; reduced dependence on prescription medicine
	MEDITATIVE, AFFIRMING, REGENERATIVE, COMFORTABLE, COMPASSIONATE, PEACEFUL	

FIGURE 12.6: Five emotional zones

problem, and often the emotions and effects become more ominous. I hope that you'll use my "Daily Emotional Load Scorecard" as a personal check-in—and avoid that possibility altogether.

DAILY EMOTIONAL LOAD SCORECARD

For each of the following ten questions, use a 10-point scale to rate your emotions, where a "1" represents the most positive response and a "10" represents the most negative response. You'll notice some overlap with physical and metabolic fitness.

1. **How do you feel you are doing with the challenges in your life?**
   Doing well . . . overwhelmed
2. **How do you feel about the blessings of gifts that you have in your life?**
   Thankful . . . resentful
3. **How do you feel about your loved ones and supporters?**
   Loving . . . unloved
4. **How much time do you feel you have?**
   Lots of time . . . no time
5. **How motivated do you feel today?**
   Highly motivated . . . completely unmotivated
6. **How do you feel about your level of fitness today?**
   Very fit . . . not at all fit
7. **How is your body feeling?**
   Fantastic . . . painful
8. **How do you feel that your training program is going?**
   Right on target . . . missing workouts
9. **How do you feel emotionally?**
   Happy . . . unhappy
10. **How did you feel when you first woke up?**
    Energetic . . . exhausted

REALIZING THE ENLIGHTENED STATE

If gaining fitness and losing weight was easy, then two out of three Americans would not be overweight, nor would one out of three be obese. If the formula "calories in equals calories out" worked, then we wouldn't have a weight-problem epidemic in the United States. And if maintaining fitness gains and weight loss was achievable without much effort, then people would get fit and stay fit. But for most people, increasing fitness and reducing body fat, and losing and maintaining weight, are very difficult tasks to accomplish. But I know you can find success.

Start your new program for a healthy, active lifestyle today. Training for a triathlon will take you a long way. And once you cross that finish line, don't stop! By lightening the physical load (working out in the aerobic zones to maximize fat burning), lightening the metabolic load (eating in the first four food zones), and lightening the emotional load (thriving in emotional zones 1–3), you get the results that you deserve: better health, more energy, and a longer, lighter life.

13

Wellness
and Triathlon

I have often said that there is a wellness continuum that flows from health to fitness to optimum performance. Health is often defined as the absence of injury or disease. Fitness takes you a step beyond health, and optimum performance is a step beyond that.

Living the triathlon lifestyle means living on the upper end of that wellness continuum daily. It means forging connections for your body, mind, and emotions as you discover a whole new high-energy way of living.

But that doesn't mean you will never find yourself struggling with a health problem. As you strive for fitness and optimum performance, you are placing a lot of stress on your body, and that means sometimes you will need to give it some extra tender loving care. In this chapter, we'll look at some of the common health issues that triathletes face in training, some of which are unique to women and some that every athlete will face.

WELLNESS IN TRAINING
Common Discomforts

Minor discomforts are associated with any exercise program. The thing to remember when you experience them is that they are your body's way of letting you know that something is slightly out of balance. Toughing it out and ignoring pain is not a wise move, because willful ignorance can turn a minor problem into a major one. If you experience any symptoms that worry or puzzle you, consult your physician promptly to ensure that you receive proper treatment.

SIDE ACHES

Side aches, or "stitches," generally seem to be caused by overexertion. The exact cause of side aches is unknown, but it is suspected that gas caught in the upper intestine might be a frequent culprit. There are a few tricks that sometimes work to stop the pain:

- Put pressure from your fingers directly on the place that hurts.
- Massage the general area with your whole hand.
- Straighten your back and stretch tall.
- Relax your breathing and slow down the number of breaths you are taking per minute.
- Lean forward, bending at the waist.

POST-WORKOUT NAUSEA

Nausea after a workout can be caused by eating too much just before the workout, but it can also be caused by not eating enough, so that your body doesn't have enough easily accessible calories to work with to provide fuel for your muscles. Nausea can also be caused by dehydration. Experiment with your drinking and eating patterns and see what helps.

If there is a possibility that you are pregnant and the nausea is caused by morning sickness, check this out with a home pregnancy kit or see your doctor.

BLISTERS

Blisters can be caused by shoes and/or socks that don't fit well, that have tight spots, that don't match your running style, or that are wet. Small blisters can be covered with medicated cream and a bandage. Large blisters should be drained with a sterilized needle, then treated with medicated cream and a covering. Pay attention to them; if they're not treated correctly, they can get infected.

MUSCLE CRAMPS

What feels like painful knots are actually involuntary contractions of the muscle. It is not known what causes them—it could be a lack of sodium, potassium, calcium, or a vitamin complex. To help get rid of the pain from muscle cramps, stretch the joint, massage the area, and walk it off by gently moving the muscle. Then, evaluate your diet, and if cramps happen frequently, change your drinking and eating habits and see if that helps.

Common Training Injuries

Tri-training can help you avoid many of the overuse injuries that plague single-sport specialists, because you alternate muscle groups in your workouts. On the other hand, triathletes also have to be wary because they're at risk for three times the injuries that single-sport athletes face—we can get swimmer's shoulder, cyclist's knees, and runner's feet.

The most common injuries are the result of overuse and are generally of one of two types: stress fractures or inflammation (of the tendons, ligaments, bursa, cartilage, connective tissues, or nerve tissues). Overuse injuries share the same common causes: repeated stress on a given structure that overwhelms its capacity to respond and repair itself. Or, quite simply, they can be caused by repetitive trauma from training.

Among runners, the most common cause of problems is excessive mileage, or the overtraining syndrome. Other causes are also in the too much or too fast categories:

- Too fast an increase in the distances in your training schedule
- Too much of an increase in resistance training, such as climbing hills
- Too much interval training too soon
- Too many bounding or jumping exercises or doing them too intensely
- Too much time running on hard surfaces

Other injuries are caused by training errors, such as training in the wrong shoes, inadequate stretching/warming up, lack of adequate flexibility and/or strength, imbalanced muscle development, and uncompensated leg-length differences.

ARE WOMEN MORE AT RISK OF OVERUSE INJURIES THAN MEN?

When I competed in the 1984 U.S. Olympic Marathon trials, my competition and I were surveyed, and researchers found that a high number (44 percent) of the 210 Olympic marathon contenders reported that they had suffered from a musculoskeletal problem that they considered significant. Of those

CONTINUED →

← ARE WOMEN AT RISK? CONTINUED

who qualified in these first Olympic Marathon trials for women, 10 percent were unable to compete because they were injured at the time of the race.

It appears from published reports that there is a higher rate of injury among female athletes, but that it is predominantly caused by their lower initial levels of fitness. As women become more active and competitive, their rates of injury approach those of men.

There are some indications that women may have a higher overall incidence of injury, but the injury patterns are the same. Women appear to have a higher incidence of shin splints and stress fractures, but they also seem to have a lower incidence of certain types of tendonitis.

Most people believe that women suffer from more knee problems than do men because of the wider female pelvis and greater joint flexibility. In fact, knee pain among runners is the most common injury for both sexes, occurring in 24 percent of the men and 27 percent of the women runners, which is not a significant difference.

It appears that women suffer from more stress fractures overall than do men, but some specific kinds of stress fractures may occur less often in women. Studies indicate that stress fractures of the iliac crest (the bone you feel when you put your hands on your hips) and the tarsal navicular (one of the bones in the middle and inside of the foot) are more predominant among men. Again, the increased rate of stress fractures in women, similar to other overuse injuries, is likely to be related to the initial lack of proper conditioning.

Another orthopedic stress trauma is swimmer's shoulder (pain from repeated trauma to the head of the upper arm bone). The incidence is higher among women (reported by 68 percent, versus 50 percent of men).

In conclusion, injuries are common in both sexes and have been found to be more sport-specific than sex-specific. If it's true that women are more injury-prone due to lower levels of initial fitness, then a sensible program that builds fitness, strengthens areas of personal weakness, and gradually adds in distance and endurance is the best prevention. It's my hope that this book will help you do just that.

The most common problem for swimmers is ear infection, which is not gender-dependent. Ear infections are caused by exposure of the tissues in the ear canal to prolonged irritation. The best treatment is prevention—wearing earplugs and drying out any water that gets in the ears (there are over-the-counter products that can do this). Once symptoms are present, you must decrease the inflammation and simultaneously treat the infection.

For overuse injuries, rest is the best treatment. However, if your condition is serious, then casting, crutches, anti-inflammatory drugs, or physical therapy may be required. It's permissible to treat less serious injuries yourself first by using the RICE formula: rest, ice, compression, and elevation of the injured part.

If you have continued or chronic pain, visit your doctor for diagnosis and treatment. With your physician's help, try to pinpoint the cause. You can't keep the problem from recurring if you don't know why it happened to begin with. Every overuse injury is caused by exerting a force on a tissue that is greater than the tissue's basic strength, and every injury-causing force can be traced to one of the following:

1. Training plans that do not allow for adequate recovery
2. Tissues that are weak and susceptible to injury
3. Biomechanical weaknesses that put excessive stress on certain parts of your body

When you know what caused an injury, you can begin to fix it. Follow your doctor's instructions for recovery—and don't start working out again before you have permission, because you could end up reinjuring the same area, ultimately causing delays in healing.

When you have your doctor's okay to resume working out, be sure to follow his or her recommendations or consult a physical therapist. Rehabilitation using flexibility, strengthening, and aerobic/anaerobic conditioning is the key to returning to your training program. Crosstrain in a different skill or sport that doesn't hurt, if necessary, until the pain disappears. If you continue to train with pain, you only exacerbate the problem.

Colds and Other Short-Term Illnesses

It's a tough call whether to exercise when you are sick. But it's better to be safe than sorry, so it's generally not a bad idea to take a few days off when your immune system is impaired by illness. If you must continue to train when you are ill, do so at a reduced amount and intensity.

For a cold, if you can take a few days off, do so. There is no proof that complete bedrest cures virus colds any faster, nor is there any proof that training extends the duration of a cold, but do take it easy, drink lots of fluids, and get some rest.

If you have a fever, don't work out. Your heart is already working double time by maintaining metabolic function as well as pumping blood to the skin's surface in order to reduce the heat from the fever. Don't add a third load on your system.

SAFETY IN TRAINING AND RACING

Triathlon can be a dangerous sport. Once after a bike wreck I was being treated for lacerations and abrasions in the medical tent. My friend Scott Molina, a pro triathlete, was nearby, and I overheard him in a moment of utter exasperation releasing a few choice expletives regarding the bike leg of the event. The bike course was on the streets of the city, through major intersections that were closed to traffic. He had been in the lead, spinning through the streets at high speed, trusting that the course marshals had stopped all vehicles. However, just as Molina entered one intersection, a fire truck also sped through, responding to an emergency. The two missed by an inch. It rattled him for a long time. Please take to heart my advice for riding safely in traffic and improving your visibility on the bike (see Chapters 6 and 10).

Women have to think about safety when training on another level, too. We are prime targets for physical abuse in its many forms. Your responsibility (and it's unfortunate that you have to do this) is to reduce your risk of being a target. One of the most important things you can do to ensure your safety is to take a self-defense course specifically for women. They are usually inexpensive and will give you invaluable strategies to fall back on in dangerous situations.

Here are fifteen rules of safety that all women should put into practice when they train. Think carefully about each one and ask yourself, "Do I do that?" Follow all fifteen—they are so important that you should think of them as laws, not suggestions.

1. *Beware of daily ruts.* It may seem logical to always run or ride at the same time of day, on the same course, in the same way, but don't. Assailants will often plan their attack around such habits, so vary your patterns and never allow them that opportunity.

2. *Don't train alone on the bike or on a run, unless you are in a populated area with plenty of people around to help out if you run into some sort of trouble, and never swim without a buddy in open water.* Train with a partner. You are safest when someone else is with you. I once had an accident when I was alone—I tripped while running and broke

my ankle. The damage from walking home and dragging my bad foot caused months of delay in my recovery and left me an easy target.

3. *Stay alert.* Never trust that you are perfectly safe, because you aren't. Never block your senses while out training, such as by wearing headphones. It's vital for your safety that you are able to see and hear what is going on around you.

4. *Stay visible.* Wear reflective gear whenever the lighting is insufficient: dusk and nighttime, early mornings, in fog or inclement weather. Purchase reflective patches and stick them on your shoes, your hat, everywhere, and always try to train in well-lit areas.

5. *Practice prevention.* Always be prepared for the worst-case scenario. Carry a cell phone, have identification on you when you are out on the roads, and tell someone where you are going before you leave. An ounce of prevention may save your life.

6. *Be aware that trouble can come anytime, from anybody.* Attacks can happen at any time of day, and the perpetrator can be anyone. There is no average assailant; there is no profile to help you predict who has the potential to be an attacker—the only common denominator is that they are almost always male.

7. *Know your turf.* Become familiar with the area in which you swim, bike, and run, and get to know some of the folks along the way. Know where there are police call boxes or telephones, and recognize where there is dense foliage or places for attackers to hide.

8. *Have a plan.* Make a decision about what you will do in different circumstances. For example, if someone enters your safety zone, that personal space that strangers may not violate, move away quickly.

9. *Don't assume anything.* Just because you have ridden a certain course for years without mishap doesn't mean it will be safe tomorrow. A local resident might have just adopted a stray dog that likes to attack cyclists.

10. *If your assailant is unarmed, assert yourself and fight back if you can do so safely, especially if you have taken a self-defense class* (and this is definitely something you should do—don't put it off). Scream "fire," "police," or create a disturbance that will attract attention.

11. *Use something.* Carry a whistle, a can of mace, pepper spray, or any deterrent—something so that you can alert people around you or, if you have to, fight. Have more than your hands and feet for weapons.

12. *Don't talk with or stop for strangers.* It is a rule you learned as a child

but may have dismissed as an adult: Don't strike up a conversation unless you know the other person. If you are verbally harassed, ignore the individual involved. If you're being followed, you have several strategies to employ. One of them is to stare at the person to let him know that you are aware of what he looks like and would be able to describe him. If he's asking you for "help," he may be trying to get you alone so that he can attack you. Don't fall for it—get to a safe place as quickly as possible.

13. *Never wear expensive jewelry or watches when you train* (well, the exception is an expensive heart rate monitor)—it's amazing what people will do to take them from you. The less you have, the less likely it is that you'll become a target.

14. *Fighting against someone with a weapon could be dangerous.* If you are threatened by someone with a weapon, try and convince your attacker to put the weapon down. Every assailant is different, so use your intuition. Some will respond to sympathy and understanding; for others, an aggressive response will work better. If it's a material item your assailant wants, by all means give it to him.

15. *Turn an attacker in.* If you are attacked, memorize everything—facial features, size, clothes, anything unusual. Call the police immediately, and do everything you can to help the police capture and prosecute your assailant. Your ordeal may be over, but you'll be doing other women a favor.

The best cure for violence is prevention—and responding with brainpower to the situation. So be smart and play by these rules of safety.

RESPONDING TO A DANGEROUS SITUATION

Your safety is a personal issue but one that I take very seriously. When I was serving in Vietnam in 1970, an American GI attempted to rape one of my fellow Red Cross volunteers who was sleeping in the quarters several doors away. She feigned an epileptic attack, and he fled. Anger may be your best weapon, because it can intimidate, buy you precious time, and make a potential attacker have second thoughts. If you have to fight, target sensitive areas, such as the eyes and the groin, and remember that with all your triathlon training, you have very strong legs that can kick.

WOMEN'S HEALTH ISSUES
Gynecological Concerns

The past two decades have brought millions of women into the world of exercise and athletic training. The medical experts have given them the green light—regular exercise can only improve the quality of women's lives. When I first began running seriously in the mid-1970s, strangely enough, some doctors were suggesting that women's breasts would droop and our ovaries would be impaired if we ran long distances. It seems strange today to think that, even then, without any science, these undocumented threats would be given any credence at all.

Here are some of the conditions that *can* affect any woman, athletic or not, and the facts that relate to these conditions as they pertain to training.

VAGINITIS

Training itself does not cause vaginitis, nor does it cure it. However, wearing nonbreathable training apparel can cause a moister than normal vaginal environment, which can encourage the overgrowth of yeast, the major cause of vaginitis (one of the common forms is known as a "yeast infection"). If you have a recurring problem with vaginitis (or even if you don't), it would be a good idea to wear training apparel made of breathable fabrics, such as cotton or rayon blends. In any case, if you notice the onset of vaginitis (the common symptoms are discharge, itching, odor, and discomfort), treat it with appropriate medication or consult your gynecologist.

STRESS URINARY INCONTINENCE

This is a condition involving involuntary urine leakage, which occurs when there is an increase in abdominal and bladder pressure such as from exercise, straining, or even coughing and sneezing. It is usually found in those who have given birth or in older women. Training can cause an increase in abdominal pressure and, as a result, involuntary leakage symptoms, but exercise does not worsen a condition if it is already present.

If you experience these symptoms, consult a urogynecologist or urologist to determine the cause. Emptying your bladder before you train can help. So can strengthening the muscles involved—the pelvic floor muscles—by doing exercises called "Kegels." Don't let this problem stop you from training. You can wear a minipad to prevent embarrassment from leakage and go ahead and train.

CONTRACEPTION

It's your call. Contraceptives will not affect your training, so you may make a decision based solely on what you think will be the most safe and effective way to prevent conception.

MENSTRUAL IRREGULARITY

Any woman who has irregular menstrual cycles should consult a gynecologist to determine the cause. Irregular periods (amenorrhea) are indeed more common among athletically active women than among sedentary women, but it is not known why. Athletic amenorrhea is a condition of menstrual irregularity caused by exercise. It may be caused by the physical stress of training, the emotional stress of competition, hormonal changes, possible loss of body weight due to increased physical activity, or a change in eating patterns and regimens. However, recent studies indicate that athletic amenorrhea may be primarily caused by eating disorders, not exercise, so don't stop training and don't stop eating.

If you experience frequent, prolonged, heavy, or unexpected menstrual periods and there are no associated gynecological problems, it is not recommended that you try to manipulate your periods using hormones. Menstruation is an inconvenience, but it's just one of the things you deal with as a woman.

In athletic amenorrheic women, normal periods usually resume once training is reduced. Likewise, fertility is restored to normal upon resumption of a normal menstrual cycle.

MENSTRUAL CRAMPS

For women who suffer from menstrual discomfort or pain, exercise has been shown to help alleviate symptoms. These strong and intermittent lower abdominal pains do not preclude working out. It's perfectly safe to exercise at all times during the month. If your menstrual cramps are severe or debilitating, consult your gynecologist and try to keep training.

PREGNANCY

One of your greatest athletic achievements may be getting fit before becoming pregnant and staying fit during pregnancy. If it isn't your greatest athletic achievement, it can still be one of your life's high points.

A program of general conditioning is desirable for moms-to-be; your pregnancy, labor, and delivery will all likely be easier for your efforts.

IS IT SAFE TO TRAIN FOR TRIATHLONS DURING PREGNANCY?

By Dr. Jeffrey Sankoff, MD, FRCP(C) The short answer: Pregnancy does confer risks to both mother and fetus in the setting of high-intensity exercise. However, most of these are only an issue after the first trimester—or three months. A modified exercise routine in the first trimester is generally accepted to be safe for both mother and baby.

The long answer: Pregnancy can be the source of enormous physiological stress for a woman. Prior to conception, all of her body's functions are geared toward her own survival. Once pregnant though, there is a dramatic change to almost every organ system so the primary focus is the development and protection of the fetus as well as the allowance of passage of a mature baby through the birth canal.

It is strongly recommended that all pregnant women consult with their own physician, specifically an obstetrician, prior to embarking on or continuing any exercise routine while pregnant. That said, speaking in general terms, and addressing the case of a supposed healthy individual with no complications, exercise has long been recognized as being extremely beneficial to both mother and baby. Women who are physically active give birth to bigger, stronger babies and tend to have fewer complications during pregnancy and childbirth. Exercise during pregnancy does need to be modified though, so as to accommodate for the physiological and physical changes associated with the gravid state. Furthermore, expectant mothers need to protect their growing babies and prevent them from being exposed to the risks that may be associated with a pre-gravid exercise routine.

Maternal exercise tolerance will be very different during pregnancy compared to before. Pregnancy-related hormones change both cardiac and pulmonary reserves so that peak exercise performance is decreased, often dramatically. Fatigue is also a predominant symptom of early pregnancy and can have obvious deleterious effects on exercise performance.

Structural changes to the maternal skeleton must also be considered. Ligaments, specifically those of the pelvis, become softer and bones tend to spread more, causing a change in how weight is distributed. Although running is not specifically contraindicated during pregnancy, most experts agree that it should be limited after 20 weeks or so and replaced with non-weight-bearing forms of exercise.

CONTINUED →

Several effects or risks of exercise may adversely affect the fetus. Sustained periods of higher maternal core temperatures are associated with problems with the neurological developmental of the fetus. Thus, hot tub or sauna use is discouraged. Furthermore, prolonged exercise in a hot environment at high levels of exertion is also inadvisable.

Until about 12 weeks of gestation, the maternal pelvis protects the uterus. After this point, the fetus has grown to a point that the uterus rises into the abdomen, where it is vulnerable to impact injury. For this reason, any exercise involving contact or with the risk of contact is contraindicated after the first trimester. This includes cycling, which can put both mother and baby at risk from falls.

Triathletes are notoriously meticulous about their nutritional intake. Although this may be perfectly acceptable in the non-pregnant state, pregnant triathletes need to remember to increase their caloric intake to provide for their growing baby. Furthermore, vitamin supplementation, including folate, is very important to fetuses' normal neurological development. Those women who do not sufficiently increase their caloric intake will actually lose weight as their own stored energy in the form of fat or muscle is broken down and shunted to the fetus.

Lastly, fetal metabolism does not handle maternal acidosis very well. Lactate production seen at high levels of intense exercise can be detrimental to fetal well-being. For this reason, it is recommended that expectant mothers maintain their exercise level in the aerobic range as much as possible.

With all this in mind, [this] question can be answered in general terms. Because the effects of pregnancy on any individual are unpredictable and widely variable, [each woman] may have to modify them to her own specific case.

All in all, exercise during the first trimester of pregnancy, including racing a triathlon, is not contraindicated and actually confers important benefits to both mother and child. However, the following adaptations should be made to a pre-pregnant routine: stay well hydrated, don't overheat, reduce maximal exertion levels to stay well within aerobic capacity, and increase nutritional intake including pre-natal vitamins to ensure body-weight maintenance.

After the first trimester, triathlon training and racing is clearly inadvisable, and open-road cycling should be stopped at this point.

However, always check with your obstetrician before starting or continuing a vigorous conditioning program. If you weren't training before you became pregnant, you might choose to start on a program, but for the cardio-endurance portion of a total fitness regimen, stay in the lower three aerobic zones. Weight training, stretching, and calisthenics are good conditioning activities for pregnant women.

Menopause

Undoubtedly, women (and men) experience major physical changes that affect their athletic performance as they age. Nevertheless, after a 20-year career of racing as an Ironwoman in Ironman triathlons, I set a personal best time of 10 hours and 42 minutes, 15 minutes faster than I have ever raced before, after the age of 40. It proved to me that as I get older, I can get better and even faster.

The statistics may show that, on average, athletic performance declines as people age, but that's *on average*, taking everyone together as a single group. It does not say anything about what happens at the personal level. If you are working out more, taking care of yourself with a good diet, and the like, your individual performance can still improve as you age. In addition, the midpoint in life, formerly around the age of 40, is being pushed further toward the age of 50 as we live active lifestyles in healthful environments, supported by proper food and medical care.

The physical changes of aging for women include those that come with menopause. On average, around the world, women begin menopause at the age of 50; women in the Western world, on average, begin a year later, at 51 years old.

Menopause is a natural phenomenon: Menstruation stops and your hormone levels change, causing numerous physical changes that you will start to notice in your daily life—such as those "personal summers," or hot flashes, that can occur several times a day. Another change may be osteoporosis, the loss of bone density. Some women experience insomnia, mood swings, memory loss, and other symptoms as well.

You can do a good deal to allay osteoporosis: Certain exercises (for example, weight-bearing activities such as running), nutritional supplements, and lifestyle changes can help to prevent significant bone loss, so check with your doctor for advice. Training can also reduce the symptoms of depression, insomnia, memory loss, and anxiety that are associated with menopause.

Once you hit menopause, you will have to make a decision on hormone-replacement therapies (HRT). HRT is a controversial treatment. A large clinical trial called the Women's Health Initiative conducted in 2002 found that hormone therapy actually posed more health risks than benefits. Many women discontinued use of HRT at this time, concerned about the links to breast cancer and heart problems. Despite the risks, there are certain groups of women who may still benefit from hormone replacement therapy. If the symptoms of menopause are severe for you, do your own research and then speak to your doctor about it.

The bottom line for you as an older triathlete is that aging and menopause do not need to slow you down. In fact, you may well speed up in swimming, biking, and running. Be safe, but don't be afraid to get out there and reach new levels of personal achievement.

Anemia

A common affliction of female athletes, anemia is a disease characterized by an abnormally low number of red blood cells (RBC). It is usually caused by the loss of iron that occurs in menstruation or by not eating a sufficient amount of iron-rich foods. Sometimes heavy training can cause a loss of iron through the intestines and in your stools. In athletic anemia, the low RBC count is due to an increase in the volume of blood without a corresponding increase in the number of red blood cells. When you are training, your blood volume may increase up to 10 percent faster than your RBC concentration. This is not true anemia, but it nevertheless has real symptoms that must be addressed, such as fatigue.

Taking anemia from all causes into account, one out of every four women in America is iron-deficient, and one out of twenty is anemic. To be iron-deficient means that your iron reserves (iron that is stored in your liver, spleen, bone marrow, and other tissues) are low. Once your iron stores are depleted, you become anemic. If you think you may be anemic, check with your doctor. Self-medicating with large doses of iron can lead to other problems, some of which have to do with absorption of other nutrients.

OTHER HEALTH CONCERNS
Cancer

Facing a diagnosis of cancer can evoke many responses, including fear, anger, depression, confusion, and hopelessness. Many cancer patients search for ways to take an active role in their treatment and recovery. One way a cancer patient can regain some sense of control in the direction of her health is through daily exercise.

Individuals who have exercised regularly prior to cancer treatment have a higher tolerance to cancer treatment and recover more quickly. Breast surgeon Paula Oliver, MD, of the Capitol Surgeons Group in Austin, Texas, has found that "the stronger a patient is at the point of diagnosis, the better chance they have of tolerating the most effective treatment." Lisa Talbott, MPH, one of America's experts on cancer and exercise, who is also author of *Breast Fitness: An Optimal Exercise and Health Plan for Reducing Your Risk of Breast Cancer* and founder of Team Survivor USA, believes that exercising throughout treatment keeps a patient's energy level up and, more important, hastens postsurgery and treatment recovery time.

After receiving a diagnosis of cancer, one doesn't always feel like going for a run or heading out for the gym. The focus shifts to survival. Women do not always know how to begin their recovery from cancer or how to begin or continue an exercise program following the initial stages of re-covery. Furthermore, it is impossible to give general advice on this mat-ter, because every cancer patient has different needs and circumstances. If you find yourself in this situation, check with your doctor about when and how to begin, because exercise can have multiple health benefits for cancer patients:

- Improved healing and recovery from surgery
- Decreased lymph edema
- Higher energy levels, less fatigue
- Weight loss/weight gain
- Decreased nausea
- Less pain
- Improved body image and self-image
- Decreased anxiety
- Improved social interactions
- Better sense of control
- Less depression, improved mood
- Better sleep patterns

Cancer patients may consider continuing their regular workout pro-grams throughout cancer treatment. Retaining as much of your lifestyle as you can, such as your exercise program, can be a powerful coping tool. Some patients may need to modify their exercise regimen, but it is not necessary to "just walk." Regardless of your exercise mode, you may need to change the intensity level.

Chemotherapy often lowers blood counts, which may decrease oxygen delivery throughout the body. Lisa Talbott recommends engaging in mild aerobic exercise, starting out with zone 1 and zone 2 efforts at 50 to 65 percent of maximum heart rate. A slower pace will not only allow for longer workouts but will also improve daily energy levels. Another good way to start an exercise routine without increasing fatigue is to do shorter bouts of exercise twice a day. Rather than aiming for a 20- or 30-minute walk, try walking just 10 minutes two or three times a day. These shorter sessions will begin to increase your endurance without depleting your energy reserves.

Exercise for cancer patients is most effective when approached on a holistic level. Yoga, for example, is the perfect complement to aerobic and energy-producing exercise such as walking. Yoga increases muscle flexibility and strength and is highly meditative. Many hospitals, cancer wellness centers, and fitness facilities are now offering yoga and other exercise and movement classes specifically for cancer survivors. If you are recovering from cancer, I encourage you to join a yoga class, a tai chi class, or something similar, and then increase the level of your workouts as you regain your strength and stamina.

Varicose Veins

The enlarged veins that appear near the skin's surface are not caused by exercise but by malfunctioning blood vessel valves. Exercise not only helps relieve the pain from varicose veins but also can help treat the condition. Do not confuse athletic veins with varicose veins. Some athletes have large veins because their bodies must carry larger amounts of blood to the skin's surface for its thermoregulatory (cooling) effects.

~~~~~

There is a long list of reasons why women, more than men, start and stop exercise programs. My hope is that neither injury, nor fears for your personal safety, nor existing medical conditions will prevent you from training for a lifetime and racing as often as you choose. I hope you will overcome every barrier and challenge to exercising and training so that I can meet you on the roads or at the starting line at a triathlon. I want to give you a high five when you cross the finish.

Epilogue

The end of this book, *Triathlons for Women,* is really just the start. Even after 30 years of professional racing, coaching, and advanced degrees in exercise science, I continue to be amazed at how much more there is to learn and how many new ways there are to improve. The science of triathlon training and racing continues to evolve, as do the technologies, apparel, nutrition, and gear that will help you go farther faster and to gain strength and endurance.

Now that you have reached the final chapter, it's time to start applying what you've learned so far. Application is a personal experience. You'll need to test what works for you—after all, you are unique.

With every passing year, continue to try something new, whether it be a new race,

a more challenging race, or racing for a faster time. Let the information in this book and the stories of countless women triathletes guide your way. Design your own personal training plan; invest in equipment to help you further enjoy the sport; or, best of all, mentor someone else. Watch your body, your mind, and your heart respond.

And as you swim, bike, and run, I hope you can sense that I'm behind you all the way. The best way I know to do a triathlon is this way—together.

I look forward to giving you a high five as you cross the finish line. *You did it. You did it better. Do it again. Let's do it together.*

—SALLY EDWARDS

The Queen of Finisher High Fives
The Head Heart, Heart Zones USA, The Training, Education, Coaching, Program Company
CEO, The Sally Edwards Company, the Professional Speaking Company
130-plus-time finisher of women's triathlons
Ironman master record holder, 16-time Ironman finisher
Triathlon Hall of Fame member

Appendix A:
Finding Your Maximum Heart Rate

This is a strenuous fitness test. The heart rate that you sustain for these two 4-minute intervals will help you arrive at a good estimate of your maximum heart rate. You can use the same test for swimming, cycling, or running.

If you are beginning this test with little to no fitness, don't push yourself to total exhaustion in this test. You can repeat the test from time to time to better define your heart rate zones. Your maximum heart rate does not fluctuate, but if you have less experience you will likely find that you are able to push harder as you become more familiar with your limits.

2 × 4 MINUTES SUBMAX TEST

1. Warm up adequately for 5–10 minutes.
2. Increase your exercise intensity quickly until you reach a high heart rate that you believe you can sustain for an extended period. Hold this heart rate for 4 minutes.
3. Slow or decrease your effort and recover for 2 minutes.
4. Again, increase your heart rate and intensity quickly until you reach the same intensity. Hold this heart rate (which may be slightly different) for a second 4-minute interval.
5. Cool down adequately.
6. Take an average of your two heart rates for the 4-minute intervals and record your results.
7. Using the table that follows, find your current fitness level and add your average heart rate (average HR) to the corresponding number to find your estimated maximum heart rate.

Your Current Fitness Level				
	POOR	**AVERAGE**	**EXCELLENT**	**FIT ATHLETE**
Fitness factor	50 bpm	40 bpm	30 bpm	20 bpm
Average HR*				
Est. max HR				

Note: bpm = beats per minute

* Average HR was obtained in the 2 × 4 minutes submax test.

For example, if you took the fitness test and found your average heart rate to be 120 bpm, you would add this number to the appropriate fitness factor to obtain your maximum heart rate. If you consider yourself pretty fit, you would add 30 bpm, for a maximum heart rate of 150 bpm.

Once you find your estimated maximum heart rate, refer back to Table 3.2. Identify your personal heart rate zones by calculating each range as a percentage of your maximum heart rate.

Appendix B:
Bike Maintenance

Many people ride their bikes without knowing even the basics about maintenance—such as how to fix a flat when you're out on the road. Women, in particular, are often not encouraged to learn maintenance skills and may feel less adept at looking after the machinery. I hope we are at the end of that era. More women are entering bike events, working at bike shops, and buying women-specific bikes. And let's face it: You don't have to be a rocket scientist to fix a flat or replace brake pads. You can do this. Once you do learn these skills, you will feel much more in control of your bike and safer on the roads. Like so many skills, if you allow yourself to have some confidence in your ability to learn, you are halfway there.

Your bike is a major investment, so you should maintain it properly for that reason alone. But you should also maintain it for the sake of your own health and safety. Fixing a flat is one of the most important skills you can learn. One reason is that you don't want to end up being stranded 10 miles out of town on a training ride. Another is that it could mean the difference between completing a race or not. In triathlon, there is rarely a bike mechanic on the course.

You can practice fixing a flat at home using the instructions in the side-bar "How to Change a Flat." If you encounter any difficulties, ask questions at a local bike shop until you understand what to do, then try again. Some shops offer bicycle repair classes, and this is an easy way to learn a variety of skills. You can easily find bike-maintenance tutorials on the Internet as well. Never leave home for a training ride without your flat repair kit, a spare tube, and the ability to change a flat, and never race without a simple repair kit in your saddlebag.

HOW TO CHANGE A FLAT

Step 1. Remove the Wheel
Front:
- Open up the brake quick-release.
- Shift to the smallest cog.
- Open up the wheel's quick-release. Push the wheel out.

Back:
- Shift so that your chain is on the smallest sprocket and the smallest chainring.
- Loosen your brake calipers so that the tire can be released from the brake pads.
- Open up the rear axle quick-release.
- Lift the chain from the teeth on the sprockets.
- There should be enough slack in the chain to easily remove it from the sprockets.

Step 2. Remove One Side of the Tire
- Insert the "scooped" side of the tire lever under the lip (bead) of the tire.
- Slide the lever around the rim until one side of the tire is off.

Step 3. Remove the Inner Tube
- Reach inside the tire and pull out the tube. Leave the valve *in* the rim.
- Inspect the tire for the cause of the puncture. Remove it. Fill the tube with air, if necessary, to find the hole.
- Patch and reuse the tube if you wish. Or you can pull the valve out and replace the tube with a new one. I recommend replacing the tube; if you get a second flat on the same ride, though, you should be prepared to patch it.

Step 4. Reinstall the Tire and Tube
- Put about three pumps' worth of air into the tube and tuck it inside the tire, if possible.
- Starting at the valve, wedge the bead of the tire into the edge of the rim for about 3 inches on each side of the valve. Push the valve up into the tire to make sure it is free.
- Continue to work the tire into the rim until you cannot do it with your fingers anymore.

- Insert the straight edge of the tire lever between the rim and the tire. Gently work it around until the tire pops on. Try to keep the tube tucked inside the tire.
- Check to see that no part of the tube sticks out under the edge of the tire.
- Inflate the tire to full pressure.

Step 5. Reinstall the Wheel

Front:

- Hold the wheel between your knees and grasp the bike frame with your left hand.
- Place the top of the chain on the smallest cog and work the wheel into the frame.
- Close the wheel's quick-release. Close the brake's quick-release.

Back:

- Place the wheel onto your bike frame, lining the rim up between the brake pads (it is sometimes easier not to inflate the tire fully yet if you have not disengaged the brakes). Do not insert the axle into the slots (called the "dropout") yet so you have room to get the chain on.
- Pull the chain back onto the small sprocket and make sure the links are securely positioned on the teeth of the cog.
- Firmly seat the axle back in the dropouts and tighten the nuts or quick-release. Tighten each side in increments, making sure that the wheel is balanced between the brakes (you can check this by giving the wheel a gentle spin—you will be able to see if it is not "true").
- Reengage your brakes and fully inflate the tire.

Step 6. Brag to Your Friends That You Can Change a Tire!

Voilà—you did it. Celebrate: Brag to a friend, teach another gal what you just learned, and give yourself a treat.

Besides knowing how to fix a flat, you will need to put some effort into the machine on a regular basis. Bikes do not require a lot of maintenance, but if they are neglected the results can affect your training and racing. Routine maintenance should take fewer than 5 or 10 minutes a week, on average.

Some maintenance tasks need to be completed every time you go out for a ride (see sidebar "Before Every Ride"). Others can be done once a

BEFORE EVERY RIDE

You wouldn't run without tying your shoes, or swim without your goggles in place. The equipment is a little more complicated with cycling, but it only takes a few minutes to make sure it's in good working order. Here's a quick checklist to go through before each and every ride:

- Check the tires for proper inflation with a gauge. On the outside of the tires, you'll find the number of psi (pounds per square inch) recommended for each tire.
- Inspect the tires for cuts or bulges.
- Clean and lube the chain.
- Listen for sounds of rattling when you start off on the bike.

week or less. Figure B.1 identifies the different parts of the bike that you should check on a regular basis. Here's what to do:

☐ *Seat post and clamp:* Twist and rock the seat. It should not move. If it does, tighten the binder bolt and saddle clamp.

☐ *Handlebars and stem:* Check bolt and tighten it if it's loose.

☐ *Spokes:* Check for broken or bent spokes and replace as needed. (You might want to have a mechanic do this one.)

☐ *Tires:* Check treads for wear or puncture dangers, such as glass fragments. Keep them at the proper inflation (or psi, for pounds per square inch).

☐ Crank arms: Rock them from side to side. If there is any give, the bearings inside the bottom bracket shell need tightening.

☐ *Gears and chain:* Does the bike shift into all gears? Check the chain for excessive grease, dirt, dryness, or rust. Clean, lubricate, or replace the chain as needed.

☐ *Brake cables:* Check for fraying.

☐ *Brake levers:* If you have to pull either brake lever more than an inch to stop the wheel, the brake cables or pads need to be adjusted.

☐ *Brake pads:* Check for cracking. Pads should contact the rims squarely.

FIGURE B.1: Parts of the bike

ESSENTIAL BIKE TOOLS

Make sure you always carry the following with you on training rides and in races:

- Frame pump
- Spare tube
- Folding tool
- Speed Lever or tire iron
- Patch kit
- Cell phone
- Identification, medical insurance information, and emergency contact phone number

All of this can be kept in a saddle bag (a small cloth bag that attaches beneath the saddle). For more information on how to perform bike maintenance, see http://bicycletutor.com, a great site with online tutorials.

Patching Tubes

When riding, you should at all times have a spare tube that fits your wheel size. The side of your rubber tread tire usually will indicate what the tube size is for your wheel. Carrying a spare tube is even more important than remembering your frame pump, because there's a much better chance that some other biker riding by will have a pump (or a patch kit). The chances of someone having the exact tube size you need are not very high.

If you want to patch your tire tube, my advice is to do it after the ride, if possible. Don't waste time looking for that hole to patch when you're flat; instead, just replace the tube so you can get back in the saddle faster. Carry the glueless patch kit, though, in case you get a second flat on your ride.

The hardest part of patching a tube is often finding the puncture. The usual way is to inflate the tube and listen for the sound of hissing air. If you cannot locate the puncture this way, hold the tube up to your eye and pass the length of the tube in front of your eye. No, you're not looking for the hole! Your eye is one of the most sensitive parts of your body, and you will feel the air coming out of the tube where the puncture is. Once you've located the puncture, follow the instructions on your patch kit. (But try this at home first so you can do it with confidence out on the road, if necessary.)

Cleaning Your Chain

Clean your chain as needed. Many women ask how often this needs to be done, but it depends on the conditions where you ride your bike. It's easy to see when the chain is dirty or dry. Clean it once and you'll know what it looks like clean. Because chains wear out, you're going to need to replace your chain and freewheel as needed.

Appendix C:
Other Books by Sally Edwards

Heart Zones Cycling, with coauthor Sally Reed

The Heart Rate Monitor Book for Cyclists, with coauthor Sally Reed

The Heart Rate Monitor Workbook, with coauthor Sally Reed

The Complete Book of Triathlons

Triathlon: A Triple Fitness Sport

The Triathlon Log Book

Triathlon Training and Racing

Heart Zone Training

Fit and Fat

The Equilibrium Plan

Snowshoeing

Triathlons for Kids

Triathlons for Fun

Caterpillars to Butterflies, with coauthor Maggie Sullivan

Health in a Heartbeat: 6-Week Emotional Fitness Training,
with coauthor Dan Rudd

Healthy Heart in the Zones: High School, with coauthor Deve Swaim

Healthy Heart in the Zones: Middle School, with coauthor Deve Swaim

Appendix D:
Heart Zones USA

Heart Zones® USA is the premier provider of training services and programs for fitness enthusiasts, athletes, coaches, personal trainers, indoor cycling instructors, weight management consultants, and health and physical education teachers. Triathlon and running legend Sally Edwards, MA, MBA, is the founder and CEO of the company as well as the creator and developer of the branded and proprietary cardiovascular training system, Heart Zones Training (HZT). HZT is practiced worldwide. The company offers a broad range of products and services for anyone practicing, coaching, or teaching cardiovascular training. Currently HZT is taught in 10,000 schools in the United States, Canada, Asia, and Western Europe and has certified over 5,000 individuals and coaches in the company's branded and proprietary training system.

The following products and services are available through Heart Zones:

- Books, DVDs, workout cards, and wall charts
- Coaching services for individual athletes
- Seminars, workshops, and conferences
- Certifications in indoor cycling, advanced personal training, coaching, triathlon, metabolic training, and power cycling (including home study certification programs)
- Coaching packages including training plans for individuals and teams
- Physical education curriculum and materials for schools
- Heart rate monitors, pedometers, power meters, and metabolic carts
- Training apparel: headwear, singlets, shorts, jerseys, and gear bags
- E-newsletters, blogs, and webinars

Visit www.heartzones.com and www.heartzonescoaching.com for free web site articles, training logs, and workouts.

Heart Zones USA
2636 Fulton Avenue Suite #100
Sacramento, California 95821
USA
916-481-7283 phone / 916-481-2213 fax
www.HeartZones.com
E-mail: Staff@HeartZones.com

Index